What are people sa   T0278257

*Dis*Connected

In his powerful new book, Steve Taylor sets out clearly how
hyper-disconnected people are responsible for a large proportion
of the brutality and suffering which has filled human history.
He provides a stark warning that, in our time of "Strongmen"
leaders, hyper-disconnected people make the worst possible
leaders in every conceivable way. In vividly demonstrating
how protecting ourselves from such dangerous leaders is now
the most urgent task facing humanity, *DisConnected* is essential
reading in these frightening times.

Ian Hughes, author of *Disordered Minds: How Dangerous
Personalities Are Destroying Democracy*

This may be the most important book you read this year.
Documenting how increasingly sophisticated disinformation
campaigns are fuelling the rise of pathocracy – literally rule by
the disordered – Dr. Taylor explains why malignant narcissists
are taking over the world in the 21st Century.

John Gartner PhD, Founder, Duty To Warn

Dr. Steve Taylor is a creative psychological thinker who has
consistently enlarged our understanding of human experience
and its highest possibilities. I recommend his newest book,
DisConnected, a lively and important work on politics and
leadership. I recommend it to all who are concerned with
humanity's future in our increasingly connected world.

Edward Hoffman PhD, author of *Visions of Innocence and The
Way of Splendor*

The task of linking modern psychological insights, the character of human societies, and perennial spiritual wisdom is crucial. Continuing his contribution to this work, through the lens of connection and disconnection, Steve Taylor does us a great service. He will aid those who are confused about the nature of enlightenment, those who suffer because their lives are distorted by disconnection in themselves or those around them. He will also help others who perceive the fundamental connection that is our ground and seek to understand more, practically and experientially, about the depths and intimacies of our being.

Dr Mark Vernon, writer and psychotherapist

*Dis*Connected

The Roots of Human Cruelty and How
Connection Can Heal the World

*Dis*Connected

The Roots of Human Cruelty and How
Connection Can Heal the World

Steve Taylor

IFF
BOOKS

Winchester, UK
Washington, USA

JOHN HUNT PUBLISHING

First published by iff Books, 2023
iff Books is an imprint of John Hunt Publishing Ltd., No. 3 East Street, Alresford,
Hampshire SO24 9EE, UK
office@jhpbooks.com
www.johnhuntpublishing.com
www.iff-books.com

For distributor details and how to order please visit the 'Ordering' section on our website.

ISBN: 978 1 80341 030 2
978 1 80341 031 9 (ebook)
Library of Congress Control Number: 2022931296

A CIP catalogue record for this book is available from the British Library.

Design: Matthew Greenfield

UK: Printed and bound by CPI Group (UK) Ltd, Croydon, CR0 4YY
Printed in North America by CPI GPS partners

We operate a distinctive and ethical publishing philosophy in
all areas of our business, from our global network of authors to
production and worldwide distribution.

Contents

Other Books by this Author

Out of Time
ISBN: 978 0 94665 079 8

Making Time
ISBN: 978 1 84046 826 7

Waking from Sleep
ISBN: 978 1 84850 179 9

Out of the Darkness
ISBN: 978 1 84850 254 3

Back to Sanity
ISBN: 978 1 84850 547 6

The Meaning
ISBN: 978 1 78099 303 4

The Calm Center
ISBN: 978 1 60868 330 7

Not I, Not other than I
ISBN: 978 1 78279 729 6

The Leap
ISBN: 978 1 78180 921 1

The Fall
ISBN: 978 1 78535 804 3

The Clear Light
ISBN: 978 1 60868 712 1

Spiritual Science
ISBN: 978 1 78678 158 1

Extraordinary Awakenings
ISBN: 978 1 60868 767 1

Introduction

From Gandhi to Hitler

In 1939, at his ashram near the city of Wardha in central India, Mahatma Gandhi was growing increasingly concerned about events in Europe. Now 69 years old, Gandhi had spent his life as an advocate of non-violence, so was disturbed by the conflict that seemed about to erupt thousands of miles away. When the news reached Gandhi that Hitler had invaded Czechoslovakia, he decided to write to the German dictator. In a letter dated July 1939, Gandhi addressed Hitler as "Dear Friend", and wrote, "It is quite clear that you are today the one person in the world who can prevent a war which may reduce humanity to a savage state. Must you pay that price for an object however worthy it may appear to you to be? Will you listen to the appeal of one who has deliberately shunned the method of war not without considerable success?"[1]

Gandhi's appeal to Hitler was perhaps not as far-fetched as it might at first seem. Several years earlier, Gandhi had a friendly private meeting with Mussolini in Rome, while in Europe for a peace conference with the British government. The Italian leader was impressed with Gandhi – mainly because of his opposition to the British Empire – calling him a "genius and a saint." Perhaps Gandhi hoped that Hitler was aware of his activities too and was similarly well-disposed to him.

It is not known whether this letter reached Hitler – perhaps it never even left India. But if Hitler did read it, he ignored it. Just a few weeks later, he invaded Poland, triggering the outbreak of World War II.

A year into the war, Gandhi tried again. This time he wrote a more detailed and reasoned letter to Hitler, imploring him to "stop the war." He appealed to Hitler's sense of humanity,

1

writing that, "My business in life has been for the past 33 years to enlist the friendship of the whole of humanity by befriending mankind, irrespective of race, color or creed." Gandhi praised Hitler's bravery and his "devotion to your fatherland" but then sternly reprimanded him for his invasions of other countries, which he called "monstrous and unbecoming of human dignity." Then he came to the point: "I, therefore, appeal to you in the name of humanity to stop the war... If you attain success in the war, it will not prove that you were in the right. It will only prove that your power of destruction was greater."[2]

Again, it is not known whether Hitler ever read Gandhi's second letter. If he did, we can imagine him flying into a rage and throwing the pages into the fire. At any rate, Gandhi's attempt to reason with Hitler was doomed to failure.

One striking thing about Gandhi's letters to Hitler is their naivety. Gandhi was nothing if not a man of reason. His philosophy of non-violent resistance was eminently rational, based on his realisation that violent resistance to oppression is counterproductive, since it always leads to more violence. Because of his ability to appeal to the reason and humanity of others, Gandhi's approach had been strikingly successful.

In his letters, Gandhi assumes that Hitler is a man of reason too, capable of understanding the rationale of his arguments. Like the lawyer that he originally was, Gandhi assumes that if he states his case clearly enough, Hitler will reconsider his actions. But Gandhi was completely wrong, of course. Trying to reason with someone as deeply disordered as Hitler is like speaking to them in a language they can't understand. It was pointless appealing to his sense of humanity because he had no sense of humanity.

Gandhi's naivety was also evident in his belief that the best way to defeat the Nazis was through non-violent resistance. Writing to the Jewish philosopher Martin Buber, Gandhi suggested that German Jews who were being terrorised by the Nazis could "melt" the hearts of their persecutors with non-resistance. Clearly, this would have been a disastrous strategy against the Nazi regime, which was far too psychopathic and brutal to acquiesce to moral principles. If the rest of the world had practised *satyagraha* against them, the Nazis would no doubt have taken full advantage by causing even greater mayhem and conquering the entire planet.

However, perhaps the main reason why Gandhi's interaction with Hitler is so significant is because as human beings they were polar opposites, standing at opposing extremes on the vast continuum of human nature.

Disconnection vs. Connection

As his naivety suggests, Gandhi was certainly not a perfect person. As a young man in South Africa, he made some contentious statements about the country's indigenous black population. At the age of 37, he treated his wife with a startling lack of consideration by taking a vow of celibacy without consulting her. Nevertheless, in many ways Gandhi was an exceptional human being. In his philosophy of non-violence and his capacity for altruism and self-sacrifice (as exemplified by his public fasts, which brought him close to death), he represented an ideal of goodness. In his willingness to sacrifice his own desires and interests (and even his own life) for universal principles of justice and peace, he embodied the selflessness of pure spirituality.

In contrast, Hitler had a severely disordered personality, with traits of psychopathy, narcissism and paranoia. With no capacity for empathy, he was unable to form any emotional bonds with other people, whom he regarded as mere objects. In reverse to Gandhi, Hitler was monomaniacally obsessed with the pursuit of his own goals (which by extension became the goals of the Third Reich) and unconcerned if millions of human beings perished in the process. He was completely indifferent to the pain and destruction his actions caused. In fact, because of his sadistic tendencies, Hitler relished causing suffering and witnessing the pain of others. Devoid of conscience, he was unable to feel emotions such as guilt, shame and responsibility. As a result, Hitler and his coterie of similarly disordered Nazis (such as Himmler and Goering) were capable of limitless brutality and depravity.

The fundamental difference between Hitler and Gandhi is one of *connection*. The "goodness" of Gandhi – or of any highly altruistic and spiritually developed person – is the result of a highly connected sense of self, which experiences a high level of empathy and compassion towards others. With a highly connected sense of self, you can take other people's perspectives and sense their suffering, which generates an impulse to alleviate their suffering. You become capable of altruism – which literally means, other-ism. You can subsume your desires and sacrifice your well-being for the sake of others. You may even be willing to sacrifice your life for others. You become aware of the importance of justice and equality, knowing that all human beings are entitled to the same rights and opportunities.

In contrast, Hitler represents a state of extreme *disconnection*. The brutality of a figure such as Hitler – or any person with strong psychopathic and/or narcissistic traits – stems from a self that is so disconnected that it has no capacity for empathy. This type of self is completely enclosed within itself, completely walled off and cut off from others. As a result, it is unable to sense the suffering or to take the perspective of others. It is unable to look beyond its own desires and ambitions, and unable to curtail these if they cause suffering to others.

Without empathy, hyper-disconnected people (as I will refer to them from now on) such as Hitler don't have any qualms about inflicting suffering on others. The suffering of others is immaterial to them. People only have value to the extent they can help them attain their goals, or (in the cases where hyper-disconnected people have strong narcissistic tendencies) help satisfy their need for attention and admiration. If this is the case, hyper-disconnected people exploit and manipulate others in order to extract as much gain as possible. If others don't have value in this way, hyper-disconnected people see them as obstacles who can be persecuted and mistreated – and in extreme cases, even killed – without remorse.

In fact, like Hitler, hyper-disconnected people often have a strongly vindictive and sadistic aspect to their personality which derives enjoyment from mistreating others, and from observing suffering. In extreme cases, such as Stalin or Mao Zedong, there is an enjoyment of inflicting or witnessing torture. This destructive aspect of their personality also impels hyper-disconnected people to create conflict and chaos, and to wage war.

It goes almost without saying that hyper-disconnected people have no interest in justice or equality. Without the capacity for empathy, they don't care about other people's rights, or about oppression or inequality. If they have any notion of morality, it is purely self-centred. What is good and right – and deserving of reward – is whatever serves their interests and helps them satisfy their desires and goals. What is bad or wrong – and liable to be ruthlessly punished – is whatever frustrates or conflicts with their desires.

In extreme cases, this skewed sense of morality extends to what is *real* or not. Hyper-disconnected people have a tendency to self-delusion, due to their tenuous connection to reality. They aren't just disconnected from other human beings, but also from reality itself. So if a real event doesn't conform to their desires or ambitions – and is therefore "bad" in terms of their moral framework – they may simply pretend it didn't happen. Negative information is treated as fraudulent, or manufactured by their enemies, as a part of a conspiracy.

The Origins of Evil

Theologians, philosophers and scientists have pondered over the origins of evil for centuries.

Why do some people purposely inflict suffering on others, and even seem to take pleasure in doing so? Is evil the result of the devil's influence, as some Christians believe? Is it caused by genetic factors, or abnormal neurological functioning, as some scientists believe? Is it the result of social conditioning, as some psychologists believe – for example, when children aren't taught moral values and are brought up to view violence and cruelty as normal?

In my view, however, the issue is quite simple. What we normally refer to as human goodness – with aspects such as kindness, altruism, fairness and justice – is the result of psychological connection. Essentially, goodness is the result of the ability to empathise – to sense other people's suffering and take their perspective. Conversely, what we normally refer to as evil – with aspects such as brutality, cruelty, exploitation and oppression – is the result of psychological disconnection.

In my view, there are two main ways in which disconnection gives rise to evil behaviour. The first is a lack of empathy, which means that disconnected people can't sense other people's suffering or take their perspective. The second factor is the state of extreme separation that hyper-disconnected people experience. This means that they have a continual sense of incompleteness, together with a feeling of fragility and insignificance. These feelings generate a desire to accumulate power and wealth, and to dominate others. Essentially, they try to strengthen – or complete – themselves by gaining power. At the same time, their sense of separation creates frustration and discontent, which in turn creates a general sense of malevolence, with a desire to create conflict and chaos, almost as if they're trying to take revenge on the world.

The Continuum of Connection

One of the most amazing things about human beings is that what we call "human nature" covers such a wide spectrum, from the psychopathic evil of Stalin and Hitler to the selfless goodness of Gandhi, Nelson Mandela or Martin Luther King. I illustrate this in a model that I call "The Continuum of Connection" (which you can see as a diagram at the back of this book, as Appendix 1). At the far left side of the continuum, there is a state of complete disconnection. This is where people with strong psychopathic and narcissistic traits are situated. Alongside Hitler and other brutal tyrants, here we can place serial killers, violent sadists and other extreme criminals. In other words, this is where human evil is situated.

At the far right side of the continuum, there is a state of intense connection. Here we find people with a very strong sense of empathy, and a high level of altruism. In other words, this is where human goodness is situated. Such "hyper-connected" people also feel a strong sense of connection to the natural world, to animals and other living beings – to the whole cosmos, even. In especially intense cases, they may even feel that they are *one with* the whole world, with no sense of separation at all.

Every human being has a sense of identity, of being "somebody" living inside their own mental space. But hyper-connected people have a soft and fluid sense of self. Although their sense of identity is rooted in their own mental space, it expands *outside* them too. As I will explain towards the end of this book – when we look at the exact nature of the connection between human beings – there is a sense in which all human beings (and other living beings) *are* deeply interconnected, since we share the same fundamental consciousness or being. Because their sense of self is soft and fluid, hyper-connected people can sense this interconnection strongly, which gives rise to their empathy and altruism. On the other hand, hyper-disconnected people have a very solid, rigid and strong sense of self that encloses them in their mental space. They are unable to sense their fundamental connection with others.

In the terminology of spirituality, we can refer to highly connected people as "awakened". This is where this book links to my research as a psychologist, and also to my previous books. In my research, I have found that one of the main characteristics of the spiritually awakened state is a strong sense of connection – to other human or living beings, nature or the universe in general. Other major characteristics are high levels of compassion and altruism. When people undergo spiritual awakening – either as a gradual process or in a sudden and dramatic transformation – they switch from a mode of accumulation (trying to *get* as much as they can from the world) to a mode of contribution (trying to *give* as much as they can to the world). In this sense, "wakefulness" – or enlightenment – is the polar opposite of the hyper-disconnected state.

As we will see in Chapter 1, psychologists often use the terminology of personality disorders to describe hyper-disconnected people, diagnosing them with conditions such as psychopathy or narcissistic personality disorder. So we could also see psychopathy or NPD as polar opposites of spiritual wakefulness, situated at the opposite ends of the continuum of connection.

Most human beings are in the middle of the continuum of connection, somewhere between the extremes of psychopathy and wakefulness. We are a combination of good and evil, capable of both selfishness and selflessness. Our behaviour may fluctuate from day to day, from mood to mood, and situation to situation. In our most connected moments, we feel empathy and compassion and act selflessly. In our most disconnected moments, we are dominated by our own needs and desires and act selfishly and cruelly. Sometimes our position on the continuum of connection may even fluctuate from moment to moment. For example, imagine if you're in a bad mood and someone irritates you. You might respond aggressively, by insulting them or even pushing or kicking them. Then the person shows that they're upset and you suddenly shift into a state of empathic connection. You sense the suffering you've caused, feel ashamed of your behaviour and apologise.

Our position on the continuum of connection might simply depend on how tired or stressed we are. Research has shown that people tend to be more empathic and altruistic – in other words, more connected – when we feel relaxed and calm.[3] We might also shift to a different point along the continuum during crises and emergencies. Emergency situations – such as accidents, natural disasters and even warfare – often bring out an impulsive selflessness in people, leading to many courageous and heroic acts. (We will see some examples of this in Chapter 11 of this book.) Periods of crises also have a strong bonding effect on communities as a whole, shifting them up to a higher level of integration.[4]

From another perspective, our position on the continuum of connection may fluctuate at different times of our lives. Some people become more connected and altruistic in their senior years, as they let go of personal ambitions and goals. For other older people, the opposite phenomenon occurs, and they become more embittered and self-centred.

Our position on the continuum of connection may also vary according to gender. Generally speaking (of course there are many exceptions), women tend to be slightly further along the continuum of connection than men. For reasons that are difficult to establish precisely (although I will examine some theories later) men appear to be generally more disconnected than women. This has been well established by research showing that women have higher levels of empathy and altruism. These empathy differences are evident from a young age. Studies of children's styles of play have shown that girls are much more likely to allow turn-taking than boys, and that boys show much more competitiveness. As adults, women give much more money to charity than men – around twice as much, according to some studies.[5] This trend is also evident in the fact that men are much more likely than women to have psychopathic traits.[6] As the psychologist Simon Baron-Cohen has stated, using neurological language, "the female brain is predominantly hard-wired for empathy. The male brain is predominantly hard-wired for understanding and building systems."[7]

It's also important to note that we have some *control* over our position on the continuum. As we will see towards the end of the book, one of the main themes of all the world's spiritual traditions and paths – from Hindu and Buddhist spirituality, Chinese Taoism to Christian and Judaic mysticism – is to transcend separation and move towards connection and union. They are effectively *paths of connection*. These traditions encourage us to uncentre ourselves from the ego, letting go of selfish desires and personal ambitions. They encourage us to follow a life of service, helping those in need and radiating good will.

In other words, the primary goal of spiritual development – whether it occurs in the context of the above traditions or in a more spontaneous or eclectic way – is to move further along the continuum of connection.

The Structure of this Book

The structure of this book roughly follows the continuum of connection itself. We begin in a state of extreme disconnection, before moving towards states of increasing connection.

In the first part of the book, we examine hyper-disconnected minds in detail. In Chapter 1, we examine the states of hyper-disconnection that psychologists usually describe as personality disorders, such as psychopathy and narcissistic personality disorder. Nowadays most psychologists agree that such disorders overlap to a large degree and are difficult to distinguish. As a result, it's common to speak of a "dark triad" of psychopathic, narcissistic and Machiavellian traits. However, I prefer to use the more general term "disorders of disconnection."

In Chapter 2, we examine the link between disconnection and crime. If a person with a disorder of disconnection is from an underprivileged background, their lack of empathy and conscience makes it almost inevitable that they become criminals. We will also see that a lot of crime is related to a state of "shallow disconnection" caused by social deprivation, environmental conditioning or drug addiction, bringing a temporary "switching off" of empathy and conscience. We'll also look at the "selective disconnection" of terrorists, who absorb ideologies which persuade them to switch off empathy towards certain groups.

However, hyper-disconnected people may also follow more conventional career paths. In Chapter 3, we'll see that some gravitate toward the business or corporate world. The corporate world attracts them because it's so competitive and hierarchical, with power and wealth strongly concentrated at the highest levels. Hyper-disconnected people use their ruthlessness and manipulative skills to rise quickly through hierarchies and attain the power and wealth that they crave.

In Chapters 4 to 7, we examine the major way that hyper-disconnected people inflict suffering on the majority of normal people: through political power. With their strong desire for power, it's inevitable that hyper-disconnected people feel attracted to politics, and often become senators, ministers, governors or advisors, as well as presidents and prime ministers. Their ruthlessness and lack of empathy make it relatively easy for them to attain political power. As a result, the governments of countries – at a national and local level – are often made up of "dark triad" personalities with psychopathic and narcissistic traits.

This is the problem of "pathocracy" – government by hyper-disconnected people – which in my view is one of the biggest problems in the history of the human race. The people who rise into the highest positions of power are often precisely the kind of people who should *not* be entrusted with power. For every Nelson Mandela or Thomas Jefferson, there have been legions of ruthless, unprincipled and disordered leaders like Hitler, Stalin or Saddam Hussein, who have wreaked havoc on their countries, and on the wider world. A large proportion of the brutality and suffering which has filled human history – including warfare, oppression, injustice and even modern-day environmental destruction – is due to the actions of these hyper-disconnected people.

In Chapter 4, we examine the problem of pathocracy generally, with a historical overview. I suggest that, in pre-modern times, leaders and rulers were slightly less likely to be hyper-disconnected, due to a lack of social mobility and the hereditary nature of power. In Chapter 5, we examine the devasting effects of pathocracy during the 20th century. Due to the collapse of traditional social structures and a lack of democratic systems, hyper-disconnected people took control of societies all over the world. As a result, the 20th century was by far the most violent and murderous century in history. As we see in Chapter 6, in the 21st century there are some promising signs, such as the smaller number of dictatorships in Africa and South America. However, traditionally democratic parts of the world such as Europe and North America have actually moved closer to pathocracy. A new type of hyper-disconnected leader has emerged, with strongly narcissistic traits (in contrast to leaders with strongly psychopathic traits, such as Hitler, Stalin and Mao Zedong).

In Chapter 7, we examine how the personality traits of hyper-disconnected people manifest themselves in politics. Hyper-disconnected leaders are inevitably nationalistic and authoritarian. The nation becomes an extension of their own identity, and they are obsessed with increasing national prestige and power as a way of increasing their own power. They always follow "hard-line" policies, persecuting minorities and taking away rights and civil liberties. They always try to take control of the media, and to clamp down on dissent. All of this "fascist" behaviour is the inevitable consequence of their narcissistic and psychopathic traits. Over time, these traits always grow stronger, resulting in more extreme authoritarianism and oppression. Hyper-disconnected leaders also tend to grow more and more paranoid over time. As a result, the longer they remain in power, the more malevolent and destructive they become.

In Chapter 8, we examine one further avenue that hyper-disconnected people sometimes use to try to satisfy their need for power and prestige: religion and spirituality. I describe how hyper-disconnected people sometimes establish themselves as spiritual gurus or cult leaders, in isolated communities where they can indulge their needs for dominance and admiration. The unconditional worship of disciples is a perfect way for hyper-disconnected people to satisfy their narcissistic traits.

In Chapter 9, we discuss why many people are so willing to give their allegiance to hyper-disconnected people. Why do disconnected leaders hold so much appeal, both in the fields of spirituality and politics? There are countless cases of spiritual gurus who behave appallingly, and yet their corruption and immorality are denied or explained away by their adoring followers. Nothing seems to be able to dent the disciples' unconditional worship. In a similar way, many people seem to be strongly attracted to hyper-disconnected politicians, no matter how corrupt and incompetent they are. I explain this in terms of the "abdication syndrome" – an impulse to return to a childhood state of irresponsibility, in which an infallible parental figure (in the guise of an authoritarian leader or a spiritual guru) takes control of our lives.

Towards Connection

In Chapter 10, we take a slight detour from individual psychology, and examine disconnection from a social perspective. We see that the continuum of connection can be applied to societies too, and that social progress can be measured in terms of how far we move along the continuum. (You can see a diagram of "The Social Continuum of Connection" at the back of the book, as Appendix 2.) We begin by travelling back to the prehistory of the human race, examining the simple hunter-gatherer way of life which our ancestors followed for tens of thousands of years. Based on anthropological and archaeological research, I argue that our prehistoric ancestors lived in a state of connection, without a sense of separateness to their immediate environment or their community. This was reflected in their social and sexual egalitarianism and their power-sharing practices, including measures to ensure that dominant, power-hungry people didn't take control.

However, at some point a "fall" into disconnection occurred. This may have been partly connected to a shift to a sedentary lifestyle, with the advent of agriculture and the development of settlements and towns. Perhaps most fundamentally though, it was connected to a psychological change: the development of a more individuated sense of self. The fall into disconnection was severe. Most pre-modern societies – up to the beginning of the 18th century – were highly disconnected, with high levels of cruelty, violence and social oppression.

Moving towards the other side of the social continuum of connection, we find modern connected societies which are egalitarian, democratic and peaceful. Such societies are usually led by responsible and conscientious figures without psychopathic or narcissistic traits. Women have high status and often (in contrast to disconnected societies) take leadership roles. Over the past 300 years or so, there has been a trend towards increasing connection in many societies – particularly in Europe

– with greater compassion, democracy and quality. Although most of the world's population still live in disconnected societies, there are some grounds for optimism.

This takes us into the final section of the book, where we move further along the continuum of connection. In Chapter 11, we look at the phenomenon of altruism. In its purest sense, altruism is the result of connection. The fundamental connection between human beings creates empathy, which generates the impulse to alleviate other people's suffering. Often this connection is obscured by our sense of separation, but in moments of connectedness, we feel the impulse to relieve other people's pain in the same way that we feel the impulse to alleviate our own pain.

This leads to a discussion of the *nature* of the fundamental connection between human beings. If we are connected, what is the basis of our connection? When we sense each other's pain and suffering (or each other's joy), what is the basis of this shared experience? In the materialist worldview that prevails in modern Western cultures, there is an assumption that separateness is fundamental. Human beings are seen as biological machines, made up of selfish genes, who are enclosed inside our own bodies and brains. However, in my view, *connection* is fundamental, not separateness.

In Chapter 12, we examine the hyper-connected people who feel a powerful ongoing sense of empathy and compassion, and spend their lives serving and helping others. We look at some examples of highly connected leaders, who use their influence to alleviate suffering and oppression, and to promote justice and well-being. In Chapter 13, we examine the main way in which "hyper-connection" manifests itself: spirituality. Connection is the defining characteristic of spirituality. Spiritual experiences are essentially experiences of connection, and spiritual traditions (such as yoga, Taoism and Buddhism) lead us further along the continuum of connection.

In the final chapter, we discuss some practical measures to move towards connection, both individually and socially. I point out that what we consider "progress", both individually and socially, is a movement towards connection. This movement towards increased connection is our greatest hope for the survival of our species. Without connection, it is impossible for us to live in harmony with our own selves, with one another, and with the world itself.

A word of warning: the first few chapters of this book won't make pleasant reading. We'll be exploring the darkest aspects of human nature, and the most brutal and violent types of human behaviour. But in the later chapters, the darkness clears and light emerges. In this way the progress of this book mirrors human progress itself, moving from separateness to connection, and from evil to goodness.

Chapter 1

Hyper-Disconnected People

Let's begin with a thought experiment. I want you to put yourself in the shoes of a different person.

If you're a relatively normal person, you no doubt feel sensitive to other people's emotions. When your friends are sad, you feel sad too. When your friends are happy, it puts you in a good mood. And if you happen to hurt other people – intentionally or accidentally – you feel guilty and feel the impulse to apologise or make amends. No doubt there are some desires and ambitions you would like to fulfil, but you're not ruthless in your pursuit of them. If your desires and ambitions are likely to hurt and exploit other people, then you'll abandon or modify them.

But imagine that you're someone who lacks these traits. When people around you are sad (say, about the end of a relationship or the death of a pet), you find it hard to comfort them. You find it hard to comprehend their emotions and aren't sure how to react. When they receive good news, you can't share their happiness. Other people seem somehow distant and foreign to you, like members of a different species. You find their intense emotions puzzling, since you have never experienced them yourself.

Another aspect of your character is that you're highly confident. Other people seem to be held back by fear, guilt and embarrassment, but those feelings don't seem to affect you. When you feel the impulse to do or say something, you go ahead and do it straight away, without considering the consequences. Others seem to be impressed by your directness and decisiveness, and you find that you can control them. You can manipulate them, charm them, and usually persuade them to follow your wishes. You feel superior to them, and enjoy the sense of control.

Most seriously of all, you don't have any qualms about hurting other people. Other people seem like objects to you, without sentience or feelings. You use and abuse them as you wish, just as you would any inanimate objects. If people have any value to you, it is only as vehicles who can help you satisfy your desires or ambitions, or perhaps as followers who can help satisfy your need for power and admiration.

If you did imagine this person's inner world, it shows that you are not that type of person. People who live in the state of extreme disconnection I've just described find it impossible to put themselves in other people's shoes. They are so locked up inside themselves that they can't see the world from any perspective besides their own. They're so locked up inside themselves that they have no sense of other people's feelings or experiences.

It's normal for human beings to experience some degree of separation. Most of us have a sense that we are "somebody" who lives inside our own bodies and brains. Our own thoughts and feelings occur within our mental space, and the events of the world seem to take place "out there" in the world. This sense of separation can be uncomfortable, bringing a sense of isolation and incompleteness. In my book *The Fall*, I referred to this state as "ego-separation" and suggested that it is at the root of psychological problems such as loneliness and boredom, and social problems such as warfare, patriarchy and sexual repression. But our normal sense of separateness isn't so strong that it completely disconnects us. Most of us still feel a sense of empathy and responsibility towards others. Even if we sometimes behave selfishly, irresponsibly or even cruelly, we are also capable of compassion and altruism.

However, in a minority of people, this normal sense of ego-separation becomes extreme. They are trapped inside their own mental worlds like prisoners in solitary confinement, alone with their own impulses and desires. The world outside their own minds is a shadowy, unreal place, which they feel little responsibility towards. Other people are alien creatures to whom they feel no attachment. Nothing matters to them except the fulfilment of their own desires and ambitions.

Disorders of Disconnection

In conventional psychology, such hyper-disconnected people are usually described in terms of personality disorders such as psychopathy and narcissistic personality disorder.

The first major investigator of the "psychopathic" personality was the American psychologist Hervey Cleckley, who published a book called *The Mask of Sanity* in 1941. Cleckley's findings became the basis of the well-known "Psychopath Test" devised in the 1980s by the Canadian psychologist Robert Hare. Cleckley described psychopaths as efficient emotionless machines, who can't form intimate relationships, and are incapable of loving anyone (apart from themselves). Their relationships are usually based on manipulation and exploitation, rather than healthy emotions such as respect, trust or love. Cleckley spoke of "self-regulatory mechanisms" like guilt, shame and embarrassment which restrain the behaviour of normal people, making us reluctant to harm one another or commit crimes. Psychopaths lack these mechanisms, so they are much more likely to behave in damaging ways. Despite their deep abnormality, psychopaths usually masquerade as normal people, aping conventional behaviour and manipulating others with their charm and charisma.

Narcissistic personality disorder (or NPD) overlaps with psychopathy to some degree. It's also associated with superficial charm, a lack of empathy, and the inability to love or respect other people. There is the same sense of superiority and entitlement, and the same manipulation and exploitation of others. However, unlike psychopaths, narcissists have a powerful need for admiration and attention. They need to be liked, to feel that they are respected and envied, which regulates their behaviour to some degree. Although they're also free of guilt or shame, they are restrained somewhat by their fear of the judgement of others. In other words, like psychopaths, narcissists feel superior to you and want to exploit and manipulate you, but they also want you to like them, which means that they are less likely to be aggressive and cruel.

Because of the similarities between psychopathy and NPD, it's difficult to draw a dividing line between the two conditions. In fact, nowadays psychologists normally study psychopathic and narcissistic traits together, combined with a third trait, Machiavellianism. This has become known as the concept of a "dark triad" of personality traits. Wherever you find psychopathic traits, it is inevitable that you find narcissistic and Machiavellian traits too (although the three traits may vary in intensity, and one in particular may be more prevalent).[1]

However, my own preferred approach is to set aside labels like psychopathy and narcissism (and related labels such as antisocial personality disorder and sociopathy) and simply speak in terms of "disorders of disconnection". Rather than using labels like psychopath or narcissist, I prefer to simply use the term "hyper-disconnected person". After all, the primary characteristic of both psychopaths and narcissists (or dark triad personalities in general) is their extreme disconnection. Disconnection is the underlying condition which gives rise to both psychopathy and narcissism, with the same symptoms of a lack of empathy, self-centredness and inability to form authentic relationships.

The Significance of Empathy

A lack of empathy is the primary way that disconnection manifests itself. Empathy is sometimes described as the ability to put yourself in another person's shoes and to see the world from their perspective (as in the exercise at the beginning of this chapter). It has also been described in terms of being able to read other people's emotions. For example, there is a well-known "empathy test" where participants are shown pictures of different pairs of eyes and try to guess the emotion that they are displaying.[2]

However, empathy is more than just a cognitive or imaginative ability. It's also the ability to *feel* what other people are experiencing. Here we could think in terms of "shallow" and "deep" empathy. Shallow empathy is when we guess or read other people's feelings, whereas deep empathy is when we actually *sense* their feelings. Deep empathy is the ability to enter the "mind space" of another person. The separateness between you and them fades away. In a sense, your identity merges with theirs, which enables you to feel what they are experiencing.

In other words, deep empathy is an experience of *connection*. You could even consider it a spiritual experience, since spirituality is about transcending separateness and connecting to a wider and deeper reality. In this sense, it's probably the most common type of spiritual experience that human beings can have.

To some extent, shallow and deep empathy function independently. Hyper-disconnected people can't experience deep empathy, but they can develop a degree of shallow empathy. With practice and experience, they can guess what emotions people are experiencing based on their facial expressions and general behaviour. Conversely, some people may have a high degree of deep empathy yet lack shallow empathy. For example, people with autism are sometimes described as lacking empathy, although it may just be that they lack *shallow* empathy. They may find it hard to read social signals, and so may have difficulty responding to people in an appropriate way, sometimes appearing emotionless and impolite. At the same time, they may be deeply empathic in the sense that they pick up on other people's emotions and react strongly when people or animals are in distress.

Empathy – deep empathy in particular – is the source of altruism. Sensing other people's suffering triggers an impulse to take action to try to alleviate their suffering. It's because we can *feel with* other people that we are motivated to help them when they are in need. (Although we'll see later that this doesn't apply to *all* acts of altruism, some of which may have hidden selfish motives.)

On the other hand, hyper-disconnected people can't be altruistic because they can't feel with other people. They completely lack deep empathy. This is the basis of the ruthlessness, exploitation and cruelty that defines disorders of disconnection. Robert Hare gives the example of a psychopathic rapist who was unable to sense the terror and trauma he was causing his victims. As the rapist put it, "They are frightened, right? But, you see, I don't really understand it. I've been frightened myself, and it wasn't unpleasant."[3] In other words, what made it possible for the rapist to commit his offences was his inability to connect with other human beings. And this is true of all the brutality caused by hyper-disconnected people.[4]

For hyper-disconnected people who lack empathy and conscience, there are no internal checks to prevent them exploiting and abusing – and even torturing and killing, in extreme cases – other human beings. There may be some external checks such as fear of punishment or of losing power and wealth (or fear of losing the respect of others, in the case of narcissists). But without internal checks, all normal human notions of morality, responsibility and justice dissolve away.

Lack of Emotion

Since they can't experience or understand emotions, hyper-disconnected people denigrate emotional expressions, viewing them as weakness or cowardice. Toughness and ruthlessness are seen as superior masculine traits, while emotion and compassion are inferior feminine qualities. "Real" men are fearless and callous, whereas "soft" men are empathic and sensitive. In line with this, hyper-disconnected people also see women as weak and inferior, and tend to be patriarchal and chauvinistic. This is why, as we'll see later, disconnected societies in general are always highly oppressive to women. Similarly, when they become political leaders, hyper-disconnected people are always authoritarian "strongmen" who pride themselves on their toughness and lack of emotion.

Their lack of emotion and empathy is a huge asset for hyper-disconnected people, helping them to attain positions of power. Without emotion, they experience little or no fear, which allows them to take risks and face dangers that other people shy away from. And without empathy, they have no qualms about manipulating and persecuting other people in their pursuit of power. If people can help them on their way, they exploit and manipulate them. If people stand in their way, they persecute and eliminate them.

In fact, hyper-disconnected people's lack of fear is one of the main ways that they gain the admiration and loyalty of ordinary people. People whose behaviour is regulated by fear of failure or embarrassment admire the hyper-disconnected person's lack of inhibition, his tendency to speak his mind and to confront and even humiliate others. People who take a long time deliberating over their actions admire the hyper-disconnected person's ability to make quick decisions. As a result, hyper-disconnected people are often viewed as courageous, confident and decisive. However, the absence of a quality does not necessarily entail the presence of the opposing quality. To be fearless doesn't necessarily mean that you possess courage. In fact, hyper-disconnected people are simply emotional ciphers. Their apparent courage is simply emotional blankness.

Other Traits of Hyper-Disconnected People

One of hyper-disconnected people's defining characteristics is their compulsive need for power, wealth and success. This is a major reason why they are so dangerous and destructive – because once they attain positions of power, either in business or in politics, they use their power malevolently, inflicting massive amounts of suffering on ordinary people. (We'll see some graphic examples of this later, when we examine hyper-disconnected political leaders in detail.)

Hyper-disconnected people's lives are dominated by their need to *accumulate*. They feel a constant need to *add more* to their lives. On the most basic level, this might mean more material possessions – more money, jewellery, cars, or clothes. It might also mean more achievements, success, fame, higher social or professional status or more romantic conquests. On a more everyday level, it might mean a constant demand for attention and deference from colleagues and peers, alongside a need to always be the centre of attention. For hyper-disconnected business tycoons or CEOs, the need to accumulate might mean acquiring more companies or properties. For hyper-disconnected political leaders, it might mean more national prestige and territory, or more personal power, leading to a fascist dictatorship.

This struggle to accumulate is so all-consuming that it leaves little room for other aspects of life. This is why most hyper-disconnected people are strangely narrow and shallow personalities, with few (or no) cultural interests or hobbies. They may even seem to be strangely *empty* people, since their preoccupation with their surface needs and desires prevents them developing deeper aspects to their personality. They aren't interested in travel, creativity, self-development or relaxation. Like drug addicts, all they care about is satisfying their craving for accumulation and attention. (Unfortunately, this is another reason why they are often very successful – because they work harder and longer than everybody else.) For example, when the hyper-disconnected business magnate Robert Maxwell – who we'll hear from later – was featured on BBC Radio's *Desert Island Discs*, he asked his family to choose his music for him, as he had no interest in music. As one close confidante of Maxwell stated, "He had no hobbies, no private activities, no friends."[5]

This is also part of the reason why hyper-disconnected people are usually lonely and isolated figures. They aren't interested in other people, just as they aren't interested in culture or travel. They don't spend time nurturing relationships, in the same way that they don't spend time cultivating hobbies. They only relate to other people on a utilitarian basis, like generals instructing soldiers in a war. As a result, their relationships are only ever superficial, never intimate and loving. Loneliness is their fundamental condition, because of their extreme ego-separateness. Even if they never spend a moment of the day in solitude, they are always alone.

This relates to another common trait of hyper-disconnected people: they hate solitude and inactivity. In the words of Robert Maxwell's confidante again: "What drove him more than anything [was]... the desire to generate activity, no matter how pointless it was. Above all, he dreaded being on his own with nothing to do."[6] When they are alone and inactive, hyper-disconnected people feel a painful sense of unease, due to their extreme sense of separation. They feel a compulsive need to be active – and to be in the company of others – to avoid experiencing their inner discord.

The hyper-disconnected person's struggle to accumulate never ceases and is never satiated. In fact, this is another of the hallmarks of hyper-disconnected people: they are never satisfied. No matter how much power or wealth they gain, it is never enough. Even if they were on the front page of every newspaper in the world, it wouldn't be enough attention. Even if they owned every building or company on the surface of the planet, it wouldn't be enough property. (They would probably immediately start planning to build properties on other planets.) No amount of achievement or accumulation brings them contentment. The only happiness they ever experience is short-term pleasure – most often, the egotistical thrill of defeating, humiliating or hurting others. Otherwise they live in a perpetual state of restless discontent.

Why Do Hyper-Disconnected People Feel a Strong Impulse to Accumulate?

In fact, hyper-disconnected people's desire to accumulate power and wealth stems from their extreme sense of separation. Subconsciously, even if they project an image of confidence and self-sufficiency, they feel incomplete, like fragments that have been broken off from the whole. As a result, they hanker after power, status, and wealth as a way of trying to complete themselves.

This also explains why hyper-disconnected people are never satisfied or content: because no matter how much power, attention and wealth they accumulate, the sense of lack still remains. Often, as they grow older, they are forced to try ever more extreme ways of accumulating power and wealth, like drug addicts who have to keep increasing their dose to get the same high. And sometimes, the ongoing failure of these strategies leads to an increasing sense of disillusionment and bitterness, which usually expresses itself as hatred and aggression towards others.

As I showed in *The Fall*, a need to accumulate is common to almost all human beings. Most of us experience some degree of ego-separation, and therefore some degree of lack. This sense of lack fuels the mad materialism of modern life, with the need to buy unnecessary possessions, to accumulate more money than we need, and to strive for ever more success and status. However, in most of us, this need to accumulate isn't so extreme, and is mitigated by empathy and conscience.

The strength of our need to accumulate correlates with our degree of disconnection. This means that you can judge how disconnected a person is, by how strong their need to accumulate is. When a person – like Robert Maxwell or Donald Trump – devotes their whole life to accumulating wealth, power and fame, it's a sure sign that they live in an extreme state of disconnection. Conversely, as we'll see towards the end of this book, highly connected people feel very little desire for power and wealth.

Having said all this, it's important to remember that there is no clear dividing line between hyper-disconnected and normal people. Psychologists sometimes speak about psychopaths (and also narcissists, to a lesser extent) as if they're members of a different species, walking secretly amongst us. This attitude reminds me of Philip K. Dick's famous novel, *Do Androids Dream of Electric Sheep?* (later adapted as the film *Blade Runner*). In the novel, androids are almost impossible to distinguish from real human beings. They look and act perfectly normally, with the exception that – like hyper-disconnected people – they lack empathy. They can't form emotional connections, can't sense other people's feelings or see the world from anyone else's perspective. The protagonist of the novel, Rick, is a kind of detective who is employed to find androids. He gives people empathy tests to ascertain whether they are androids and kills them if they fail the test.

However, disorders of disconnections are not like this. They aren't physical conditions, which you either have or don't have. They range from very mild to extreme. They may also be latent until they are triggered by situations or events. For example, some people may not show any hyper-disconnected traits until they take on leadership roles or attain some success. At that point, power "goes to their head" and they start to behave narcissistically and callously. In fact, disconnective traits are almost always intensified by power and success. As we'll see later, this is a problem that sometimes arises with spiritual teachers, particularly when they set themselves up as gurus at the centre of a community.

The Causes of Hyper-Disconnection

What causes hyper-disconnection? Are some people simply born with an innate lack of empathy and conscience, in the same way that some people are born with certain physical conditions? Or is disconnection environmental in origin, due to our early life experiences? Or is it a combination of both of the above – that is, are some people born with a tendency to disconnection which is intensified by environmental experiences?

Most researchers believe that psychopathy is at least partly heritable, but there is no clear link to any specific genetic or neurological disorders. As a recent study pointed out, "the genetic background [of psychopathy] is unclear. The underlying molecular mechanisms have remained unknown."[7] In contrast, the environmental aspects of disorders of disconnection are very clear. Put simply, disorders of disconnection appear to be strongly linked to negative early life experiences. People who have experienced childhood trauma, or simply a prolonged lack of attention and affection during early childhood, are highly likely to become hyper-disconnected.

This links to the "attachment theory" of the British psychiatrist John Bowlby. After studying children brought up in orphanages and other institutions in the 1930s and 1940s, Bowlby developed his "maternal deprivation hypothesis". He suggested that if a child's attachment to a mother figure is broken, this damages their social, emotional and intellectual development. Most pertinently, Bowlby found that a lack of attachment resulted in what he called "affectionless psychopathy", the inability to empathise with other people, or to form meaningful relationships.[8]

This is a common theme of hyper-disconnected people. From

serial killers and other violent criminals to hyper-disconnected political leaders or business magnates, there is a pattern of childhood trauma and neglect. In some cases, this is due to parents' alcoholism or drug addiction, mental or physical illness, or the death of one or more parent. In some cases, there is severe trauma due to physical and sexual abuse. Less severely, hyper-disconnection may be linked to a childhood environment of authoritarianism and fear, with harsh punishments and a lack of emotion and affection. It may also occur when young children from privileged backgrounds are taken away to a boarding school at a young age, before they have developed a sense of security or autonomy. Generally, the more traumatic a person's childhood is, the more intensely disconnected they become. As we'll see, most serial killers have chaotic and violent upbringings, as do the most brutal dictators (such as Hitler and Mussolini, whose fathers were both violent alcoholics).

This doesn't mean that everyone who has a traumatic childhood becomes hyper-disconnected, but it certainly increases the likelihood. Put simply, if a person receives little empathy and affection during their early years, it usually impairs their ability to experience empathy and express emotion during their later years. As a defence mechanism, some children respond to deprivation and trauma by "closing in" on themselves, unconsciously disconnecting themselves from other people and from the world. They don't allow themselves to form emotional bonds with others, as this could be a source of further pain and trauma. They also become disconnected from *themselves*, by repressing their feelings and their memories of traumatic experiences. They build a kind of armour around themselves, to protect themselves from emotional pain, and from other people. This armour also helps them to cope with the challenges of their lives, giving them a sense of autonomy and self-sufficiency. This is why some young people who have been through early life trauma often project confidence and independence, as if they are unusually mature.

Effectively, then, some children who go through deprivation and trauma unconsciously "switch off" the ability to empathise. And once empathy has been switched off, it usually stays off. Once a psychological armour has been built, it usually stays in place, leading to permanent disconnection. In my view, this is the main way in which hyper-disconnection develops.[9]

Social Forces and Values

Beyond a child's upbringing, there are some wider social factors that encourage hyper-disconnection. As I noted in the introduction (and as we'll see in more detail in Chapter 10), the continuum of connection can be applied to societies as well as individuals. And societies that are highly disconnected are much more likely to produce highly disconnected people. This links back to childhood deprivation and trauma: highly disconnected societies are characterised by harsh, authoritarian child-raising practices, with a lack of affection and emotion, which inevitably lead to more individual disconnection. At the same time, disconnected societies are strongly hierarchical and patriarchal. They have high levels of violence and warfare, and a lack of justice and democracy. All of these factors encourage a general atmosphere of ruthlessness, with a lack of empathy, which inevitably encourages psychopathic and narcissistic traits.

It is also significant that, in disconnected societies, disconnective traits are *valued*. Children (especially boys) are brought up to be tough and emotionless. They are taught to view empathy and sensitivity as signs of weakness. The latter traits are associated with women, and therefore devalued, whereas ruthlessness is idealised as a male quality. This is partly because, in disconnected societies, disconnective traits bring success. If you're born into a competitive, hierarchical society, psychopathic and narcissistic traits are a distinct advantage. An attitude of ruthless competitiveness will help you to become successful, powerful and wealthy. Empathy and conscience will actually be a hindrance, reducing your capacity to manipulate and exploit others.

Disconnection is Aberrational

All of this shows that hyper-disconnection doesn't emerge in a genetic vacuum. Although there may be some biological factors that predispose people to disconnection, for the most part hyper-disconnected people are *made*, not born.

This is important because it implies that disconnection isn't natural. Some psychologists and scientists believe that extreme disconnection is human beings' essential and most natural state. In his recent study of serial killers, *Sons of Cain*, the Canadian historian Peter Vronsky suggests that all human beings have the capacity to be killers, but that the "primal instinct" of murder is moderated by more developed parts of the brain. Or to put it another way, we are "unmade" as serial killers by good parenting and socialisation. But when these are lacking, the killing instinct is free to express itself.[10] The eminent science writer Richard Dawkins made a similar argument in his book *The Selfish Gene*, where he described human beings as ruthless "survival machines" who live in a state of complete disconnection. As Dawkins expresses it:

> To a survival machine, another survival machine (which is not its own child or another relative) is part of its environment, like a rock or a river or a lump of food. It is something that gets in the way, or something that can be exploited... Natural selection favours genes that control their survival machines in such a way that they make best use of their environment. This includes making the best use of other survival machines, both of the same and of different species.[11]

Dawkins is effectively saying that all human beings – and living beings in general – are psychopathic, with a natural impulse to use and abuse each other. Serial killers see other people as valueless inanimate objects, and Dawkins is suggesting that this is fundamentally true. We *are* just objects to each other. According to Dawkins, our only hope is to try to override our fundamental psychopathy by *learning* to be kind and selfless. He believes that this is the basis of any civilised society.

Fortunately, all of this is nonsense. The fact that psychopathic traits emerge from dysfunctional upbringings and negative social influences suggests that they are not innate. Hyper-disconnection arises when something *goes wrong* with human nature, not when human nature expresses itself directly. Hyper-disconnection is not an expression of human nature, but a *distortion* of it. In other words, disconnection is aberrational. Human beings are not isolated biological machines who only care about their own survival and reproduction. We are fundamentally interconnected beings who are innately predisposed to care for each other.

In other words, we aren't naturally psychopaths, but *empaths*.

Chapter 2

Hyper-Disconnected People as Criminals

Let's return to the thought experiment I described at the beginning of the last chapter.

Imagine again you're a hyper-disconnected person who lacks empathy, guilt and shame, and feels highly confident and superior to others. Imagine that you're young and reach the point – perhaps in your final year at school or college – when you need to decide what to do with the rest of your life. What career path would you choose? What profession would most appeal to you? Which job would best suit your personality? Perhaps you visit a careers advisor, who gives you a personality test and recognises your dark triad traits. They might feel a little uneasy in your presence, but still feel obliged to help you. What profession would they recommend?

A caring profession probably wouldn't be a good fit. Without empathy, you probably wouldn't make a good childminder or nurse or teacher. A technical or manual profession – such as electrician or car mechanic – probably wouldn't be right either, since those careers don't normally offer much opportunity to climb a hierarchy and attain a position of dominance. However, there are a number of better career options open to you. In fact, there are three main options: crime, business and politics. In this chapter, I will deal with the first of these options.

Crime isn't a career in the conventional sense, and it certainly wouldn't be recommended by a careers advisor. However, depending partly on their socio-economic background, many hyper-disconnected people gravitate to a life of crime. Research has shown that crime is strongly associated with both psychopathic and narcissistic traits. Studies of prison populations have found that between 15% and 25% of prisoners have psychopathic traits, compared to .5 to one per cent of the general population.[1] Psychopathic traits are also linked to lower levels of rehabilitation. Criminals with psychopathic traits almost never change their ways and become law-abiding citizens. Perhaps because they often appear charming and know how to manipulate other people (presumably including prison officers and parole boards), psychopathic prisoners tend to be released earlier than others. However, there is a higher likelihood of them returning.

Hyper-Disconnected Crime

Why are hyper-disconnected people so likely to become criminals? To answer this, we need to consider what it is that prevents most of us from committing crimes. No matter how hungry we are, most of us would never consider threatening a passer-by with a weapon and stealing their wallet or purse. Even if we were poor and facing bankruptcy, most of us wouldn't consider stealing from another person's bank account or from the funds of the company we work for. No matter how sexually frustrated they might feel, the vast majority of men would never contemplate assaulting or raping a woman.

What is it that stops us responding in these ways? Or conversely, what is it that allows some people to commit such crimes? Of course, there are many complex sociological and psychological reasons for crime (some of which I will discuss later in this chapter), but in my view, there is one fundamental, overriding factor: a lack of empathy. This is the major reason why hyper-disconnected people are liable to become criminals.

Most types of crime involve inflicting harm on other people – for example, stealing their money or possessions, physically violating, injuring or killing them. Most of us recoil from these types of behaviour because of our empathy and conscience. We're reluctant to make other people suffer because we can *sense* their suffering. When other people do suffer due to our actions, we feel intensely uncomfortable. Even if we harm them thoughtlessly or accidentally, we feel guilt and shame.

On the other hand, if you can't empathise with other people, then you are much more liable to commit crimes against them. You can't sense their suffering and so have no qualms about harming them. You don't feel any guilt or shame, whether you hurt them accidentally or intentionally. (This doesn't mean that all criminals are innately incapable of empathy – as I will suggest in a moment, it may just mean that a person's empathy is "switched off" temporarily and superficially, due to environmental factors or addiction.)

It's therefore not surprising that research has shown a strong link between a lack of empathy and crime. A low level of empathy is associated with all types of crime, from minor juvenile delinquency to murder. Conversely, research shows that people with a high level of empathy are less likely to commit crimes.[2] It's also significant that most crimes are committed by men. In the UK, men are nearly seven times more likely to be arrested for a crime than women, and women make up only 5% of the prison population.[3] In particular, women are much less likely to commit violent or sexual crimes. Research has suggested that around 90% of serial killers are men, and around 95% of sexual offenders.[4]

Many reasons have been suggested for these gender differences – for example, that men are genetically predisposed to risk-taking and violence, that men have higher social status and so more opportunity to commit crimes, or that justice systems are more lenient to women. However, in my view, the most important factor is women's higher level of empathy. This means that they are less capable of inflicting suffering on others – and therefore less capable of committing crimes, particularly violent ones.

However, a lack of empathy isn't the only reason why hyper-disconnected people are likely to become criminals. In fact, almost every characteristic of highly disconnected people predisposes them to crime. Their lack of regulatory emotions like remorse, guilt or shame is a major factor. These emotions are a retrospective empathic response to actions that harm others. We feel guilty because we're aware of the harm we have caused, and because we have fallen below the standards of our conscience and morality.

The same is true of other hyper-disconnected traits such as impulsiveness, recklessness, grandiosity and a sense of entitlement. Impulsiveness and recklessness mean that hyper-disconnected people are prone to rage and violent outbursts. Their sense of superiority and entitlement means that they are prone to take short cuts. They see no reason why they should "work their way up" slowly like everyone else. They crave for wealth and power and feel that they deserve to have them now, even if it means attaining them through unconventional illegal ways.

Rape and A Lack of Empathy

The more disconnected a person is, the more serious their crimes are likely to be. The most serious types of crime – such as murder, violent crime, rape and other kinds of sexual abuse – are committed by the most severely disconnected people, who are completely devoid of empathy, guilt and shame.

In 1976, the psychologist Samuel Smithyman – then a PhD student at Claremont Graduate University in California – conducted one of the first psychological studies of rape. He placed a newspaper advertisement that read: "Are you a rapist? Researcher interviewing by phone to protect identity." He didn't expect to receive any responses, but the advertisements led to detailed interviews with 50 undetected rapists. (He titled his PhD thesis "The Undetected Rapist".) Smithyman found that the rapists' backgrounds were so diverse that it was impossible to make any generalisations about them. There didn't seem to be any link to any particular social background or status. He interviewed an artist who had raped an acquaintance's wife, a computer programmer who had raped his girlfriend, and a school caretaker who had committed multiple rapes. The only trait that seemed to link them was a lack of remorse and concern for their victims. They didn't seem to view rape as a serious crime.[5]

More recent research has supported Smithyman's findings. Rape doesn't seem to be connected to demographics such as race, class or marital status. However, there is a strong connection with certain personality traits – in particular, a lack of empathy, narcissism, and feelings of hostility towards women. The latter two factors are linked, in that some highly narcissistic men commit rape in revenge for rejection by women. In the modern age of the Internet, exposure to rape porn is also a factor – although significantly, research has shown that men who watch rape porn are much less likely to commit sexual assault if they score highly on empathy tests.

Some evolutionary psychologists have crudely suggested that rape is an evolutionary adaptation. Evolutionary psychology is a field which attempts to explain modern human behavioural traits as genetic adaptations from our species' past. It assumes that every common trait has been genetically "selected" for evolutionary or genetic reasons. In these terms, rape has been seen as a desperate attempt at reproduction by low status men who can't attract consensual sexual partners.[6] However, this theory is both absurd and offensive. The vast majority of men would never be able to commit rape, even if they can't attract a sexual partner. Rape isn't caused by a genetic compulsion to reproduce, but by an absence of empathy. The defining characteristic of rapists, beyond any social demographics, is their extreme psychological disconnection.

Serial Killers

Of all types of criminals, serial killers represent the most extreme point of disconnection. In terms of the continuum of connection, they stand at the furthest possible point to the left, as the most psychopathic of psychopaths, the most disconnected of all disconnected people.

As mentioned at the end of the last chapter, the defining trait of serial killers is that they treat other people as inanimate objects. To them, destroying another person's life is equivalent to smashing an object that has no more use. The pain and suffering of their victims is as inconsequential as the creaking and grinding of a machine that has broken down. This is why serial killers typically don't show any remorse after they have been caught – because they don't believe that their victims' lives had any value. The German serial killer Rudolf Pleil – who was convicted of ten murders in 1950 but admitted to 15 more – viewed murder as his "hobby" and claimed: "What I did is not such a great harm, with all these surplus women nowadays. Anyway, I had a good time." Similarly, the American serial killer John Wayne Gacy – who murdered at least 33 boys and young men in the 1970s – said of his victims, "They were just a bunch of worthless little queers and punks."

In other words, serial killing is only possible through a complete lack of empathic connection to other human beings. In view of the link between childhood trauma and disconnection, it isn't surprising that most serial killers stem from severely abusive backgrounds, from unstable families with histories of criminality, addiction and psychiatric problems. One study found that 50% of serial killers experienced psychological abuse during childhood, while 36% experienced physical abuse, and 26% experienced sexual abuse.[7] Serial killers such as David Berkowitz, Ted Bundy and Joel Rifkin were rejected or abandoned by their mothers, while others (such as Edmund Kemper) were tormented, abused and even tortured by their mothers. The female serial killer Aileen Wuornos (portrayed by Charlize Theron in the film *Monster*) was abandoned by her mother at the age of four and brought up by her grandfather, who abused her physically and sexually. In other words, serial killers starkly illustrate that the more emotionally deprived and abusive a person's childhood is, the more disconnected (and therefore potentially violent and brutal) they are likely to become.

While a complete lack of empathy *enables* them to commit murders, the actual *motivation* of serial killers may be a general sense of hatred or humiliation, and/or a desire for power and attention. Like rapists who irrationally "take revenge" on women in general after rejection by an individual woman, some serial killers may irrationally take revenge on human beings in general after feeling humiliated or embarrassed by their peers. In the introduction, I mentioned that hyper-disconnection creates a sense of incompleteness and insignificance which people try to alleviate by accumulating power, status and wealth. Serial killers may kill as a way of exercising power – in this case, the ultimate power to take away another person's life.

This urge may also manifest itself in serial killers as a desire for fame or prominence. They may be highly insecure and inadequate young men who feel a desperate desire to "make a mark on the world." In 1966, an 18-year-old student named Robert Smith killed seven people in a beauty parlour in Arizona, simply because – as he told the police – "I wanted to get known, to get a name." John Lennon's killer Mark David Chapman also told the police that his motivation for the murder was to become known as "the man who shot John Lennon."

Many people assume that serial killers are insane, but this usually isn't the case. As with dark triad personalities in general, most serial killers don't suffer from psychosis or schizophrenia. After killing ten people in the 1960s and early 1970s, Edmund Kemper – known as the "Co-Ed Killer" because most of his victims were college students – gave himself up to the police and was indicted on eight counts of first-degree murder. His legal counsel entered a plea of insanity, but three court psychiatrists found him to be legally sane. They reported that he was fully cognizant of his actions and appeared to be relishing the infamy he had gained. Similarly, the British serial killer Peter Sutcliffe killed 13 women in the late 1970s, becoming known as the "Yorkshire Ripper". His legal team also made a defence of insanity. Sutcliffe had previously worked as a gravedigger and claimed that he heard the voices of spirits instructing him to kill women. However, psychiatrists found no evidence of insanity, and the defence was rejected.

The difference between most serial killers and normal people isn't that they are insane, but that they are completely disconnected from other human beings, and from the world itself.

Terrorism

Another type of violent crime that can only be understood in terms of disconnection is terrorism.

As a child, I remember being with my mother at a train station, eating a chocolate bar and looking around for somewhere to put the wrapper. I asked my mum, "Have you seen a bin anywhere?" "There are no bins in train stations anymore," she replied. "They took them all out because of the IRA. That's one of the places where they put bombs."

Growing up in England in 1970s, the threat of IRA bombings was always in the background, creating a sense of anxiety. You always had to be vigilant and look out for unusual-looking packages. In the 1970s, there were bombings almost every month, and as my mum noted, the IRA often targeted train stations and the London Underground, because of the high density of people.

Even people who were sympathetic to the IRA's cause of ending British rule in Northern Ireland were appalled by the indiscriminate brutality of some of their attacks. There was widespread outrage in November 1974, when two pubs in the centre of Birmingham were bombed, killing 21 people and injuring 182 others. In 1987, a Remembrance Day parade was bombed in the Northern Irish town of Enniskillen, killing 11 people, mainly old men. There was similar outrage in 1993, when bombs in litter bins exploded in Warrington (a small town near Liverpool), killing two children and injuring 56 people.

Such attacks undermined the IRA's support and led to a determined effort to end "The Troubles" (as the period of conflict in Northern Ireland was known). Peace negotiations between the IRA and the British government began in the mid-1990s, leading to a ceasefire agreement (the Good Friday Agreement) in 1998. However, shortly afterwards a dissident Republican group calling themselves the "Real IRA" carried out the worst single atrocity in the history of the Troubles. On a Saturday afternoon, a massive car bomb exploded in a crowded shopping area in the small Northern Irish town of Omagh, killing 29 people and injuring 229 others. Ironically, revulsion to this attack increased support for the Good Friday Agreement, and peace has held ever since (despite occasional small-scale attacks by the Real IRA and other dissident groups).

Unfortunately, it wasn't long before a different kind of terrorism emerged: the religious terrorism of groups such as Al-Qaeda. In the UK, this began in 2005, with the 7/7 bombings in London, when terrorists blew themselves up on the London Underground, and on buses, causing 52 deaths. More recently, my home city of Manchester suffered a horrific terrorist attack in 2017. Just a few hundred metres from the site of a massive IRA bomb 21 years earlier (in which miraculously no one was killed after the police received a warning and managed to evacuate the city centre), a suicide bomber blew himself up at the Manchester Arena after a concert by Ariana Grande. Twenty-two other people were killed, most of them children and teenagers waiting to be picked up by their parents. The bomber was a 22-year-old man called Salman Abedi, who wanted to kill "infidels" in revenge for the Muslims who had been killed by Western forces around the world. As a relative of Abedi reported, "I think he saw children – Muslim children – dying everywhere and wanted revenge. He saw the explosives America drops on children in Syria, and he wanted revenge."

Selective Disconnection

As with serial killers, it's a mistake to simply to think of terrorists as psychologically deranged or insane. While some terrorists may show signs of schizophrenia or psychosis, this isn't the normal pattern. Psychologists who have studied members of terrorist groups – from the "Red Army" terrorists of 1970s Germany to members of the IRA through to contemporary members of groups like Al-Qaeda – have repeatedly found them to be psychologically stable, rather than paranoid or delusional.[8] What separates terrorists from psychologically normal people is not a lack of sanity, but a lack of empathy. As with serial killers, acts of terrorism are only possible through a complete lack of empathy for victims, which allows terrorists to treat people as disposable inanimate objects, who can be sacrificed for a cause. In other words, the root cause of terrorism is the same as that of crime in general: disconnection.

However, whilst some terrorists probably do have the same type of hyper-disconnected personality of serial killers, the best way to understand terrorism is in terms of *selective* disconnection. Serial killers in the normal sense (such as Ted Bundy or Peter Sutcliffe) experience an *all-encompassing* lack of connection and empathy. They can't even connect with people close to them, even their own families. On the other hand, most terrorists do feel a sense of connection with their own ethnic or religious group. The group provides them with a sense of identity and belonging, and they feel an allegiance to its other members. They may sometimes even act altruistically towards other members of the group, showing sensitivity to their needs. But that's as far as their empathy stretches. They are completely disconnected to anyone outside their group – and particularly members of one or more groups who they perceive as enemies. Members of other groups are dehumanised and can be justifiably killed for their cause.

Selective disconnection occurs when a political or religious ideology encourages people to *switch off* their empathy and conscience in relation to other groups. This is what the process of "radicalisation" – as associated with Islamic extremism – aims to do. Followers of extremist ideologies are encouraged to see the world in an abstract, conceptualised way, where human beings are separated into distinct categories. They are encouraged to hate certain national, political or religious groups *in toto*, and to believe that the enemy group is responsible for the suffering of their own group. Through absorbing the ideology, they become divorced from the immediacy of human experience – and in particular, the reality of other human beings. They see their "enemies" not as individuals but as units in an abstract, conceptual game.

In these abstract terms, *any member* of the enemy group can be punished for the crimes of the group as a whole. For example, since US foreign policy was responsible for the deaths of Muslims in the Middle East (for example, through the Gulf Wars), Osama bin Laden and the Al-Qaeda movement believed that *any* American civilians could be justifiably killed in retaliation. As we saw above, the Manchester bomber Salman Abedi adopted this kind of rationale. Similarly, when Chechnyan terrorists bombed Moscow apartment blocks in 1999, killing more than 300 people, the Egyptian-British extremist Islamic leader Abu Hamza declared that the attacks were justified as "a Muslim revenge for the Russian criminal policies in Chechnya."

The Psychological Roots of Extremism and Terrorism

In 2014, a number of Western journalists and aid workers were killed in Syria, apparently by a young British man known as

"Jihadi John". Jihadi John was a part of a four-man terrorist group, all of whom had English accents. As a result, their hostages referred to them as "The Beatles" and gave them each the name of one of the real Beatles (hence John for John Lennon). At that time, a steady stream of young British men of Asian descent were travelling to Syria to fight for Islamic State. According to some estimates, 500 travelled to Syria or Iraq to become *jihadis* in extremist groups. David Cameron, the then UK Prime Minister, blamed the phenomenon on the "poisonous narrative" of Islamic extremism which was being fed to young people.

There's no doubt that extremist ideologies and those who propagate them are partly responsible for terrorism. But Cameron's explanation is simplistic in that it ignores the psychological reasons why people are vulnerable to these ideologies, and willing to adopt them. The most common personality profile of terrorists is a young man with a history of problems with integration and identity, who has long felt alienated and disenfranchised. Terrorists are typically young men who have spent years in a state of existential instability, with a sense of disorientation and confusion. They frequently have backgrounds in petty crime.

Even in the best circumstances, adolescence and early adulthood can be a psychologically difficult period. People become aware of themselves as separate individuals – they become aware of their own psychological disconnection, if you like. There is often a sense of vulnerability and fragility, which creates a need for identity and belonging. This is why adolescents often join gangs or become followers of fashion or of pop groups. Belonging to a group helps alleviate their sense of separateness and strengthens their identity. And young men whose identity is especially unstable – including people from immigrant families, who feel caught between two different cultures, belonging wholly to neither – may be drawn to religious extremism for similar reasons.

This was true of the terrorists who committed one of Europe's worst ever modern atrocities in 2015, when 90 people were killed in Paris after a concert by the Eagles of Death Metal. Investigations showed that the attackers had a general profile of drifters, with no sense of meaning and purpose, who hadn't managed to find a place for themselves in society. Similarly, Salman Abedi spent his childhood being shunted back and forth between Manchester and Libya. When he was a teenager, his father settled permanently back in Libya, and he was often left alone in Manchester with his brother. From that time, he became wild and delinquent, drinking a lot, smoking cannabis and often getting into fights.

For such alienated people, a terrorist group provides a like-minded community, with supporting beliefs, common goals and a family-like structure. There is a sense of status for people who may feel anonymous and insignificant in ordinary life. The group's ideology brings a sense of certainty: its goals provide a sense of purpose. All of these psychological benefits are so great that people are prepared to commit murders to gain them. In effect, at an unconscious level, people allow themselves to become psychopathic killers in order to alleviate their psychological discord.

In a paradoxical way, then, terrorism is a reaction to disconnection. It's a horrifically misguided attempt by disconnected people to try to gain identity and certainty.

Shallow Disconnection

However, I certainly don't want to imply that *all* people who commit crimes are innately hyper-disconnected. Some – usually less serious – crimes are linked to what I call *shallow disconnection*. This is when a state of disconnection is caused by social conditioning or addiction, but isn't deep-rooted, and can (under the right circumstances) be overcome.

For example, it's clear that crime is strongly linked to social deprivation and poverty. In hierarchical societies, there is always a higher concentration of crime amongst groups with lower socio-economic status, due to lack of opportunity, education, employment and social mobility. Crime is also gestated by hostile environments (usually crowded, deprived urban environments) that encourage ruthlessness and devalue connective traits such as empathy and altruism.

Social conditioning is clearly an important factor. Aside from the effects of childhood abuse and emotional deprivation, if a child is brought up in a family – or a wider environment – where illegal behaviour is seen as normal and acceptable, and often demonstrated by their parents and peers, then it's highly likely that they will get involved in crime too. As social learning theory has shown, the behaviour of parents and peers becomes "encoded" into children, simply through observation.

In such environments, even people who have had a stable and attached upbringing may take on disconnective traits. However, these traits may only be superficial. A person's empathy and conscience may only be temporarily "switched off", covered up by a superficial layer of callousness which leads to delinquency and crime. It is likely that this applies to a good proportion of the prison population, who may show psychopathic and narcissistic tendencies, but whose disconnection is shallow rather than deep-rooted.

In such cases, it may not be so difficult to "switch on" a person's empathy, especially if they are taken away from their home environment and their peers. In fact, this is one of the aims of the "restorative justice" programmes that have been adopted by many justice systems around the world. Restorative justice aims to help offenders understand the impact of their actions, by bringing them into contact with their victims (or relatives of their victims). Typical restorative justice programmes include "empathy seminars" and empathy training for offenders, to help them understand crime from the perspective of victims.

In some cases, when offenders hear first-hand about the

suffering they've caused, it generates empathy and guilt. Some offenders – especially those who've been brought up in hostile environments or socially conditioned to view crime as normal – have never developed the ability to see beyond their own impulses and desires. So an encounter with their victims may break through their self-absorption. They take the perspective of their victims and face the consequences of their actions. This is one reason why restorative justice programmes are successful, significantly reducing rates of reoffending. Once empathy is switched on, it often stays on, and acts as a check on future criminal behaviour.

This may apply to some terrorists too. A proportion of terrorists are no doubt *deeply* disconnected individuals with innate psychopathic traits who simply use the framework of religious extremism as a conducive environment to express their brutality. This certainly applies to the extremist demagogues and ideologues who attract vulnerable young people to their cause and persuade them to commit atrocities. However, the disconnection of some younger extremists may be less deep-rooted. Underneath their psychological discord and their ideology, they may still have an innate capacity for empathy. This is supported by the fact that a significant proportion of young extremists "grow out of" their fanaticism. Presumably, as they reach their late 20s or so, they no longer feel as vulnerable and fragile, and so longer have the same strong psychological needs for identity, certainty and purpose. As a result, they lose the urge to commit acts of violence. (This is analogous to the way that most young gang members "grow out" of their gangs by their late 20s.) But of course, deeply disconnected terrorists never lose the impulse to commit acts of violence, just as serial killers rarely lose the motivation that drives them to murder.

It's also important to remember that a large proportion of crime is linked to drug addiction. An overpowering need for drugs or alcohol often creates a state of shallow disconnection.

The addiction overrides a person's natural empathy, enabling them to behave with a callousness that would be impossible otherwise. In other words, the addiction effectively generates a temporary disorder of disconnection, with psychopathic and narcissistic traits. The addict's empathy and conscience are (at least largely) switched off by their addiction, and they become ruthless and self-centred, disregarding the needs of others. As a result, they become capable of committing crimes, impelled by the need to feed their addiction. But usually, once a person becomes free of addiction, their empathy and conscience return, often bringing a strong sense of remorse for their behaviour and a desire to make amends.

As with terrorists, many criminals undoubtedly *do* have deeply ingrained psychopathic and narcissistic traits, as opposed to shallow and temporary ones. (Although obviously there aren't clear distinctions between shallow and deep disconnection, but varying degrees of depth.) In deprived socio-economic backgrounds, these are likely to be the hardcore criminals who are deeply immersed in a life of drug dealing, extortion, robbery and violence. And the deeper a person's state of disconnection, the more difficult it is to rehabilitate them. Deeply disconnected people rarely become rehabilitated. Restorative justice programmes rarely help them, because they are unable to take the perspective of their victims or contemplate the consequences of their crimes. They are so irreparably disconnected that it's almost impossible to switch on their empathy.

Chapter 3

Hyper-Disconnected People in the Corporate World

The last chapter showed how hyper-disconnected people – especially if they are from a lower socio-economic class – often become a part of society's "underclass". They live apart from normal society, beyond its laws and conventions, often in conflict with authority. However, sometimes the opposite is the case. Hyper-disconnected people may be very much a part of normal society, especially if they come from a more privileged background, with access to education and social opportunities. In fact, hyper-disconnected people frequently attain the most high-status social positions, taking on leadership roles and even becoming authority figures.

Let's return briefly to the careers advisor we met at the beginning of the last chapter. If she recognised that a client had a disorder of disconnection, her best advice would be to pursue a business or corporate career. (Politics would be another possibility, but we'll save that for the next chapter.) The corporate world is an ideal outlet for hyper-disconnected people's antisocial impulses. Rather than being punished for their ruthlessness and cruelty, they are likely to be handsomely rewarded.

The corporate world appeals to hyper-disconnected people as a congenial place to satisfy their desires for dominance and wealth. It offers a quick and easy route to success. The hierarchical nature of businesses and corporations – with high level managers who have a massive amount of power and control thousands of employees – suits them perfectly. Indeed, research confirms that people with disorders of disconnection gravitate to the upper echelons of the business world. This attraction is even evident at university level: research has shown that students with psychopathic traits gravitate towards business and commerce degrees.[1] In line with this, Professor Simon Croom of the University of San Diego has suggested that 12% of corporate senior managers display psychopathic traits.[2] One of the world's foremost investigators of the phenomenon of "corporate psychopathy", the Australian professor of management Clive Boddy, has found that around a third of employees have been managed by a psychopath at least once during their working life. Boddy has also estimated that between a third and a quarter of workplace bullying is caused by corporate psychopaths.[3]

Disconnected Magnates and Tycoons

In the last chapter, we saw that the more disconnected criminals are, the more brutal and violent they tend to be, culminating in serial killers. In a similar way, the more disconnected corporate criminals are, the wealthier and more successful they tend to be, culminating in avaricious and amoral CEOs and tycoons.

An archetypal example was Czech-British business magnate Robert Maxwell, who died mysteriously in 1991. In some ways, Maxwell (who we briefly discussed in Chapter 1) was an impressive figure. He came from a severely deprived background and managed to completely reinvent himself through pure willpower. He was so ruthless, cunning and desperate for dominance that he overcame massive social disadvantages to become one of the most prominent businessmen of his time.

Maxwell was born in 1923, to a poor Jewish family in the then Czechoslovakia. Not surprisingly given his later life, he had a traumatic childhood, blighted by poverty and an abusive father. (He said that he was once so hungry that he ate a dog.) Aged 16 when the Second War World broke out, Maxwell fought with the Czechoslovakian army in exile in France, then joined a regiment of the British Army. By the end of the war, he was promoted to the rank of captain, and was later awarded the Military Cross for bravery. However, his conduct as a soldier also illustrated his hyper-disconnection. He shocked and appalled his fellow British soldiers by killing German civilians – including a mayor who he executed in the town square – and shooting soldiers who were trying to surrender.

Settling in Britain after the war, Maxwell became a publisher, owning several publishing houses and newspapers. He founded and bought so many different companies that it was difficult to keep track of them all. Eventually he owned language schools, TV stations and football clubs. (He even owned shares in MTV.) His business dealings were marked by deceit and bullying. He mocked and humiliated his employees and became so suspicious of them that he had his newspaper offices bugged, to listen out for disloyalty and disrespect. As his most recent biographer, John Preston, has noted, Maxwell took great relish in "humiliating other people, publicly grinding them into the dust... [I]t was as if he needed to devour his victims on a regular basis in order to replenish himself."[4]

Maxwell loved to show off his wealth and travelled around the UK by helicopter, even for short trips. Wherever he went, he expected to be treated like a head of state, flying into a rage if he wasn't shown sufficient respect. In order to sustain his grandiosity, he loved to fraternise with politicians and became a confidante of many Eastern European communist dictators, such as Nicolae Ceausescu of Romania. Significantly, he also tried his hand at politics himself, joining the UK Labour Party and serving as a member of Parliament between 1964 and 1970, before losing a local election.

Hyper-disconnected people are rarely faithful to their partners. Their lack of empathy and conscience means that they have no loyalty, and their grandiosity means that they feel entitled to have extramarital affairs. In addition, for them seduction is a matter of conquest and power, which helps to sustain their inflated self-esteem. Maxwell certainly conformed to this pattern. He was constantly unfaithful to his wife, whom he also regularly mocked and humiliated.

He had a similar attitude to his children. Working 15 hours a day and often travelling, Maxwell spent little time with them, but when he did, he was a harsh disciplinarian who constantly berated them. A friend of mine, Serge Beddington-Behrens, often visited Maxwell's mansion as a child, since his father was a close friend of Maxwell's. Serge would often observe "the crooked old monster booming at his children and all of them feeling cowed by him."

In 2021, Maxwell's daughter Ghislaine was convicted of recruiting and trafficking young girls to be sexually abused by her close friend Jeffrey Epstein. It's probable that Ghislaine Maxwell's appalling behaviour – showing a complete lack of empathy and conscience – stems from disconnection caused by her childhood experiences. This shows how hyper-disconnected people – themselves the product of traumatic childhoods – often pass on trauma to their children, who themselves become hyper-disconnected. So disconnection passes from one generation to the next.

Towards the end of his life, Maxwell's business dealings dissolved into massive debt, when he took out huge loans that he couldn't repay. This led to speculation that his death – by apparent drowning – was suicide. After his death, it was found that he had embezzled hundreds of millions of pounds from the pension fund of his most popular newspaper, the *Daily Mirror*.

There are many other well-known examples of hyper-disconnected corporate figures with similar patterns of behaviour, including Bernie Madoff, Dick Fuld (former CEO of Lehman Brothers) and Fred Goodwin. (Another example is Donald Trump, who has many parallels with Robert Maxwell. However, since Trump's main role is now as a politician, I'll discuss his case a little later in this book.) As CEO of the Royal

Bank of Scotland, Fred Goodwin obsessively acquired other companies, expanding the reach of the bank throughout the world like a Roman emperor expanding his territory. His peers accused him of megalomania and recklessness, and of wasting company money on vanity projects (such as a £350 million company headquarters, with his own enormous penthouse office). Goodwin's colleagues reported feeling terrorised by him, describing him as a bully with a constant need to find victims. He was unable to admit to mistakes, or to show empathy and compassion. As one former colleague put it, "I seriously don't think I ever saw him be compassionate... I don't think that compassion is in his makeup." Another colleague commented, "If there was an issue or a problem, Fred was more interested in finding a victim and having them crucified."[5]

Like all hyper-disconnected people, Goodwin was highly sensitive to slights, and enjoyed taking revenge on anyone who he felt disrespected by. He kept a list of employees who asked awkward questions, describing them as "toast". His employees learned not to discuss any awkward issues for fear of incurring his wrath. Eventually, Goodwin's banking career came to crashing halt when the Royal Bank of Scotland collapsed with losses of £24 million and had to be bailed out by the UK taxpayer. At that point, Goodwin retired with a pension worth £16 million.

Hyper-disconnected people such as Maxwell and Goodwin rise quickly and easily through the corporate hierarchy because of their recklessness (which is often misinterpreted as confidence), their ruthlessness (often misinterpreted as decisiveness), and their manipulative charm. Whereas empathic and moral people are reluctant to harm others, hyper-disconnected professionals routinely trample over anyone who stands in their way.

Another factor is that, due to their grandiosity and sense of superiority, hyper-disconnected people feel that they *deserve* power (in the same way that they think they deserve to have affairs). As far as they're concerned, they are more intelligent and competent than everyone else. They feel that they deserve to rise above the rank and file, into positions of authority and power. In extreme cases of disconnection, they believe that they are infallible, incapable of making wrong decisions. They believe that they possess a vast range of expertise which in reality they lack.

But even more fundamentally, the reason why highly disconnected minds rise into positions of power – and why they so often attain them – is simply because of their desperate *need* for power, wealth and success. Their intense ego-isolation creates an insatiable, obsessive need to *accumulate* which impels them to climb to the top of business hierarchies.

However, despite their seeming confidence and decisiveness, hyper-disconnected people make the worst possible leaders. Corporate psychopaths always have a catastrophic effect on businesses. They create conflict and mistrust, and promote a culture of ruthless competition and bullying, which damages staff morale and the company's reputation. They cause low levels of job satisfaction, reduced productivity, and high staff turnover. Part of the reason for this – on top of their psychopathic and narcissistic traits – is that hyper-disconnected businesspeople aren't even particularly *good* at their jobs. In many cases, they aren't particularly intelligent or astute. Unfortunately, there is no correlation between desire of power and intelligence and ability. Whereas some business or political leaders may slowly work their way to the top due to their ability and determination, hyper-disconnected leaders simply push their way to the top with their ruthlessness and cunning, like thugs who push themselves to the front of a queue, knowing that other people are too scared to stop them.

Social and Environmental Factors

At the same time, as with traditional criminality, it's important to consider the social aspects of the success of hyper-disconnected leaders. Part of the reason why hyper-disconnected people thrive in the modern world is because our societies are hierarchical and competitive. In more connected, egalitarian societies, hyper-disconnected people wouldn't have the same opportunities to gain power and wealth. They wouldn't feel so impelled to become business magnates or CEOs (or politicians, we'll see in the next chapter) simply because those roles wouldn't offer the same level of power.

At the same time, the prevalence of hyper-disconnected CEOs illustrates how much the values and structures of contemporary societies *favour* disconnective traits. Like a sports match where the weather conditions or the pitch suit one of the teams, our social conditions are perfectly suited to hyper-disconnection. If you want to "get on" in individualist-capitalist societies, you have to be single-minded and self-centred, cold and calculated, willing to make sacrifices and tough decisions. You have to use charm and charisma to manipulate others, and ruthlessness to exploit opportunities. When company shareholders or directors list the ideal qualities of a CEO, these are often very closely matched to the traits of hyper-disconnected people, such as ruthlessness, competitiveness, calmness under pressure, the ability to make quick decisions, and so on. In such an environment, it's inevitable that hyper-disconnected people rise into leadership positions.

It's also important to remember that attaining a position of power can be detrimental to a person's character. In competitive, hierarchical societies, the sheer concentration of power in higher status positions often has the effect of triggering or intensifying disconnective traits. Disconnected people usually become even more disconnected once they attain power. And even people who previously seemed relatively empathic and responsible – who become leaders on the basis of ability or through being chosen by others – sometimes become callous and display narcissistic traits once they attain power.

In psychological theory, this is described as the "leadership trap".[6] In situations where success is due to the combined efforts of a group, a leader figure might be singled out for credit and admiration, which feeds his or her narcissistic tendencies. The leader starts to think of himself as special and superior, due to the status difference between himself and others. The other members of the group begin to feel resentful, and the creative dynamic of the group is disrupted, which ultimately undermines their success.[7]

About 20 years ago, I took a part-time job at a college, assessing students with dyslexia and other learning difficulties. The principal of the college was a tall and handsome man, who seemed unusually young for such a high-ranking position. I felt wary of him from the start. He had a harsh piercing stare which unnerved me, and I did my best to avoid him. My only contact with him was our weekly staff meetings, when he would pace up and down in front of the teaching staff, flailing his arms and complaining about why the college performance wasn't good enough. I heard from colleagues that at management meetings he would bang his fists on the table and shout at the top of his voice, "We need to do better! Why aren't our results improving?"

Shortly afterwards, the principal was suspended after allegations of bullying. This didn't surprise me at all, but what did surprise me was when I talked to a colleague who had known him for several years. "It's a shame what happened to him," she told me. "He used to be such a nice guy, so friendly and approachable." Other people told me a similar story. Before he became a principal, he had been a science lecturer, who was popular with his students and colleagues. He was renowned for coming up with innovative ideas for lessons and sharing them with other lecturers. It was because he was so impressive as a lecturer that he was rapidly promoted through the ranks. "But he just changed when he became principal," another of his long-time colleagues told me. "He distanced himself from us all, as if he wasn't allowed to be one of us. And this horrible, controlling side of his personality came out."

This is certainly a common phenomenon (I could give you some other examples from my own working life!) which is probably linked to insecurity. When inexperienced people are thrust into positions of authority, they often feel exposed and isolated. In hierarchical organisation structures, there is too much distance between them and their employees. And this insecurity manifests itself in authoritarianism and bullying.

All of this is reflected in the famous saying of the 19th century British historian and politician, Lord Acton, "Power tends to corrupt, and absolute power corrupts absolutely." Lord Acton went on to clarify, "Great men are almost always bad men." (One might quibble about the use of the term great here – in fact, Lord Acton was referring to great in the sense of prominent or notable.) However, the situation is made much worse, by the fact the power attracts corrupt people in the first place. So people who were already corrupt become even more corrupt – or in my terms, disconnected people become even more disconnected.

As my example above shows, the problem of hyper-disconnected leaders and managers runs through the whole of society, not just the business or corporate worlds. In any organisation with a hierarchical structure, there is a tendency for disconnected people to rise into high status positions. Even if they might not have the high level of disconnection that would bring a diagnosis of a personality disorder, people with lower levels of empathy and conscience are inevitably drawn to managerial or leadership positions. This applies to schools (where they may become head teachers), universities (where they may become deans or vice-principals), hospitals, law firms and town councils. As a rule, the higher ranking the position – both within society as a whole and within individual organisations – the more likely it is to be occupied by a hyper-disconnected person.

Other Types of Leaders: Involuntary and Altruistic

Obviously, this doesn't mean that *all* leaders and managers (even in the corporate and political worlds) are hyper-disconnected. And clearly, not all leaders and managers fall victim to the leadership trap once they attain power. In my view, we can think in terms of three general categories of leaders: hyper-disconnected, involuntary and altruistic leaders.

Across society there are many *involuntary leaders* who gain power without a large degree of conscious intention on their part, due to merit or privilege (and frequently a combination of the two). There are two different types of involuntary leaders: meritorious and privileged. *Meritorious* involuntary leaders slowly work their way up their organisation's hierarchy through talent and diligence, without a particularly strong sense of ambition. They are usually quite benevolent and effective as leaders. They feel a sense of responsibility towards other workers (partly because they used to belong to their ranks) and are usually cooperative and approachable. In other words, they are often connected people, with empathy and conscience.

Privileged involuntary leaders attain their positions largely through advantages of wealth, education, connection and influence. In the pre-modern era, monarchs are an obvious example of privileged involuntary leaders. In modern times, such leaders often emerge from a background of elite private schools and universities, and from families with connections to other powerful or influential individuals. Privilege gives people more access to education and wealth, so that they are more likely to gain the qualifications that lead to high level positions. In addition, people from privileged backgrounds – such as, in the UK, a private school followed by Oxford or Cambridge University – often have an inbred sense of superiority and confidence that creates an expectation that they will attain high status positions. While both types of involuntary leaders are vulnerable to becoming corrupted by power, this is more likely in the case of privileged involuntary leaders.

There are certainly a good number of *altruistic leaders* across society too, motivated by the impulse to improve conditions and alleviate suffering. Such leaders often feel a passionate attachment to their particular field – perhaps education, law, environmental issues or race relations – with an idealism or sense of altruistic missions which propels them to high status positions. Once they attain power, they become (or at least try to become) instruments of change, often battling with conservative forces who are reluctant to shift. Altruistic leaders can also be referred to as "connected leaders." (We'll look at them in more detail in Chapter 12.)

The presence of both altruistic and hyper-disconnected leaders within an organisation often brings conflict, since their approaches are completely antithetical. Altruistic or connected leaders treat their employees with respect and fairness, and try to create a positive atmosphere, with a sense of trust and belonging. Without a psychological need for power, they try to give their employees a sense of autonomy and encourage them to contribute ideas. This contrasts with the authoritarianism of hyper-disconnected leaders, who relish their dominant position and take every opportunity to impose their power. Hyper-disconnected leaders enjoy making their employees feel inferior and insecure. Ideally, altruistic leaders (and involuntary leaders too) protect their employees from the worst excesses of hyper-disconnected leaders. However, it's also common for disconnected leaders to attempt to undermine and remove altruistic and involuntary leaders, whom they perceive as a threat.

The nature of the relationship between hyper-disconnected and altruistic leaders depends on how disconnected a society is as a whole. The more disconnected a society is – with more hierarchical and competitive social structures – the fewer number of connected altruistic leaders there will be. And when they do arise, connected altruistic leaders are likely to quickly be quashed by the Machiavellianism of disconnected leaders.

In the next chapter, we're going to look at an area where hyper-disconnected leaders are even more common, and where they cause the greatest harm of all. This is the third career avenue that is well suited to people with disorders of disconnection: politics.

Chapter 4

Hyper-Disconnected People in Politics: The Problem of Pathocracy

In communist countries, psychology could be a dangerous profession. As with any role, if you didn't use your expertise in service of state propaganda, you were in danger of falling foul of authorities. The Polish psychologist Andrzej Lobaczewski was persecuted especially harshly, since the focus of his research was political power, and how it can be misused.

After spending his early life suffering under the Nazis, and then under the Soviet rule of Stalin, Lobaczewski recognised that ruthless and disturbed individuals – like Hitler and Stalin – were strongly drawn to political power, and often constitute the government of nations. He began to study the relationship between power and personality disorders – like psychopathy – and coined the term "pathocracy" to describe the phenomenon. As he put it, pathocracy is a system of government "wherein a small pathological minority takes control over a society of normal people."[1] Since he was living under a pathocratic regime himself, Lobaczewski took great risks studying this topic. He was arrested and tortured by the Polish authorities, and unable to publish his life's work, the book *Political Ponerology*, until he escaped to the United States during the 1980s.

According to Lobaczewski, the transition to pathocracy begins when a disordered individual emerges as a leader figure. While some members of the ruling class are appalled by the brutality and irresponsibility of the leader and his acolytes, his disordered personality appeals to some psychologically normal individuals. They find him charismatic. His impulsiveness is mistaken for decisiveness; his narcissism is mistaken for confidence; his recklessness is mistaken for fearlessness.

Soon other people with psychopathic traits emerge and attach themselves to the pathocracy, sensing the opportunity to gain power and influence. At the same time, responsible and moral people gradually leave the government, either resigning or being ruthlessly ejected. In an inevitable process, soon the entire government is filled with people with a pathological lack of empathy and conscience. It has been taken over by members of the minority of hyper-disconnected people, who assume power over the majority of psychologically normal people.

Soon the pathology of the government spreads amongst the general population, like an epidemic. The pathocratic government presents a compelling simplistic ideology, promoting notions of future greatness, with a need to defeat or eliminate alleged enemies who stand in the way of this great future. The government uses propaganda to stoke hatred towards enemies, and to create a cult of personality around the leader. In the general population, there is an intoxicating sense of belonging to a mass movement, inspiring loyalty and self-sacrifice. Present sacrifices become immaterial in the movement towards a glorious future. In addition, the mass movement inspires acts of individual cruelty, including torture and mass murder.

Once they become leaders, pathocrats devote themselves to entrenching, increasing and protecting their power, with scant regard for the welfare of others. However, Lobaczewski also noted that pathocracies never become permanent. Ultimately, they are destined to fail, because their brutality and amorality aren't shared by the majority of the population, who are psychologically normal and possess empathy and conscience. This was certainly true of the two pathocracies that Lobaczewski himself experienced, Nazi Germany and the communist regime of Poland.

Pathocracy

Pathocracy is one of those hidden concepts that, once uncovered, suddenly helps to make sense of the world. In my previous writings on the topic, I have found that it's one of those topics that brings an "Of course!" response from readers. It certainly helps to explain much of the chaos and suffering which has filled human history, and which still sadly afflicts the world today.

There are many different forms of government – democracy, for example, which literally means rule by the people. There is also autocracy, which means government by one person with absolute power, such as a monarch or dictator. Another form is oligarchy, which means rule by a small number of extremely wealthy and influential people. Pathocracy should certainly be added to this list, since it is so common. It obviously overlaps with some of the systems too. For example, many oligarchies and autocracies could also be classed as pathocracies.

Pathocracy takes us into the world of dictatorships and fascism. Dictators are simply hyper-disconnected people who use their cunning and brutality to become leaders of their nations. Dictatorships are the wider government that has gathered around the hyper-disconnected leader, usually consisting of other hyper-disconnected people. Rather than a coherent political philosophy, fascism is really just a term that describes the behaviour and the policies of hyper-disconnected people in power, with traits such as authoritarianism, nationalism, repression of free speech, oppression of minority groups, and so on – all of which follow inevitably from their disconnective personality traits.

At the same time, it's important to remember that pathocracy doesn't just manifest itself in dictators and fascist regimes. There are degrees of pathocracy just as there are degrees of disconnection. Some pathocracies may be less extreme, especially when a country has some degree of democracy. A country's democratic institutions and systems may prevent the emergence of a fully-fledged dictatorship, but still permit the formation of a milder form of pathocracy. Such governments may superficially abide by democratic principles (with elections, parliamentary debates and votes on legislation, and so on) and yet – especially if they have the support of the mass media – quietly subvert and circumvent democracy when it suits them. As I'll point out in the next chapter, this less overt form of pathocracy has become common in the 21st century, and usually involves leaders with prevalent narcissistic traits, whereas 20th century pathocracies usually involved leaders with prevalent psychopathic traits.

Most of the conflict that fills the world isn't between groups of ordinary people but between different pathocratic regimes, acting malevolently and pursuing power and prestige. When journalists speak about the nefarious actions of countries like Russia, Iran or China, they are just referring to the actions and attitudes of a small number of hyper-disconnected individuals who constitute the governments of those nations. When wars break out, it's not because the majority of ordinary people want them, but because the small groups of hyper-disconnected individuals in government provoke them, through their malevolence and desire of power. (Although of course, in some cases, the governments do have popular support, at least for a time, even if this is largely due to the propaganda that they bombard their citizens with.)

Two Pathocracies

To illustrate the concept of pathocracy, let's briefly examine the two pathocracies that Lobaczewski experienced himself, Nazi Germany and Soviet Russia.

Nazi Germany is a salutary example of how quickly and easily a democracy can degenerate into pathocracy. In the 1920s and early 1930s, Germany was a functioning democracy, with a parliament and elections. For many years, the Nazi party was seen as an extreme fringe group, and not taken seriously. In the 1928 elections, it only received 2.6% of the national vote. But then the German economy went into recession, following the Wall Street Crash. This created instability and public discontent, which the Nazis exploited with their keen political instincts and propaganda skills. In the 1932 elections, they increased their vote to 37%. As leader of the party with the largest share of votes, Hitler was made chancellor. This was the point where the descent into pathocracy began. Germany democracy was too fragile to withstand the ruthlessness and brutality of a severely disordered person such as Hitler.

Even during his lifetime, psychologists were convinced that Hitler was psychologically disordered, although in those days their opinions were couched in the language of psychoanalysis. In 1943, the American psychoanalyst Walter Langer was asked to prepare a psychological analysis of Hitler. He described him as a neurotic-psychotic, with masochistic and schizophrenic tendencies. More recently, psychologists have suggested severe traits of psychopathy, narcissism and paranoia. Certainly, one of Hitler's main traits was his grandiosity, with his belief that he was "the greatest German in history" who had been given a messianic role to fulfil the will of God and create a new civilisation. (He also remarked in passing that he could have been "one of the best architects if not the best architect in Germany.") Whatever its exact nature, Hitler's hyper-disconnection was probably linked to a traumatic and abusive childhood. His father was a violent alcoholic, while his mother was deeply traumatised by the loss of three previous children.

However, we've already seen that pathocracy isn't just about individual leaders. It's one of the basic laws of pathocracy that hyper-disconnected people in power attract other hyper-disconnected people, and some the acolytes who Hitler attracted were arguably even more disconnected than him. Figures such as Joseph Goebbels, Reinhard Heydrich, Heinrich Himmler and Hans Frank would certainly be diagnosed by modern psychologists as severe psychopaths. In a different context, they might have been serial killers – although of course they became mass murderers in a much more devastating sense, orchestrating the deaths of millions of innocent people. Himmler was the head of the SS, the elite group of the most fanatical Nazis – or as we should say, the most psychopathic and disconnected people. The SS attracted people with psychopathic traits in the same way that gyms attract athletic people. The organisation was a place where they could exercise their brutality and violent impulses in an organised, socially sanctioned setting. All over Germany, hyper-disconnected people emerged, taking advantage of the opportunity to express their hatred and cruelty.

With great rapidity, Hitler and his similarly disconnected acolytes set about dismantling democracy, suspending civil liberties, crushing sources of opposition and establishing complete control of the government and media. The so-called "Enabling Act" of 1933 gave Hitler the power (supposedly temporary, although of course it continued indefinitely) to act without the consent of parliament or following the German constitution. Exactly as Lobaczewski described, while other hyper-disconnected people emerged and aligned themselves with the pathocratic government, moral and responsible individuals were either killed or moved to the sidelines, where most were understandably too frightened to voice misgivings.

Soon, as Lobaczewski also described, the pathology of the government spread to the general population, with the aid of media and the Nazis' adroit use of propaganda. With a quasi-religious cult of worship of the Fuehrer, and the rapid conquest of territory that Germany had lost after the First World War, there was an invigorating sense of national unity, with a sense of moving towards a great future. As a result, millions of ordinary Germans – who were essentially psychologically normal – became complicit (to a greater or lesser extent) in some of the most heinous crimes ever committed by human beings.

The pathocracy of Stalin and the Soviet Union followed the Russian Revolution of 1917, when the old social order of Czarist Russia broke down. In Russia, there were no democratic systems or institutions to speak of, and so no protection at all from the brutality of hyper-disconnected people with an intense lust for power. Unlike Hitler, Stalin didn't have to set about dismantling democracy. All he had to do was use his ruthless cunning and cruelty to persecute and eliminate rivals and take such a firm hold on power that no one could dislodge him.

Stalin had a similar degree of grandiosity and psychopathic brutality to Hitler. As with Hitler, this was probably linked to his violent alcoholic father, as well as to the violence and social instability that surrounded him during his childhood in Georgia in the late 19th century. However, Stalin was different from Hitler in significant ways too. He had more severe paranoid tendencies, which resulted in the murder of countless colleagues and peers. He could also be charming and friendly in a way that Hitler rarely was. Foreign ministers – including Roosevelt and Churchill – found him congenial and jovial company, making jokes and offering hospitality. (In contrast, during such encounters Hitler was more likely to be sullen, to rant bad-temperedly, or to fly into a rage.)

Before Stalin, the communist Bolshevik party was led by Lenin, a highly disconnected personality himself. After the revolution, Lenin immediately set about generating a climate of fear, creating penal colonies for people deemed to be insufficiently loyal to the Communist cause. In reality, people were often sent to the penal colonies indiscriminately, as a way of instilling fear. Lenin also created a secret police organisation which had power to shoot anyone without charges or trial. Lenin died of natural causes in 1924, initiating a struggle for power amongst other high-ranking members of the Bolshevik party. All were hyper-disconnected people, but none were as ruthless and cunning as Stalin, who quickly outmanoeuvred them, then set about murdering them.

The atrocities of Stalin's regime are staggering. Unlike Hitler, they were mainly perpetrated against his own people. In the short period between 1930 and 1933, several million Russians died of hunger or disease due to Stalin's brutal collectivisation policies, when privately owned farms were forcibly converted to state owned communes. This created massive numbers of orphaned children, hundreds of thousands of whom were sent to the *gulags* (the prison camps that Lenin had started but which Stalin massively extended). In the "great terror" of 1937 and 1938, around 700,000 Russians were executed for suspected disloyalty, often without evidence. The total number of Russians killed indirectly or directly by Stalin – by starvation due to his policies, or through his political purges and his prison camps – has been conservatively estimated at 20 million.[2]

Like Hitler, Stalin was aided and abetted by other hyper-disconnected people with severe psychopathic traits. One of the most disconnected was Lavrenti Beria, chief of Stalin's secret police, who controlled the gulags and organised purges which killed countless innocent people. Beria was a sexual predator who would drive around the streets of Moscow with his bodyguard, looking for women to kidnap and rape. His deputy, Vladimir Dekanozov, followed the same practice, and would often rape women in his limousine, while his bodyguards kept watch.

Pre-Modern Pathocracy

A cursory overview of human history will show that pathocracy has always been a common form of government. From the earliest civilisations of Egypt and Sumer through to Ancient Rome, from the Middle Ages of European civilisation to the modern era, societies have frequently – and tragically – been governed by hyper-disconnected people.

Despite this, there's a good case for arguing that in the pre-modern world, pathocracy was less endemic than in recent times – particularly compared to the second half of the twentieth century, when pathocracy reached its zenith.

If you were a citizen of Ancient Rome, there was a good chance of being ruled by an emperor as psychopathic as Stalin or Hitler. The second emperor Tiberius (who ruled AD 14-37) was as paranoid as Stalin, and executed anybody he suspected of disloyalty. He was also a serial rapist who kept sex slaves. Tiberius was followed by the famously degenerate Caligula (who ruled AD 37-41) who proclaimed himself as a god and also ruthlessly killed his enemies. The emperor Domitian (who came to power 27 years after Nero) also demanded to be treated as a god. The Roman historian Cassius Dio provides a clear description of Domitian's psychopathic traits: "He was not only bold and quick to anger but also treacherous and secretive... he would often attack people with the sudden violence of a thunderbolt and again would often injure them as the result of careful deliberation."[3]

On the other hand, some emperors were reasonable and sensible people, with some degree of empathy and conscience. Historians sometimes refer to the "five good emperors" of Ancient Rome, who ruled for a period of 84 years, from AD 96 to 180. Not uncoincidentally, this was the period when the Roman Empire was at its peak of power and prosperity. One of the good emperors was Marcus Aurelius, a rare example of the ideal of the "philosopher-king" envisaged by the Greek philosopher Plato. As described in his famous *Meditations* (a book which still reads as a spiritual classic now), Marcus followed the philosophy of stoicism, which is akin to Buddhism in its emphasis on acceptance and detachment. Marcus attempted to embody stoic principles in his role as emperor, living simply, accepting his duties without complaint and respecting others. As the ancient historian Herodian wrote of him, "Alone of the emperors, he gave proof of his learning not by mere words or knowledge of philosophical doctrines but by his blameless character and temperate way of life."[4]

One of Marcus's role models was the earlier "good emperor" Antoninus Pius (who reigned AD 138-161). In his own writings, Marcus describes Antoninus as modest and tolerant, and dedicated to improving the lives of ordinary people. He built many aqueducts, roads and bridges. When natural disasters occurred in the empire, he altruistically suspended taxes from the affected regions.

The monarchs of pre-modern Europe follow a similar mixed pattern, although with perhaps a slightly lower ratio of "good monarchs" to bad ones. Many European monarchies could certainly be described as pathocracies. For example, Henry VIII of England was probably as highly disconnected as Stalin or Hitler, even though his brutality manifested itself on a smaller scale. Henry was sadistic and paranoid, and historians have estimated that during the 36 years of his reign he was responsible for the execution of around 60,000 people. He also famously executed two of his wives and presided over the looting and destruction of hundreds of monasteries. With the kind of self-centredness that can only arise from extreme disconnection, Henry broke with the Catholic Church and founded the Church of England simply so that he could divorce one of his wives.

However, as with the Roman Emperors, some monarchs appear to have been fairly reasonable and decent people, with a degree of empathy and conscience. Amongst British monarchs, Henry VI (who reigned for 40 years altogether during the 15th century) seems to have been a genuinely good person. A piously religious man with little interest in warfare, he had a reputation for courtesy and kindness. In the aggressive environment of the period (and especially in comparison to his warrior father, Henry V), his empathy and sensitivity were interpreted as weakness. His decency made him unpopular amongst other members of the ruling class, and led to his ejection from the throne, and ultimately to his execution.

George III (who reigned for 60 years, from 1760-1820) also has a reputation for decency and empathy, despite his role in provoking in the American War of Independence. When Senator John Adams visited the king, he was impressed by his friendliness and hospitality, and the way he doted on his children. The novelist Fanny Burney – a member of the king's court – also remarked on his kindness and fairness. George was a cultured man, with a keen interest in literature and science. He took his role as king very seriously and annoyed some of his ministers by carefully scrutinising government policy. (In his later years, George suffered from mental illness, which has clouded his reputation somewhat.) The present British monarch – Elizabeth II – also appears to be a person of integrity and morality. I'm certainly not a royalist – in my view, the Royal Family is an absurd outmoded institution – but I've been very impressed by the Queen's sense of duty and responsibility, and the dignified way in which she conducts herself.

In Europe as a whole, there have been other kings with a reputation for fairness and decency. This includes the so-called "enlightened monarchs" of the 18th century, of whom the best example is probably Joseph II of Austria. Joseph was an intelligent and cultured man, who acted as a patron of musicians, artists and philosophers. He also reduced taxes for peasants and, at a time when religious conflict was still rife, encouraged religious tolerance.

Another example – ironically and sadly, in view of what came afterwards – was the last Czar of Russia, Nicholas II. He is usually described by historians as a gentle, well-meaning person, who loved spending time quietly with his wife and family. Like Henry VI, he was ill-suited to the role of the Czar, and ill-equipped to deal with the chaotic, febrile political atmosphere around him. He attempted to be fair and just, while at the same time ruthless to his political opponents. These efforts were doomed to failure, and along with the whole of his family, he was executed on Lenin's orders in 1918.

Hierarchy as a Barrier to Pathocracy

There is a good reason why pathocracy was less common before the 20th century, and why there were some examples of decent and responsible leaders. Pre-modern societies were strongly hierarchical, and power was usually hereditary rather than acquired. As a result, power was only accessible to a small pool of people. Even when – as with Roman Emperors – the role of leader was non-hereditary, rulers were chosen from a small elite group, membership of which was itself hereditary. The entire ruling class was a homogeneous, independent group which you couldn't belong to unless you were born into it.

In such societies, there was little or no social mobility. The dividing lines between different classes were strong, and very difficult to cross. If you were born as a peasant, you would remain a peasant for the rest of your life, and your children would be peasants too. The nobles or aristocrats who owned the land that you farmed had attained their positions by birthright, and you had no chance of joining their ranks, in the same way that an animal has no chance of becoming a member of another species.

The only way of overturning hereditary power was through military force. If you had a desperate desire to attain power – for example, if you didn't like the present king and thought you had a justifiable claim to be king yourself – you could raise an army, and attempt an insurrection, which might lead to a civil war. But even in these cases, if power changed hands, it would only be passed on to other members of the aristocracy or nobility. The closest a peasant would come to the seat of power would be when they were enlisted by their landlords to fight for the king or his attempted usurper, whether they wanted to or not.

I certainly don't want to romanticise or defend pre-modern societies, which had high levels of injustice, oppression and inequality. Social hierarchy is itself a disconnective trait. As we will see in Chapter 10 (when I examine disconnected societies in more detail), the more disconnected societies are, the greater the gulf is between different classes or castes, with less social mobility and equality of opportunity. However, one paradoxical positive effect of the extreme hierarchy of pre-modern societies was that there was less opportunity for hyper-disconnected people to attain power. Like everyone else, hyper-disconnected people (assuming they weren't born into a privileged class) were constrained by their social position. They might become violent criminals who would terrorise their family and local community, but they would be unable to gain any real degree of power or authority. No matter how strong their psychopathic traits, they would be unable to start wars, to persecute minority groups, or to execute people who they suspected of conspiring against them.

If they had been born a hundred years earlier, it would have been almost impossible for Hitler or Stalin to become leaders of their countries, given their humble origins. In fact, almost all of the worst dictators of the 20th century came from very humble and even extremely deprived backgrounds. This was the case with Chairman Mao, Mussolini, General Franco of Spain, and more recent examples such as Pol Pot of Cambodia or Manuel Noriega of Panama. A century earlier, their destructive influence would have been dramatically limited.

In societies without social structures or strong democratic institutions, it's inevitable that the most disconnected people rise into powerful positions, impelled by their greed, ruthlessness, cruelty and grandiosity. Even in modern democracies such as the US and the UK, there is a strong possibility that hyper-disconnected people will become political leaders.

But in pre-modern times, there was very little possibility of *anybody* rising into positions of high power.

In other words, despite their inherent oppression, pre-modern societies kept hyper-disconnected people in check. If around one in 100 people have psychopathic traits, then a country of five million people – equivalent to England in the Middle Ages – would have around fifty thousand psychopaths. Most of those fifty thousand people would be peasants, and so would be unable to inflict much damage on their society.

Modern societies are also hierarchical to some degree, of course. However, there is certainly much *more* mobility in modern societies, and so more opportunity for the most disconnected people to attain powerful positions.

Pre-Modern Pathocracy and
Environmental Narcissism

In the light of the above, you might ask: if hyper-disconnected people were less likely to occupy positions of power in pre-modern times, why were there so many brutal and narcissistic kings, emperors, and aristocrats? Why weren't more rulers benevolent and responsible people? Why did so many aristocrats and nobles treat their serfs and peasants so appallingly?

There are many accounts from the Middle Ages of landowners exploiting and abusing their peasants and serfs. Female peasants were sometimes raped by landlords, who would also take advantage of what historians euphemistically call *le droit du seigneur* – the master's "right" to have sex with serfs' brides on the wedding night. Peasants were also liable to be brutally punished for insignificant crimes, including the death penalty for stealing any of the master's food or property. In a more general sense, landowners commonly exploited peasants with high rents and taxes, along with tithes and fines. If only one in a hundred members of the ruling class were psychopathic, why did so many exhibit so much psychopathic behaviour?

This is, in fact, a useful reminder that disconnection is

linked to social factors. One factor that can certainly intensify narcissism is an environment of privilege and indulgence. Like power, privilege has a corrupting influence. Even if biological or childhood factors don't predispose a person to narcissism, a privileged social environment can engender disconnection, creating a sense of superiority and entitlement. This "environmental narcissism" helps to explain some of the pathocratic elements of pre-modern ruling elites. Monarchs, aristocrats and nobles were brought up to think of themselves as different and superior to the peasants or serfs whose lives they controlled. As a result, most members of the ruling class probably had an ingrained lack of empathy towards ordinary people, an inability to see the world from their perspective or to apply principles of morality and justice to them.

The "leadership trap" I described in the last chapter also helps to explain the brutality of many pre-modern monarchs and emperors. One of the ways that power corrupts is through attention and admiration, which encourage narcissism. The more attention and admiration we receive, the more special and superior we perceive ourselves to be. Given that emperors and kings were constantly surrounded by fawning admirers or servants and sycophantic colleagues, it's not surprising that many of them became highly narcissistic, seeing themselves as gods, or the servant of God.

In many cases, the effects of the leadership trap were probably exacerbated by insecurity. For example, it's not surprising that many Roman emperors became paranoid, since they were in a brutal and dangerous environment, with people conspiring against them. In fact, to become an emperor was effectively to condemn yourself to an early death. Of 79 emperors, 37 were murdered or forced to kill themselves, while several more disappeared under mysterious circumstances.

Another important point is that most pre-modern societies were highly disconnected *as a whole*. Life was extremely hard for the vast majority of people, and brutality and cruelty pervaded everyday life. People treated children and animals with a level of cruelty that would shock most of us nowadays, and criminals were punished with a sadistic severity. Compassion and altruism were rare. As one historian remarked of life in 17th century England, "Pity was still a strange and valuable emotion."[5] (We will examine the disconnection of such pre-modern societies in more detail in Chapter 10.) In this context, the brutality of some Roman emperors and European kings wasn't so exceptional.

Overall, I don't think the disconnection of pre-modern ruling elites – even with the effects of environmental narcissism, the leadership trap and the general disconnection of their societies – was as severe as the leaders of twentieth pathocracies. In fact, it's striking that, even in such negative circumstances, we do find some pre-modern leaders with empathy and conscience. That such qualities could flourish even in such brutal social conditions emphasises how innate they are, stemming from our fundamental state of connection.

Chapter 5

The Most Murderous Century: Twentieth Century Pathocracy

Towards the end of the 18th century in Europe, a wave of social change began. Although some monarchs – such as Joseph II of Austria – were associated with the European Enlightenment movement, it made the inborn privileges of monarchs and aristocrats seem outmoded and absurd. Philosophers, poets and musicians expressed revolutionary ideas of democracy, equality and freedom. New vistas of opportunity seemed to open up, along with new possibilities of happiness and fulfilment. During the same era, the Industrial Revolution weakened the power of landowning nobles and aristocrats, whose peasants left their farms to work at the new factories, mills and mines. Slowly, the power and privilege of the old ruling elites began to ebb away.

In theory, this movement was an advance in social connection, leading to greater egalitarianism and social justice. However, in many cases, the breakdown of the old social structures had a dangerous side effect. Particularly when change occurred dramatically in the form of revolution, and when societies lacked democratic systems to regulate the use of power, the effects were disastrous. Pathocracy became endemic throughout the world. What should have been a movement towards social connection led to even greater brutality and oppression.

Twentieth Century Pathocracy

When future historians look back at the 20th century, they may well see it as the century of pathocracy. Certainly, it was the darkest century in the history of the human race, in terms of the sheer number of people who were murdered, and in terms of the sheer amount of suffering and destruction caused by hyper-disconnected people in power. Writing in 1994, the historian Eric Hobsbawm estimated that between 1914 and 1991, 187 million people were "killed or allowed to die by human decision"[1] – that is, through wars and other conflicts, and acts of persecution and oppression. More recent estimates have increased the figure to 231 million over the whole of the century.[2]

All over the world, as centuries-old social structures broke down, hyper-disconnected people with an insatiable lust for power were let loose, like psychopathic prisoners released into society. Now they were free to terrorise whole societies, and even the whole world. In most countries, there were no democratic institutions and processes to restrain them. As hyper-disconnected people fought against one another for power, savage conflicts erupted everywhere, and the most brutal and most disconnected people emerged victorious. Moral and responsible people disappeared from public view, often imprisoned or murdered, as hyper-disconnected people took over leadership positions.

Naturally, pathocratic regimes around the world fell into conflict with each other too. Like hyper-disconnected individuals, pathocratic regimes have an insatiable lust for power, wealth and prestige, which manifests itself in a drive to gain territory and to conquer other peoples. They are often fixated on notions of national "greatness", usually framed in terms of a return to a former – largely fictitious – state of glory and power. Military power becomes a means of both capturing territory and restoring national prestige. For example, in Nazi Germany, the drive for territory was expressed as a need to increase the German people's *lebensraum* – literally, room for living. A return to former glory (together with the promise of future greatness) were encapsulated as a movement to create the Third Reich – literally, the third empire, after the Holy Roman Empire and the German empire of the late 19th and early 20th centuries.

The competing drives of pathocratic regimes around the world to gain power and prestige resulted in the two bloodiest wars in human history. Historians have estimated that over the 150 years from 1750 to 1900, around 30 million human beings around the world died in warfare. This figure is terrible enough, but it is only half the number of people who died in the combined ten years of the First and Second World Wars.

At the same time, one of the most striking things about 20th century pathocracies is that they also declared war on their own people. In their paranoia and sadism, pathocrats such as Stalin, Hitler and Mao Zedong (better known as Chairman Mao) were determined to eliminate any potential opposition to their regimes, and also to "cleanse" their societies of impure elements. (Significantly, as an unconscious symbol of their hatred for human beings, pathocrats often use metaphors of health, purity and disease, and speak of ridding their countries of vermin, viruses or poison.) As we saw in the last chapter, Stalin was responsible for the deaths of around 20 million Russians. Even more shockingly, a 1994 report from the Chinese Academy of Social Sciences estimated that 80 million people died as the direct result of the policies of Mao Zedong from 1950 to 1976.[3]

In Europe, the pathocracy of Hitler and the Nazis, and Stalin and the Soviet Union was accompanied with the pathocracy of Mussolini's Italy and Franco's Spain. Like Hitler and Stalin, Mussolini and Franco were both from humble backgrounds, and the children of violent alcoholic fathers. From a young age, Mussolini and Franco showed signs of psychopathic cruelty, and complete indifference to the feelings of others. As a child, Mussolini was a violent thug who was expelled from school for stabbing a classmate. He also stabbed a girlfriend and led a gang which raided local farms.

Both dictators also had the same grandiose sense of self-importance as Hitler and Stalin, and the same fanatical desire for power. These traits – combined with their charisma, oratory skills and cunning intelligence – made it almost inevitable that they would become powerful figures. They are a good illustration of the rule that, in the absence of strong social structures or democratic systems, the most psychopathic and disconnected people become the most powerful people.

The same process occurred in China, a few years after the demise of Hitler and Mussolini. As with Russia in 1917, a long period of political turbulence in China led to the establishment of a communist state in 1949. The leader of the communist party, Mao Zedong, was as severely disconnected as any leader we have mentioned so far, although with some slight variations. The main traits of Mao's hyper-disconnection were his extreme narcissism and sadism. He saw himself as a "great hero" who was exempt from the rules of normal human behaviour and so could express every impulse and desire without restraint. He also had a strong impulse to inflict suffering and pain, which he did incessantly in his three decades as China's supreme leader. As a sadist, he was exhilarated by torture and murder, and realised that he could use both as a way of attaining and maintaining power. As leader of the communist party, he used mass public executions to instil fear, and once he became leader of China as a whole, he extended the practice throughout the country. The attendance of executions became compulsory for adults and children alike.

Like all hyper-disconnected leaders, once he had attained power Mao became increasingly paranoid, perceiving enemies everywhere and mercilessly eliminating them. In his first decade in power, he killed at least five million people – farmers, businessmen, university-educated people and anyone else he perceived as a potential enemy or obstacle. In 1958, Mao began his Great Leap Forward, his policy of shifting the Chinese economy from privately owned farms to communist communes. This was his equivalent of Stalin's enforced collectivisation and was even more devastating, causing around 30 million deaths due to starvation.

Pathocracy After the Second World War

After the catastrophe of the Second World War, there were some efforts to increase cooperation between countries, leading to the formation of the United Nations and the European Community. In 1948, a Declaration of Human Rights was created by the 50 member states of the United Nations, agreeing that all people had the right to life, liberty and security. In most of Western Europe, there was a retreat from pathocracy and a movement towards democracy. Countries such as the UK, Germany, France and the Scandinavian countries implemented programmes of social democracy that were designed to curb the excesses of capitalism, and to ensure a basic degree of security and equality for everyone. In the UK, this led to the creation of the National Health Service and the Welfare State. In the United States, Franklin Roosevelt's New Deal provided a similar purpose, regulating the free market and offering some protection from poverty and destitution.

However, elsewhere pathocracy spread around the world like an epidemic. After the Second World War, Stalin took control of Eastern Europe, which led to the development of many other pathocratic regimes, masquerading as communist states. The eight new communist countries were closely modelled on Stalin's own regime, with puppet leaders who blindly followed his orders. It's sadly ironic that communism was supposed to create egalitarian societies in which property and wealth were fairly distributed and power was shared. In reality, every communist regime has been a pathocracy in which an elite group of government officials and party members have dominated and oppressed the majority of ordinary people. Like Russia itself, the new communist countries all had massive secret police forces who terrorised their populations. People were arbitrarily arrested and tortured, convicted without trial (or at least a fair trial) and sent to labour camps at the slightest pretext. There was a constant bombardment of propaganda from every possible channel. Anyone whose thoughts deviated from the state-sanctioned view of reality was in danger of persecution and punishment.

Certainly, some politicians and officials from these regimes were naive idealists who genuinely believed that they were acting in the best interests of society. However, it's likely that most positions of power were filled with hyper-disconnected people without political principles, who were simply taking the opportunity to express their malevolent traits. Moral and responsible people would usually remain as lower-level workers, or else be imprisoned or exiled, with disconnected people as their supervisors or prison guards.

In South America, a lack of democratic systems meant that there was little to prevent the most disconnected people becoming leaders, who then expressed their dark triad traits through the violence and repression of their governments. The pathocratic regimes of Franco and Mussolini were an inspiration to a whole host of South American military leaders with political ambitions. In many cases, these leaders attained power with the support of the United States, whose government was so terrified of communism that they were willing to support almost any right-wing regime, no matter how repressive or violent.

By 1977, 17 of the 20 South American countries were pathocracies, ruled by fascist dictatorships who waged war on their own populations through imprisonment, torture and murder. The most enduring was the pathocracy of Alfredo Stroessner of Paraguay, who held power for 35 years until 1989. For almost all that time, Paraguay was literally in "a state of siege", renewed by Stroessner every 90 days until 1987. This meant that people could be arrested and detained indefinitely without trial, and that public meetings and demonstrations were forbidden. Although the country's constitution guaranteed freedom of the press, journalists were tortured and imprisoned, and any media outlets that criticised the government were closed down.

In Argentina, a military junta – led by Jorge Rafael Videla – ruled between 1977 and 1983 and killed an estimated 30,000 people. In Chile, General Augusto Pinochet took power in a military coup in 1973, with the support of the United States (who opposed the democratically elected socialist government of Salvador Allende). Over the 17 years of his rule, Pinochet destroyed every semblance of democracy and abused human rights on a massive scale. In an attempt to crush all opposition and dissent, over 3000 people were killed for political reasons, and 80,000 people were imprisoned.

Colonial Pathocracy

The first genocide of the 20th century was perpetrated between 1904 and 1908 by German forces against the Herero people of Southwest Africa. Under the auspices of the pathocratic Prussian government, the German commander declared a race war, ordering his soldiers to "pursue until death" all Herero men, women and children. After a domestic and international outcry, Kaiser Wilhelm overruled his commander and revoked the order, but the soldiers followed it anyway. Around 100,000 Herero people are believed to have died, along with tens of thousands of members of neighbouring tribes (the Damara and Nama) whom the German forces also attacked.

This exemplifies another way in which the pathocratic drive for power, wealth and prestige has always manifested itself: the desire to conquer other peoples and colonise their territories. Although colonialism has existed since ancient times, as far back as Ancient Egypt and Greece, European nations began to compete with each other to colonise the wider world during the 15th century. By the end of the 19th century, the native populations of the whole American continent, from Canada to South America, had been decimated, with their cultures largely destroyed and their ancestral lands stolen. The pre-colonial population of the American continent was probably around 50 million, but after European contact the indigenous population declined rapidly. By 1860, there were only 340,000 Indians left in North America, and by 1920 the figure had decreased even further, to 220,000.

As regimes became more pathocratic towards the end of the 19th century, these brutal expansionist enterprises intensified even further. Desperate to increase national prestige and to attain new natural resources, European armies invaded vast areas of Africa and the Middle East and subjugated their populations. At a conference in Berlin in 1884, the "scramble for Africa" – as historians sometimes call it – was legitimatised. The entire continent was divided between European powers as if it were a cake. To justify their occupation, the European powers told themselves they were bringing the benefits of civilisation to primitive people. But any pretence of benevolence was betrayed by the ongoing persecution and exploitation of native populations, and genocides such as the Herero massacre. Between 1885 and 1908, an estimated 10 million Congolese people died at the hands of Belgian colonialists. In 1923, Spanish soldiers were defeated in a battle by Moroccan tribesman, and took revenge by dropping mustard gas bombs over Moroccan villages indiscriminately, killing thousands of civilians. In 1935, Mussolini's desire for prestige and power led him to invade Ethiopia, resulting in one of the most murderous conflicts of the whole colonial era, in which close to three-quarters of a million Ethiopians died.

Post-Colonial Pathocracy
After the Second World War, European nations were financially crippled and could no longer maintain their colonies, which led to their independence. Naturally, the populations of these new countries rejoiced in their freedom, believing that they were

entering a new era of prosperity and harmony. However, in almost all cases, the pathocracy of European colonialism was quickly replaced by new, home-grown pathocracies.

This was almost inevitable, since these newly independent countries lacked social structures and democratic systems. Under colonial rule, traditional ways of life had been disrupted, and traditional social and political systems had broken down. In addition, the European colonists had established artificial borders, leading to the arbitrary creation of nations where none had existed before. This disrupted traditional ethnic or tribal identities, causing tension and conflict. As with Russia and China after their communist revolutions, this chaos and lack of social structure was a perfect breeding ground for pathocracy. All over Africa and in parts of the Middle East, there was nothing to stop the most psychopathic people rising into positions of high power.

In the Middle East, the country of Iraq had never existed before British colonial rule. It was created as the British Mandate of Mesopotamia after the First World War, when the British also installed a loyalist king, Faisal. The new nation was a clumsy imposition over a complex mix of different ethnic and religious groups, with no sense of unity but a great deal of enmity. So when Iraq gained independence in 1932, there was little prospect of the different groups living in harmony. An atmosphere of conflict and chaos soon arose, as power-hungry individuals and groups competed for prominence.

Saddam Hussein was born into this febrile atmosphere in 1937, to a single mother who lived in a mud hut. Saddam's father and older brother both had died shortly before his birth, leaving his mother so traumatised that she rejected Saddam, who was taken in by his uncle. As the only child of a single mother, he was constantly bullied and beaten as a child, and learned to be violent in self-defence.

In other words – like so many other hyper-disconnected

people – Saddam experienced severe emotional deprivation during early childhood, which shut down his capacity for empathy. He became brutal and violent, with a wily intelligence, which were the ideal qualities for a political agitator. Joining the anti-British Ba'ath party, Saddam quickly rose to prominence due to his eagerness to commit acts of violence. Once the British-backed monarchy was overthrown, Saddam rose rapidly through the ranks of the new government. By his mid-thirties he was already the *de facto* leader of Iraq, becoming the official leader in 1979.

For the next 24 years, he terrorised his country with a similar degree of mendacity to Stalin and Mao, with regular purges and genocides carried out by his security forces. It's estimated that around a quarter of a million Iraqis were killed under his instructions. Hundreds of thousands of other people died as a result of his military actions, such as his invasions of Iran and Kuwait.

With their incessant need for attention, and their grandiose sense of self-importance, pathocratic leaders always establish personality cults, presenting themselves as omnipotent quasi-divine figures. Saddam's personality cult was especially extreme. While terrorising his people, he demanded their adulation. His image was omnipresent, imprinted on every bank note and coin and emblazoned on the walls of schools and airports and shops. Towns, mosques and even rivers were named after him. Children were encouraged to call him "Daddy Saddam", while banners proclaimed that "Iraq is Saddam and Saddam is Iraq." Officials competed to be as sycophantic as possible to their leader.

In North Africa, a similar process propelled Muammar Gaddafi to power in Libya, which gained independence after more than 30 years as an Italian colony (and previously a colony of the Ottoman Empire). The similarities between Saddam Hussein and Gaddafi are striking – although not at all surprising, given that they were both hyper-disconnected individuals born into similar circumstances. Like Saddam, Gaddafi's background was extremely deprived. He was born in a Bedouin desert tribe, to an illiterate goat and camel herder. At the age of 8, he effectively left home to attend a school 20 miles away and would only see his parents at the weekend.

Gaddafi's rise to power was even more meteoric than Saddam's. Propelled by a cunning intelligence and fanatical lust for power, he was just 27 when he helped overthrow Libya's European-backed monarchy in 1969. He ruled Libya for the next 42 years, terrorising his people with detention without trial, torture and public executions. However, Gaddafi's most prevalent trait was his extreme narcissism. Initially, he projected this on to Libya itself, determined to make his small country of six million people a "major player" on the world stage. He attempted to achieve this by supporting terrorist organisations around the world, including the IRA and Farc in Colombia, supplying them with weapons and explosives. He staged his own terrorist attacks too, such as the bombing of an American passenger plane in 1988, in which 270 people were killed, including people in the village of Lockerbie, Scotland, where the plane crashed.

Predictably, however, Gaddafi's terrorist activities ostracised him from the world community and so deprived him of the status and attention he craved. To compensate, he directed his need for attention and reverence internally, within Libya itself. As with Saddam, he imposed his personality over every aspect of life, and his image over almost every available public space. He awarded himself increasingly grandiose titles, such as "Imam of all Muslims" and the "King of Africa's kings". He wore increasingly bizarre clothes, sometimes changing several times a day, in an apparent desire to attract attention.

At the same time, Gaddafi became more violent and sadistic. After murdering his enemies, he would keep the bodies in freezers, so that he could look at them and gloat. After his death, it emerged that he was a violent sexual predator who had raped hundreds of victims. Multiple accounts stated that his standard practice was to tour a school or university, and single out pretty girls to his security guards, by patting them on the head. The girls would then be kidnapped and used as his sex slaves.

In sub-Saharan Africa, a similar pattern unfolded in country after country. In the post-colonial chaos, hyper-disconnected people vied for positions of power, with the most brutal and violent people winning. Installed as rulers, these hyper-disconnected people became even more brutal, inflicting massive amounts of suffering on populations. One of the most well-known examples was Idi Amin, who gained power in Uganda in the aftermath of British colonial rule. Although Western media portrayed him as a harmless buffoon, Amin was a man with severe psychopathic and sadistic traits, who viewed human beings as inanimate objects. Torture and murder were to him the equivalent of pulling weeds out of the ground. In the eight years of his rule, between 300,000 and half a million of his own people were murdered.

A lesser known but equally horrific example is the dictator of the Democratic Republic of Congo, Mobutu Sese Sako. He showed a psychopathic indifference to anyone's well-being apart from his own and his family's. From the moment he attained power in 1965, Sako's sole aim was to make himself wealthy by plundering the nation's resources. After consolidating his power with the familiar tactic of mass public executions, he siphoned off vast amounts of money meant for civil and public servants, which resulted in the decay of the country's infrastructure. By 1984 his fortune had increased to $5 billion. While millions of his country struggled to keep themselves alive, Mobutu and his acolytes used a fleet of Mercedes-Benzes to travel between his various palaces, which included replicas of the Palace of Versailles and the Imperial Palace of Peking.

He regularly chartered Concorde for shopping trips to Paris, and often flew in the world's leading chefs to cook for him. For example, in 1985, Gaston Lenôtre, France's leading pastry chef, flew in on Concorde with a birthday cake for Mobutu.

There are so many examples of hyper-disconnected leaders in 20th century Africa, but it's difficult to think of a more extreme case than Francisco Macías Nguema, who ruled Equatorial Guinea from 1969 to 1979. Nguema had the typical traumatic and emotionally deprived childhood of hyper-disconnected people. Aged nine, he witnessed his father's murder, which was followed by his mother's suicide a week later. As leader, his paranoia was so extreme that (like Pol Pot of Cambodia) he ordered the death of everyone who wore spectacles, afraid that anyone who read books would pose a threat to his regime. He forbade the use of the term "intellectual" and banned fishing and sailing, to stop people fleeing his regime by boat. Like Gaddafi, he awarded himself an array of grandiose titles such as the "Grand Master of Education, Science, and Culture". Eventually he proclaimed himself as a god, changing the national motto to: "There is no other God than Macías Nguema." By 1978, around half of Equatorial Guinea's population had fled the country, due to the brutality and mismanagement of Nguema's regime.

In 1979, Nguema was ousted from power and killed by his nephew, Teodoro Obiang Nguema Mbasogo, who still holds power in 2022. Sadly, his leadership has been almost as brutal and corrupt as his uncle's. Obiang has plundered his country's oil resources, accumulating a fortune of around £600 million. Like his uncle – and most other pathocracies – his regime routinely practises torture, murder and abduction. In 2003, following in his uncle's footsteps, government-run radio stations declared that he was the country's god who possessed "all power over men and things," and had the right to "kill without anyone calling him to account and without going to hell."

Many African governments have exemplified a specific type

of pathocracy – *kleptocracy*, literally government by thieves. Many African countries have abundant natural resources – such as Angola, which has massive oil reserves and diamond mines – which could easily guarantee the whole population a reasonable standard of living, if they were shared equitably. But many governments have simply kept the wealth created by resources for themselves, at the same time as stealing public and government funds which should be used to pay officials and public servants, and to maintain infrastructure. This has resulted in enormous inequality between ruling elites and ordinary people.

After this brief survey, it seems justifiable to state that pathocracy was the world's most common system of government during the 20th century. Lobaczewski believed that pathocracies develop partly because psychopathic leaders succeed in spreading their pathology to the masses. The best example of this is Nazi Germany, and it is also true of Mussolini's Italy and Franco's Spain. But it's tempting to wonder whether there are exceptions. Although it's difficult to judge how popular they were, most of the pathocrats we've looked at in this chapter maintained their power not through spreading their pathology to the masses, but simply through oppression and violence. In most cases, they maintained power for such long periods simply because they created such a powerful climate of fear and suspicion that no one dared resist them.

Pathocracies such as these function without the support of the masses. In fact, regimes like Saddam Hussein's and Gaddafi's illustrate the resilience and independence of the human mind. Despite extreme personality cults, and the constant bombardment of propaganda from every possible source, a large proportion of ordinary Libyans and Iraqis were never taken in by their leaders, who they secretly despised and opposed. This is also true of the communist regimes of Eastern

Europe, where a healthy proportion of the population never supported their governments, despite endless propaganda.

Since pathocracies have been so common, it's worth remembering that the hyper-disconnected individuals who constitute them are actually quite rare. As we saw in Chapter 2, psychologists have estimated that between a half to one per cent of people have psychopathic traits, with a similar figure for narcissistic personality disorder. It's remarkable that such a tiny minority has dominated the world's governments and been responsible for so much of the chaos and violence that has filled recent human history. This illustrates how easily hyper-disconnected people attain power, and why we need to take measures to protect ourselves from them.

Chapter 6

From Psychopaths to Narcissists: Pathocracy in the 21st Century

So where are we now, in the 21st century? In some parts of the world, there has been a movement away from pathocracy. In 1990, the communist pathocracies of Eastern Europe dissolved, and after some years of instability, most countries have adopted democratic systems of government. In South America, there has been a resurgence in democracy, leaving just three dictatorships in 2022. Similarly, in sub-Saharan Africa there have been many positive developments. In the 1990s, multi-party elections were introduced in most African countries, along with increasing civil liberties and freedom of the press.

Elsewhere, progress has been more limited. In North Africa and the Middle East, the "Arab Spring" of the early 2010s brought a new wave of optimism, with the overthrow of pathocratic leaders such as Gaddafi, Ben Ali of Tunisia and Mubarak of Egypt. However, in most cases – as happened at the end of the colonial era – political instability has created social unrest and conflict, leading to the emergence of new pathocracies. After Gaddafi's death, Libya quickly dissolved into civil war, with various armed groups fighting over territory and power. In Egypt, a democratically elected president was driven from office in a military coup in 2013. The present government of Abdel Fattah el-Sissi has become increasingly pathocratic, rigging elections and using imprisonment, torture, sexual violence to try to silence critics.

Meanwhile, the largest countries in the world, Russia and China, are still pathocracies, with ruthless amoral leaders. While they haven't (at least so far) caused death and destruction on the same scale as Stalin or Mao Zedong, the present-day Russian and

Chinese leaders (and their regimes) show a similar antipathy to basic democratic principles such as freedom of speech and fair elections. They also show a similar enthusiasm for pathocratic practices such as imprisoning and torturing political opponents. As I write this (in early March 2022), Russian forces have just invaded Ukraine, in an expansionist desire for conquest – and an unconscious desire to create chaos and destruction – which is reminiscent of the Nazi invasions which provoked the Second World War.

A Shift to Narcissistic Leaders

It's also important to remember that, as I mentioned in Chapter 4, pathocracies don't just exist in the form of dictatorships. A milder form of pathocracy can emerge in democratic countries. Modern democratic systems regulate the behaviour of hyper-disconnected people once they are *in* power, but they aren't very effective at preventing them from attaining power in the first place. In fact, hyper-disconnected people's cunning and charisma means that they are good at winning elections. They are happy to lie, to make promises they know they can't meet, and to ruthlessly undermine their opponents. And once they attain power, there is a danger of hyper-disconnected leaders destroying democracy. They don't believe in democracy – don't understand it, even – and resent the limits it places on their authority. So they do everything they can to undermine it.

In the early 21st century, a shift to this milder and more insidious form of pathocracy has emerged in the democracies of Europe and North America. Along with this, there has been a change in the type of hyper-disconnected individuals who attain power. In politically unstable countries without democratic systems, leaders tend to have predominately *psychopathic* traits, that predispose them to brutality and sadism. In democratic societies, hyper-disconnected leaders tend to have predominantly *narcissistic* traits.

Leaders with predominantly psychopathic traits aren't suited to democratic countries with established traditions of human rights and civil liberties, since they can't give free rein to their cruelty and sadism. They may also be uncomfortable with the constant glare of media attention, preferring to operate more secretively. However, narcissistic leaders crave admiration and attention. They relish the continual attention of mass media and social media, which continually reinforces their sense of self-importance. They love to pretend to be altruistic figures who have entered politics to work selflessly for the common good, when in reality they are completely self-centred. (At the same time, as the dark triad concept makes clear, psychopathic and narcissistic traits – together with Machiavellianism – almost always exist in combination, so such leaders will certainly possess the other traits too.)

In fact, now that social media such as Twitter and Facebook have increased the amount of attention that politicians receive, the role has become even more attractive to narcissists – and arguably less attractive to ordinary people who lack psychopathic and narcissistic traits. After all, who would actually *want* to become a politician in the modern age? As a career choice, it isn't particularly attractive – long hours, a high level of stress and pressure, a heavy load of responsibility, constant complaints and criticism from the media, a lack of job security, and so on. It isn't even particularly well paid, at least compared to other high-status jobs. In the UK, the salary of members of Parliament is around £80,000, less than the average head teacher or lawyer. It's also very expensive to get a political career off the ground. If you want to stand to be a member of Parliament in the UK, it costs thousands of pounds, and is a time-consuming process. If you want to be a senator in the US, it is many times more expensive. Who would actually *want* to put themselves through such stress, pressure and expense, for relatively little reward?

Perhaps some intensely altruistic people would be willing to do this, to gain the opportunity to enact positive change. But in most cases, it would be people with a strong desire for power, prestige and attention – which means hyper-disconnected people with predominantly narcissistic traits. Only to them would the benefits of political power seem to outweigh its negative aspects.

21st Century Narcissists

Let's look at some examples of narcissists who have formed pathocratic governments in ostensibly democratic countries.

In Chapter 3, I mentioned that one of the best career avenues for hyper-disconnected people was the corporate world. However, there's no reason why hyper-disconnected people should stick with just one career, and it's not surprising that some business magnates have tried their hand at politics too. Also in Chapter 3, we discussed the publishing tycoon Robert Maxwell, who was a Labour politician in the 1960s, before concentrating fully on his business career. Usually, however, business magnates move in the opposite direction, and enter politics later in their career, when the business world has begun to exhaust its sources of power and prestige. Like conquerors who have laid waste to one country, they begin to look for other territories to dominate.

This was the case with the Italian businessman Silvio Berlusconi, who dominated the Italian political scene from the mid-1990s onwards. Berlusconi has a very similar personality profile to Robert Maxwell, with the same insatiable desire to accumulate. He built up a vast array of business interests, including property developments, TV stations and AC Milan football club. All through his business career, he was dogged by allegations of criminality, including colluding with the Italian Mafia. He was also an insatiable womaniser, who exasperated his wives with his constant affairs.

After making his fortune as a businessman, Berlusconi entered politics. He followed an unashamedly populist approach that appealed to working-class Italians, who were frustrated with the instability and corruption of Italian politics. His appeal was similar to Mussolini's several decades earlier, as an authoritarian who could provide unity and reawaken a sense of national pride. He was a fairly popular politician, in spite of (and perhaps because of) his grandiosity, his misogynism, his luxurious lifestyle, and a series of bizarre decisions, such as handing important government roles to ex-glamour models and escort girls. Throughout his periods as Prime Minister, Berlusconi promoted his own companies' interests, and undermined the freedom of the press by using his own media outlets as propaganda channels. Eventually, his habitual corruption caught up with him, and he was convicted of tax fraud in 2013.

The Case of Donald Trump

When Donald Trump emerged as a presidential candidate for the American Republican Party, his similarities with Berlusconi were noted almost immediately. Certainly, the similarities are as striking as those between Saddam Hussein and Colonel Gaddafi. But again, this isn't at all surprising, since Berlusconi and Trump are both hyper-disconnected people with predominantly narcissistic traits, born into similar circumstances and living in similar societies. (There are also, of course, strong similarities between Trump and Robert Maxwell.)

Even before Trump took office, many American mental health professionals publicly voiced concern that he was psychologically unfit for the role of president. The psychologist John Gartner formed the "Duty to Warn" organisation, which declared that Donald Trump "suffers from an incurable malignant narcissism that makes him incapable of carrying out his presidential duties and poses a danger to the nation."

In 2018, Gartner started an online petition to remove Trump from office, which was signed by over 70,000 mental health professionals. The Yale psychiatrist Bandy Lee founded the World Mental Health Coalition, bringing thousands of mental health professionals to debate the President's mental condition.[1]

Shortly before the US election in November 2021, the President's niece, Mary Trump – a clinical psychologist – offered her own assessment, largely based on her own interactions with her uncle. She agreed that Trump suffers from malignant narcissism but suggested that he also "meets the criteria for antisocial personality disorder, which in its severe form is generally considered sociopathy but can also refer to chronic criminality, arrogance, and disregard for the rights of others."[2] She also suggested that he could be diagnosed with dependent personality disorder, whose typical traits are an inability to be alone and a failure to take responsibility for one's actions or mistakes.

Mary Trump also provided a possible explanation for her uncle's disorder of disconnection: an emotionally deprived childhood, with a mother who was often physically or emotionally absent due to ill health, and a cold, authoritarian father who saw any expression of emotion as weakness. (In fact, Mary Trump describes Trump's father as a "high-functioning sociopath.") As she has written, "During and after her surgeries, [his mother's] absence – both literal and emotional – created a void in the lives of her children."[3] Donald Trump was only two and a half years old when his mother became ill, and so would have suffered from a lack of parental attachment, as described by John Bowlby. As we saw in Chapter 1, Bowlby believed that if a child's attachment to a mother figure is broken, it inevitably damages their social, emotional and intellectual development, resulting in "affectionless psychopathy". It's easy to see how this could apply to Donald Trump.

Beyond diagnoses of specific personality disorders, the

essential feature of Trump's condition is hyper-disconnection, resulting in a severe lack of empathy and conscience, and extreme self-centredness. Trump's incessant desire to accumulate property, fame and power, and his inability to be alone or to be inactive (characteristics shared by Robert Maxwell) suggest a state of extreme separateness. This is also suggested by Trump's sensitivity to slights, and the mendacity with which he responds to any perceived disrespect. At Trump's extreme level of disconnection, there is a high level of psychological fragility and vulnerability. As noted earlier, hyper-disconnected people feel a strong sense of incompleteness, like fragments broken off from the whole. They are completely isolated and alone, and as such they feel exposed and vulnerable. Any slight is a threat to their fragile sense of identity, and they respond aggressively to try to preserve their identity.

Aside from Trump's own personality, it's easy to identify many elements of pathocracy in his presidency. More specifically, it's easy to identity the stages by which pathocracies take hold over nations, as identified by Lobaczewski. First, there is a charismatic leader figure with a strong desire for power and prestige, who attracts acolytes and other disordered people through his seeming confidence, determination and fearlessness. Ordinary people are attracted to these characteristics too, perceiving him as a strong leader who can shake up the system and bring about real change. The leader and his acolytes promote a simplistic ideology – in this case, the "Make American Great Again" campaign – which both promotes an ideal of future greatness and harks back to an imaginary time of previous greatness. In particular, the strongman leader and his simplistic ideology appeal to working class people who feel disenfranchised and dissatisfied.

At the same time, the leader and his acolytes use propaganda to demonise ethnic or religious groups (in Trump's case, immigrants and Muslims), creating a sense of group identity in the face of enemies. All of this creates an exhilarating sense of unity amongst his supporters. As a result, just as Lobaczewski described, the pathology of a small psychopathic group – Trump and his acolytes – spread to large numbers of psychologically normal people. This was aided, of course, by the propaganda of media outlets and commentators, and Trump's own adept use of social media as a propaganda channel. A personality cult began to develop, with followers viewing Trump as a kind of saviour, becoming blind to his constant lying, his childish egotism and petulance, and his impulsive and incompetent decision-making. (We'll examine the reasons for the appeal of hyper-disconnected leaders more deeply in Chapter 9.)

Lobaczewski also described how, once a pathocratic leader gains power, responsible and moral people gradually leave the government – through resignation or ejection – while other disordered people join. This certainly happened over the course of Trump's presidency. Initially, a number of longstanding White House officials referred to themselves as "the adults in the room" and attempted to rein in the President's impulses and maintain some semblance of responsible government. Gradually, these conscientious figures – such as General John Kelly – were removed following disagreements with the President, until eventually the whole government was filled with ruthless and mendacious people with dark triad traits.

Thankfully, however, the last stage of pathocratic regimes as identified by Lobaczewski occurred too. As he suggested, pathocratic regimes never become permanent, because their brutality and lack of morality aren't shared by psychologically normal people. Although large numbers of people continued to support Trump, a majority of the American electorate became increasingly appalled by the President and his pathocratic regime. Despite Trump's attempts to undermine democracy – another sure indication of pathocracy – the democratic systems established by the founding fathers held firm, and he was ejected from power after one term. (The saga of Trump's political career may not be over though. At present, it seems likely that he will run for President again in 2024. Certainly, he's still a massively influential figure in the Republican Party, with a lot of popular support.)

Pathocracy in the UK

At the time of writing, a similar process seems to be playing out in Brazil, where the pathocratic regime of Joel Bolsonaro has reached record levels of unpopularity. Initially, Bolsonaro held the same strongman appeal as Trump, promising a new era of stability after years of government corruption. With his opposition to homosexuality and abortion, he gained the support of Brazil's growing fundamentalist Christian community. However, Bolsonaro soon proved to be incompetent and malevolent as a leader. He has encouraged the destruction of the Amazon rainforest and disastrously mishandled Brazil's response to the COVID pandemic, almost as if he is trying to inflict as much damage as possible during his presidency. As a result, it seems likely that Bolsonaro will lose the next election. (For the good of the world, we can only hope that this will be the case.)

Meanwhile the UK – my home country – also presently has a pathocratic government. The present prime minister, Boris Johnson, has the same type of hyper-disconnected narcissistic personality as Trump or Berlusconi. As with Trump, Johnson's hyper-disconnection can be traced back to an emotionally deprived and unstable upbringing. Born in New York (where his father was studying), Johnson moved back and forth between the US and the UK, before moving to Belgium at the age of eight. In Belgium, his mother had a psychological breakdown and suffered ongoing depression, which meant that she was largely absent, both physically and emotionally. (Johnson's father had always been largely absent, due to his studies and later his work.) At the age of ten, Johnson was dispatched to a boarding school in the UK, where he remained as a "boarder" for the rest of his education.

Besides parental deprivation, the instability and peripatetic nature of Johnson's childhood probably influenced his personality. A great deal of research shows that children who don't have a settled family home – such as the children of military families who regularly move to different bases or of diplomats who regularly move to different countries – suffer worse psychological health as adults. They are more prone to depression and anxiety and have poorer relationships.[4] They may also feel an ongoing sense of insecurity, which they compensate for with narcissism and grandiosity. They have weaker emotional ties, and may treat other people in a callous, disposable way.[5]

As with Trump, once Johnson attained power, there was an exodus of moderate, responsible people from his government, who were replaced by hard-line figures from the extreme right of his party. Again and again, Johnson and his government showed a startling disregard for the principles of democracy. They have illegally suspended Parliament, exonerated ministers who broke the ministerial code, broken international law, curbed the right to protest, and packed senior media and cultural roles with ideological allies. These measures were accompanied with increasing nationalism and populism, including hard-line measures against refugees and asylum seekers and hostility to other nations.

In December 2021, Johnson and his government were found to have held multiple parties during the coronavirus lockdown, breaking the rules they created. This exemplifies the government's lack of morality and integrity, along with their hubris and sense of entitlement. In their narcissism, Johnson and most of his cohorts seem to lack any sense of what constitutes acceptable or unacceptable behaviour. To them, moral principles are like the customs of a foreign country. No matter how long they stay in the country, they struggle to understand its ways.

There is a vast difference in morality and integrity between Britain's nominal leader, Queen Elizabeth II, and its actual leader, Johnson. This illustrates the point I made in Chapter 4, that hereditary systems of power (although intrinsically unfair) are actually more likely to produce connected leaders than modern cultures.

Like Trump and Bolsonaro, Johnson and his government have also proved to be startlingly incompetent, as illustrated by their disastrous response to the coronavirus pandemic and their mishandling of the UK's exit from the European Union. This is another unfortunate aspect of pathocracies – that leadership roles are often taken up by people who (along with all their other faults) aren't particularly competent or intelligent. There is often a massive gulf between their self-confidence and their ability. Although their grandiosity convinces them that they are superior and deserve power, hyper-disconnected people usually make very poor politicians. Although they may be cunning and manipulative, they are too impulsive to make rational decisions. They lack the mental clarity needed to evaluate evidence. They are too short-sighted to judge the long-term consequences of their actions. Their capriciousness means that they often make sudden, unexpected changes or policy reversals, without any clear strategy. (This complaint was often made of both Trump and Johnson.)

But why would we expect hyper-disconnected leaders to be good at their jobs? After all, it's not their competence or intelligence that has put them into leadership positions, but simply their intense *desire* for power, generated by their disordered personalities.

However, this is another reason why pathocracies usually don't last for long in democratic countries. In addition to the fact that their pathology isn't shared by the majority of psychologically normal people (who become appalled by their behaviour), democratic pathocracies fail because the public grows tired of their incompetence. Hyper-disconnected leaders promise to make their countries great again, but the reality of their mismanagement and chaos soon becomes clear, bringing a sense of crushing disappointment.

In fact, hyper-disconnected leaders in democratic countries are usually undone by a combination of their incompetence and corruption. Although they may initially present themselves as responsible figures, it's not long before their habitual corruption manifests itself. Besides their lack of morality and conscience – leading to a tendency to break rules – they have a narcissistic inability to sense how their actions will be perceived by others. They are surprised when behaviour that they think is normal and acceptable is perceived as corrupt by others.

Other Types of Politicians

Fortunately, not all politicians are hyper-disconnected people with a complete absence of conscience and empathy. In Chapter 3, I pointed out that there are three different types of leaders and managers, including involuntary and altruistic leaders. And this applies to politicians too. Some politicians may gain their positions without a great deal of conscious intent. In the terminology I used before, some politicians may be *meretricious* involuntary leaders, who become ministers – or even the prime minister – after working their way up through the government, due to ability and popularity. Others may be *privileged* involuntary leaders, who become politicians due (at least partly) to an inbred sense of superiority and entitlement, and due to qualifications and connections. Obviously, in some cases there may be a combination of merit and privilege. In addition, there are clearly some genuinely altruistic politicians, whose desire for power and influence stems from a non-egoic impulse to try to improve people's lives, to overcome injustice and oppression, or to help counter global problems like climate change. (We will look at some examples of altruistic political leaders in Chapter 12.)[6]

However, it's likely that involuntary and altruistic leaders are less common in politics than in other professions. Even in 21st century democracies, politics is probably the most attractive profession to hyper-disconnected people, because of the power and prestige it confers, together the opportunity to accumulate wealth. Hyper-disconnected people gravitate towards political power like moths to a flame.

Conversely, modern politics is very *un*attractive to connected people with a high level of empathy and conscience. In theory, connected people have a much better chance of attaining power in democracies than in dictatorships, where they are marginalised and often persecuted or killed. However, connected people generally don't feel attracted to power. Since they don't experience a state of separateness, they don't feel the need to accumulate power or wealth. Whilst some may feel drawn to leadership roles as a way of enacting positive change (and so become altruistic leaders), many connected people feel slightly repelled by leadership roles. After all, in hierarchical societies power itself has a disconnecting effect, elevating us above other people and creating envy and resentment from others who covet power. (This is part of the "leadership trap" I described earlier.)

Connected people like to remain on the ground, interacting with others at the same level. They don't desire control or authority, but connection. They generally like to live quietly, without too much stress and responsibility or too much attention. Unlike hyper-disconnected people, they are usually self-sufficient and inwardly content, and so have no need for constant activity and distraction. As a result, the constant barrage of media attention that accompanies modern politics holds very little appeal for them.

Unfortunately, the reluctance of connected people to enter politics leaves leadership roles free for disconnected people, who eagerly lay claim to them.

Chapter 7

Disconnected Politics: Why Hyper-Disconnected Leaders Are Fascists

I'd like to pause for a moment to play a game. I'm going to list four statements from four pathocratic leaders, and would like you to guess which statement comes from which leader. The four candidates are: Caligula (the Roman Emperor), Silvio Berlusconi, Donald Trump, and Muammar Gaddafi. The quotes are:

1. "I believe there is no one in history to whom I should feel inferior. Quite the opposite."
2. "I think the only difference [between me and other candidates] is that I'm more honest and my women are more beautiful."
3. "I don't care if they respect me so long as they fear me."
4. "Those who don't love me don't deserve to live."*

*The answers are in Appendix 4, at the back of the book.

I would hazard that most of you didn't get all the answers right. The reason for this is simple: pathocratic leaders are always remarkably similar, in terms of their background, behaviour and policies. Even if some traits are stronger than others and even if there is some variation in terms of the *overall* severity of their disconnection (with more severely disconnected people possessing more extreme traits overall), they represent a very narrow and specific type of human being, who behaves in very narrow and specific ways. Since the behaviour of pathocrats is determined by their hyper-disconnection, it's always very similar, in the same way that the symptoms of the flu are similar for everyone who has the virus.

We've already seen that, like serial killers, pathocratic leaders almost always have traumatic childhoods, often with violent fathers (such as Hitler and Mussolini) or absent mothers (such as Trump and Johnson). In most cases, their brutality becomes evident during the later stages of childhood (as we saw above with Mussolini and Franco), when they have already responded to their trauma by disconnecting themselves, shutting down empathy and developing a ruthless self-centredness.

Hyper-disconnected leaders are often described as fascists, while their political approach is often described as fascism. Like many observers of Donald Trump, the mayor of London, Sadiq Khan – one of the many victims of Trump's Twitter tirades – recognised the President's fascist tendencies. In a 2021 newspaper article, Khan described Trump as "following the playbook of fascist dictators and strongmen that came to power in the 1930s and 1940s."[1] However, in reality there is no fascist playbook, nor any ideological basis for fascism at all. Fascism is not really a political philosophy so much as a term that describes the behaviour of hyper-disconnected people in positions of power. Pathocrats may ally themselves with a political philosophy – as Stalin and Mao did with communism, for instance – but the philosophy is always secondary. It is merely a vehicle to help satisfy their drive for power and to help express their malevolent impulses. Despite purporting to occupy different ends of the political spectrum, the communist pathocracy of Stalin and Mao was fundamentally the same as the fascist pathocracy of Hitler and Mussolini.

In fact, one could extend this to extremist politics in general. Far-right politics has nothing to do with principles or ideals and doesn't follow any coherent philosophy. It's simply a malevolent worldview generated by a state of intense disconnection. The nationalism and xenophobia of far-right politics stems from a pathological lack of empathy, which allows extremists to dehumanise members of other ethnic groups (and other political and religious groups), viewing them as objects rather than fellow human beings. Far-right followers also have a general sense of suspicion and mistrust of the world, together with a general sense of resentment and anger, related to feelings of inferiority and insecurity. These traits stem from the painful sense of separation that disconnection generates. All of this makes it clear why extremist politics can give rise to terrorist acts, as it did in January 2021, when Donald Trump's supporters stormed the Capitol.

Rather than the result of ideology, the actions of pathocratic leaders (and their regimes) are simply the expression and extension of their personality traits. The chaos and destruction they cause is simply an expression of their chaotic and destructive personalities. Since they are as severely narcissistic and impulsive as young children, they can *only* act in accordance with their own personality traits, and in terms of their own self-interest.

In this chapter, I would like to highlight some of the most significant aspects of pathocratic leaders and their regimes, showing how these aspects are simply an expression of their disconnective personality traits. To an extent, this section provides a summary of the traits of hyper-disconnected people in general, providing more understanding of their experience of the world, and the reasons for their destructive behaviour.

Nationalism and Militarism

Pathocratic leaders and their regimes are always nationalistic, obsessed with increasing their nation's power and prestige. Like Trump and Hitler, they promise a great future and hark back to a mythical great past, when the nation possessed more power and prestige. In Britain, nationalists often hark back to the "great" days of the British Empire, when British colonialists subjugated and oppressed millions of people around the world and exploited their labour and natural resources.

In their nationalist fervour, pathocratic regimes see other nations as rivals in a competition for power and prestige. They withdraw from international agreements and reject offers of support and cooperation, stubbornly insisting that they can prosper alone. They have no interest in helping other people around the world, since they view people of different countries or ethnic groups as inferior and unimportant. They can't take the perspective of other nations in the same way that, on an individual basis, they can't see the world from other people's perspectives.

In pathocracies, nationalism usually goes hand in hand with militarism. Pathocratic leaders are natural allies of the military, since it represents power and violence. Leaders attach themselves to the military to enhance their own prestige, together with the prestige of the nation (which by extension enhances their own prestige further). Pathocrats almost always build up the army and increase defence and arms budgets. Even if they don't have a military background themselves, they love to pose in military uniforms and stage military parades, flexing their strength like a bodybuilder in the mirror.

Nationalism and militarism, fuelled by the desire for power and prestige, lead inevitably to war. It's impossible for pathocracies to live in peace. Sooner or later, they always provoke conflicts with other countries, or invade or attack them. Like Hitler invading Czechoslovakia and Poland, or President Putin invading the Crimea in 2014 and Ukraine in 2022, pathocracies feel driven to steal territory and to dominate other peoples. Their present territory is never enough for them. Like hyper-disconnected businessmen who keep buying up new companies, they have to keep expanding.

All of this is simply the result of pathocrats *identifying* with their nation. The nation becomes an extension of their own personality. Their nationalist zeal is simply a way of projecting strength and trying to increase their own personal sense of power and prestige. Their isolationism is simply an expression of their hyper-masculine impulse to project strength and self-sufficiency. Their expansionist desire to invade other countries and gain new territory is simply an expression of the hyper-disconnected impulse to accumulate wealth and property. Their desire to conquer other peoples and dominate the world is simply a manifestation of the hyper-disconnected desire to control and exploit other people.

Restricted National Identity

The nationalism of pathocracies always involves a very limited notion of national identity. To truly belong to the nation, you must have the right ethnic background, the right religion, even the right sexual orientation. As pathocracies tighten their grip, and as the atmosphere around them grows more paranoid and poisonous, this notion of "true nationality" becomes ever more limited. To be a patriot, you must support the government and love the leader. In Gaddafi's words, "Those who don't love me, don't deserve to live."

This restricted national identity leads to the persecution of groups who don't fit the national profile, who are seen as "impure", with a corrupting influence. Such groups are seen as obstacles to the "great future" that lies ahead. They become internal enemies, who need to be purged. The most horrific example of this phenomenon was the Nazi persecution of the Jews. A more recent example – from the 1990s – was the Serbian leader Slobodan Milosevic's desire to create a racially pure Serbian nation (including the Serb-populated areas of Croatia and Bosnia) which meant forcibly removing all non-Serbs. Milosevic's pathocratic nationalism led to the first major European conflict since the Second World War, and the deaths of around 140,000 people. A similar phenomenon is taking place now in China, with the genocide against Xinjiang Muslims.

This persecution is made possible by what psychologists refer to as "moral exclusion". People who don't conform to the national identity are excluded from morality. They are dehumanised, treated as inanimate objects who can be oppressed and murdered without remorse, in the same way that serial killers and terrorists view their victims. Such dehumanisation enabled the Nazis to kill millions of Jews, then use their skin to make lampshades and the hair to make clothes and the lining for soldiers' boots. As the psychologist Erich Fromm wrote of Hitler's acolyte Adolf Eichmann, who organised the transportation of Jews to concentration camps, "He transported Jews as he would have transported coal... He was the perfect bureaucrat who had transformed all life into the administration of things."[2] It's the same attitude that enables the present-day Chinese authorities to "harvest" the internal organs of Xinjiang Muslims and other political prisoners.

Shallow Nationalism

However, in reality pathocrats have very little loyalty to their nation. Their attachment to the nation is as shallow as their personal relationships. To them, the nation – and even their own political party – is just an instrument that helps to satisfy their impulses and further their ambitions. The same goes for the ordinary people who constitute the nation. A pathocrat may profess love for his supporters – the "true patriots" who love him – but this is only *because* they support him. Like all hyper-disconnected people in everyday life, pathocrats simply exploit and manipulate their own countrymen for their own ends.

The proof of this is that once the nation can no longer help them satisfy their needs, pathocratic leaders often turn against it. This is what happened to Hitler, when it was clear that the Second World War was lost. After presenting himself as the "greatest German" with an undying love for the country and its folk, Hitler blamed the German people for his downfall, and swore vengeance on them. He ordered the destruction of the country's remaining infrastructure and industry – train tracks, bridges, communication lines, docks, public utilities, factories and so on. (Thankfully the order was disobeyed.)

Like all hyper-disconnected people, pathocrats love no one but themselves. They're so focused on gratifying their own insatiable impulses that they don't have the slightest interest in or affection for other people. Aside from sycophantic acolytes and the supporters who supply them with attention and admiration (and their own families), they only respect people who remind them of themselves, and so offer another source of self-admiration. Often the only people they admire are the pathocratic leaders of other nations. This helps to explain why Donald Trump was so keen to curry favour with – and so reluctant to criticise – pathocratic leaders such as President Putin, President Erdogan of Turkey, or Kim Jong-un of North Korea. At the same time, Trump disregarded relationships with America's traditional democratic allies, such as Germany and Canada. Perhaps Trump even felt slightly envious of people like Putin and Kim Jong-un, since they were able to wield much more power than him, because of the constraints of US democracy.

Hitler and Mussolini also had a relationship of mutual admiration. As Mussolini's pathocracy took hold during the 1920s, Hitler was watching closely. In many ways, Mussolini's totalitarian state was a template for the Nazi regime. Hitler adopted many of Mussolini's strategies and practices, including the Roman salute, mass public rallies, striking uniforms, and the indoctrination of children. Hitler even described Mussolini as his only true friend. However, their relationship cooled during the Second World War, when Mussolini and his armies became a hindrance, and Hitler was forced to divert resources to get them out of trouble.

Of course, pathocrats often feel attachment to their families too. They often pack their governments with family members, offering them important posts even if they lack any relevant experience. This is partly because they are so suspicious of others, whereas they feel that they can trust family. At the same time, they view family members – especially their children – as embodiments of themselves. If they manage to keep hold of power until old age, they usually single out one of their children – always a son, of course – as their successor, which is an indirect way of continuing to rule themselves. This has led to absurdities such as the communist dynasty of North Korea, with Kim Jong-un as the third ruler. Another example is the Haitian dictator Papa Doc Duvalier, surely one of the most brutal and deranged people ever to rule a country. After terrorising his own people for more than 20 years, in 1971, he was mercifully close to death. Unable to face the idea of relinquishing power, he declared his 19-year-old son the next "President for Life". Donald Trump exhibited the same impulse in promoting the political careers of his children, suggesting them as future presidential candidates.

Hard-line Policies

Pathocrats always pursue hard-line policies. They see themselves as defenders of law and order and are tough on crime and immigration. They make punishments more severe and send more people to prison. They take away the rights of refugees and asylum seekers, trying to close the country's borders and to deport as many non-nationals as they can. They often cut welfare support and social services and weaken protections and regulations, increasing competition and inequality.

At the same time, pathocrats see themselves as guardians of tradition, and resist progressive developments. They often legislate against abortion, women's rights, gay rights, animal welfare, environmental protections, and so on. Although it's rare for pathocrats to be genuinely religious – again, they are too self-centred to give attention and admiration to anyone else, even God – they usually ally themselves with traditional religions, often of a fundamentalist kind. (The exception is communist pathocracies, which are almost always atheist, in line with Marxist principles. In addition, because communist pathocracies are usually founded on revolutions, they usually try to break old traditions rather than uphold them.)

Pathocrats ally themselves with ordinary people – and often become very popular with the working class – but in practice they make most people's lives more difficult. They take away rights, weaken regulations and pander to corporations and business leaders (some of whom they no doubt admire just as they admire other dictators). Their policies always favour the wealthy rather than the poor. Even if they profess to be socialists or communists, pathocrats always create greater inequality.

Such hard-line policies are simply the expression of pathocrats' malevolence and lack of empathy. They don't feel any empathy for the plight of prisoners or refugees, and so feel no compunction to treat them better. On the contrary, their general malevolence means that they want to make life harder for these groups, or to punish them more severely. In a similar way, their lack of empathy makes it impossible for them to understand the plight of ordinary people who struggle with poverty, unemployment or lack of healthcare. They are also opposed to welfare and social support because they see life as a Darwinian struggle in which the "fittest" – the most intelligent and ambitious – rise to the top. In a disconnected world, the rich deserve their wealth, the poor deserve their poverty, and there's no reason why the winners should feel sympathy – or any responsibility to help – the losers. After all, pathocrats – and hyper-disconnected people in general – view compassion and altruism as "soft" feminine traits that should be suppressed. Empathy and emotion are signs of weakness. For example, Hitler saw compassion as a "Jewish trait" and a sign of corruption. For him, life was a savage struggle in which only the most brutal survived. Compassion was therefore an impediment to survival.

This also helps us to understand why pathocratic regimes are usually patriarchal, with low status for women. As mentioned previously, in the same way that hyper-disconnected people devalue emotion and empathy, they devalue women, who they associate with these traits. With their insatiable desire for power and control, hyper-disconnected people may also unconsciously resent the sexual and romantic power that women hold over them, and so feel the impulse to punish women. The fascist regimes of Hitler, Mussolini and Franco denigrated women, largely excluding them from active everyday life, and viewing them merely as reproductive machines.

Again, the exception here is communist pathocracies, which usually did promote greater equality for women. Gender equality was a Marxist principle, and another way that communist governments could break with tradition. Both Mao and Stalin even created female units of their armies. (Nazi soldiers were shocked and amazed by the ferocious Russian female soldiers they encountered at the Battle of Stalingrad.) The principle of gender equality was also applied to the communist countries of Eastern Europe after the Second World War. This was one positive aspect of the regimes – although in reality, it simply meant that women were oppressed and mistreated in exactly the same way as men. There weren't really any women's rights because there were no rights for anyone. In addition, communist regimes encouraged women to be part of the labour force so that mothers could hand over their children to state-run kindergartens. This fitted with the communist principle that there is no personal property, and that all goods and possessions – including children – belong to the state. It also made it easier to try to indoctrinate the children.

Intolerance of Dissent

Despite their desire to appear strongmen, hyper-disconnected people are always deeply insecure. Due to their extreme separateness, they have a deep unconscious sense of fragility and vulnerability. No matter how much power or prestige they gain, they're still essentially young children who are starved of attention and affection. The constant flow of attention and admiration that they require as adults is an attempt to offset this chronic sense of insecurity.

This helps to explain another common trait of pathocratic leaders: their intolerance of dissent and opposition. Because of their insecurity, any criticism deeply wounds them. Their grandiose self-image means that they believe they are infallible, incapable of making mistakes, and so any dissent or criticism is a threat to their self-image. Since they feel they don't deserve criticism, anyone who criticises them must have an agenda, or is simply spreading malicious lies. And of course, they are brutal and violent in their attempts to silence their critics.

This is one of the reasons why pathocrats try to destroy freedom of the press. They take over the media in order to eliminate criticism and dissent, and also so that they can fill media channels with their own propaganda. It's simply too much for their fragile egos to tolerate a steady stream of commentary and criticism through different media channels. It feels overwhelming, and they are shocked that anyone has the temerity to question their perfect judgement.

Their intolerance of criticism also means that pathocrats tend to surround themselves with "Yes men". As with the media, it's impossible for them to endure the company of people who question their judgement, and so they quickly eject non-compliant members of the government. And of course, once their associates realise how brutally pathocrats punish disloyalty, they learn to keep silent. (This is one of the ways that, as Lobaczewski noted, pathocracies quickly shed themselves of moral and responsible people.) This was certainly true of Mussolini, who, according to one historian, "never believed in experts unless they agreed with him."[3] As time went by, he became increasingly isolated and out of touch with reality, surrounded by anxious acolytes who only told him what he wanted to hear, and agreed with every impulsive decision he made. (The parallels with Donald Trump are obvious here.) This is another reason why pathocratic governments are often incompetent. Good government requires a variety of different perspectives and ideas, including dissenting voices – all of which are suppressed in pathocracies.

Destructiveness and Malevolence

One of the essential traits of hyper-disconnected people is their sheer malevolence. There is a terrible destructiveness at the heart of pathocrats and their regimes, as if they are on a mission to cause as much chaos and devastation as possible while in power – to kill people, to bomb countries, to destroy institutions, to damage the environment, to roll back rights and regulations. Some of their actions appear gratuitous, purely for the sake of causing damage, like young children who trample on other children's toys or knock down sandcastles. There is no rational justification for Joel Bolsonaro's encouragement of the destruction of the Amazon rainforest, or Donald Trump's rolling back of environmental protections and his withdrawal from the Paris climate agreement. Even more blatant was Trump's determination to approve the executions of death row prisoners before he left office. Thirteen executions were carried out between his election loss and the end of his presidency, which meant that more people were executed under his presidency that any other in history.

In a related way, hyper-disconnected people distrust – and try to obstruct – any positive developments that represent social progress. They take a perverse pleasure in disparaging people who try to fight against injustice, to protect the environment, or who act altruistically in a general sense. Such people are referred to as "do-gooders" or "snowflakes". Hyper-disconnected people's malevolence and lack of empathy means that they can't understand acts of charity or altruism, so they instinctively oppose them.

Erich Fromm – in my view, one of the most profound and insightful of all psychologists – described these destructive impulses as *necrophilia*, or love of death. Whereas healthy people experience *biophilia*, or love of life, a small number of pathological individuals worship death and destruction. Fromm saw Hitler as a perfect example of the "necrophilous type". After failing to destroy his enemies, he called for the destruction of Germany as a nation, and finally destroyed himself. Franco was also a clear example of a necrophiliac who relished destruction and mistrusted love and happiness. One of the slogans of Franco's nationalist movement (attributed to one of his generals) was, "Long live Death!" Fromm described necrophiliacs as motivated by fear of life and of the future. As he put it, the necrophiliac is "deeply afraid of life, because it is disorderly and uncontrollable by its very nature... He wants to return to the darkness of the womb, to the past of inorganic or subhuman existence."[4]

In a slight variant of Fromm's explanation of necrophilia, my view is that hyper-disconnected people's destructive traits stem from their extreme states of separation. This means that they live in a permanent state of dissatisfaction and frustration, like prisoners who are trapped inside their cells. It's impossible for them to experience true happiness, because – at least to a large extent – human well-being stems from a sense of connection to others, and to the world around us. It comes from losing ourselves, giving ourselves away – from sharing other people's company, losing ourselves in natural scenes or beautiful works of art or music, giving our whole attention to challenging activities (in other words, *flow*), helping other people, and so on. Because they are trapped inside themselves, hyper-disconnected people can't give themselves away. They might experience short periods of happiness after they've won a victory or punished an enemy. But even this type of happiness is toxic, stemming from pride, gloating, and schadenfreude. And this type of happiness always fades away quickly, returning them to their familiar sense of discontent and incompleteness.

Hyper-disconnected people's experience of the world is pallid and shallow. Because they can never unmoor themselves from their own egos, the world is always a dreary, half-real place to them. They can never experience the joy of a beautiful sunset, mountain or painting. Other people are half-real to them too, so that they can never experience the joys of love and the deep intimacy of real friendship.

This is ultimately why hyper-disconnected leaders are so destructive. Like prisoners who scream and bang on the walls of their cell, they are venting their frustration, lashing out at the world because it has inflicted the suffering of separateness on them. Over time, their discontent and frustration increase, generating more malevolence and destruction. Leaders become ever more ruthless and brutal, creating more chaos, oppression, and violence – and ultimately leading to their own destruction.

Another factor is that hyper-disconnected people *need* enemies, just as they need admirers. Pathocrats need to create conflict with other nations, and to demonise certain groups within their own nation, in order to strengthen their fragile sense of identity. In this way, their enemies provide the same function as their admirers. Enemy groups are like mirrors, which remind them of their own identity, and enable them to see themselves more clearly. (At the same time, the sense of group identity that they engender – with enemies to reflect against – is part of the appeal of hyper-disconnected leaders. Their followers relish the sense of togetherness and belonging.)

It's also worth mentioning that all the traits I have mentioned above – nationalism and militarism, hard-line policies, intolerance of dissent and malevolence – are only possible because of hyper-disconnected people's most fundamental trait of all: lack of empathy. If you empathise with your fellow human beings, you can't wage war on them. You can't deprive them of their rights or social support, punish or kill them merely for disagreeing with you. You can't inflict suffering on them for your own perverse pleasure. You can't encourage the destruction of the environment either, since you can emphasise with non-human beings and the natural world in general.

Self-Delusion

There is one further trait of pathocratic leaders (and hyper-disconnected people in general) that I would like to explore: self-delusion.

Self-delusion is an inevitable consequence of the hyper-disconnected people's tenuous relationship to the external world. They're so immersed in their own subjective world that their own thoughts and desires seem as real as the world itself. So when events in the world conflict with their desires and thoughts, it's easy for them to reject the reality of the events. They can easily ignore any negative information that contradicts their own preferred vision of reality.

This is one of the reasons why hyper-disconnected leaders surround themselves with sycophants. Once they have accepted delusions as reality, they need people around them who are willing to sustain the delusions, rather than question them. Self-delusion is also one of the reasons why hyper-disconnected leaders are usually very poor at responding to crises. They are reluctant to accept negative information, which means that they don't face the actuality of perilous situations. They prefer to pretend that dangers don't exist, or at least to downplay their peril. This means that they don't take the necessary preventative action.

This became a serious issue with Hitler once the Allies gained the upper hand in the Second World War. He refused to accept failure and danger, clinging to bizarrely unrealistic hopes. This led to many poor decisions. For example, in 1944, the Allies launched a successful misinformation campaign to convince the Nazis that they would invade France at Calais. Even after the Allies landed in Normandy, Hitler wouldn't accept that he had been deceived, and kept large numbers of soldiers stationed at Calais, convinced that at least some Allied groups would land there.

Hitler's generals despaired at his delusional thinking. Occasionally some were brave enough to disagree with him, but they never managed to change his mind, even when it was clear that his decisions were leading to disaster. (Eventually, as Hitler's decisions became more irrational, his generals made attempts to assassinate him. Their failure reinforced Hitler's delusion that providence was protecting him, and that he was Germany's saviour.) Even at the end of the war, when the Russian army was advancing on Berlin, Hitler refused to surrender, clinging to the bizarre hope that a phantom German battalion would appear out of nowhere and defeat the Russians.

The tendency to prefer his own version of events to reality was a constant theme of Donald Trump's presidency. Trump's self-delusion was evident right from the beginning, when he refused to believe that his inauguration crowd was smaller than Barack Obama's, despite photographic evidence. All through his presidency, Trump refused to accept negative information – for example, low poll numbers, evidence of malpractice by other pathocratic leaders or data about the coronavirus epidemic. If information didn't fit with his preferred version of reality, he simply labelled it fake news. This also partly explains his refusal to accept the reality of climate change. Unable to accept trivial negative information such as a smaller crowd size, he was hardly likely to entertain the prospect of an ecological catastrophe.

Most overtly, Trump's self-delusion revealed itself in his attitude to the coronavirus pandemic. He constantly downplayed the danger, as if ignoring it could make it disappear. As a result, he didn't take any meaningful action, and the United States suffered more severely than any other economically developed country. Ultimately, this led to Trump's election defeat – the reality of which he was also unable to accept, of course.

Self-delusion is one of the reasons why pathocrats – and hyper-disconnected people in general – are prone to violent rages. If events conspire against their preferred outcomes, or if other people cast doubt on their preferred version of reality, they are liable to explode, like spoilt children who can't get what they want. Donald Trump was well known for such violent outbursts, as was Hitler and the Serbian leader Milosevic. In a manner reminiscent of Hitler, Milosevic was prone to "staging temper tantrums, screaming at aides, and throwing documents in the air."[5] He was also prone to self-delusion. One of his chief generals, General Perisic, voiced the same complaint as Hitler's generals – that Milosevic was disconnected from reality, and would reject "competent opinions and proposals" in favour of his own irrational ideas.[6] On another occasion, when tens of thousands of people were demonstrating against Milosevic's regime, the Mayor of Belgrade was shocked when the leader denied that the protests were happening and told him, "You must be watching too much CNN. There aren't any [protests]."[7]

As was the case with Hitler, the self-delusion of hyper-disconnected people increases as they near their downfall. Then the gulf between their wishful thinking and reality becomes painfully absurd, in an almost Shakespearean way. Like Milosevic, even as massive uprisings take place against them, they find it impossible to believe that they are not universally loved. In a 2011 interview with Colonel Gaddafi, as his army was violently suppressing mass protests around Libya, the dictator claimed that the protests couldn't possibly exist because "Libyan people love me." He claimed that al-Qaeda were turning some Libyans against him by supplying them with drugs. Several months later, Gaddafi was killed by his own people.

The Worst Possible Leaders

There's a school of thought that holds that hyper-disconnected people make good leaders. Their charisma and charm bring popularity, which has a unifying effect. They are confident and decisive and so get things done quickly. Because of the rigidity of their beliefs, they establish goals and stick to them tenaciously. Their lack of empathy promotes a single-mindedness which can sometimes lead to real achievement. On the basis of such assertions, the British psychologist Kevin Dutton has even suggested the notion of a "good psychopath" who possesses valuable leadership qualities such coolness under pressure, fearlessness, ruthlessness, impulsivity, and so on.[8]

However, there can only be a "good psychopath" in the context of a sick society that is overly competitive and hierarchical, and so perversely values negative personality traits. In addition, as I've already argued, the idea of hyper-disconnected people as decisive, fearless and confident is an illusion. They are not really decisive, just impulsive. They are not really confident, just lacking in self-awareness and self-regulation. They are not really fearless, just lacking in feeling.

In every conceivable way, hyper-disconnected people are the worst possible leaders. As history has shown with painful regularity, there is no such thing as a good psychopathic leader. On the contrary, a large proportion of the suffering that has blighted the human race's existence over recent centuries (and particularly since the end of the 19th century) has been directly caused by the malevolence and incompetence of hyper-disconnected leaders.

Even if we define "good" not in moral terms but simply in terms of success, hyper-disconnected people can't be considered good leaders. By this definition, a good business leader would be one who helps a company to make more money, to expand and increase their share of their market, to increase efficiency, and so on. Similarly, a good national leader would bring economic growth, increase employment, reduce the national deficit, deal effectively with national crises, and so on. Like chess players, a good leader should think strategically, evaluating multiple options and developing long-term goals. They should be flexible and open-minded, so that they can change their plans if events unfold differently to expectations.

Hyper-disconnected leaders completely fail in these terms too. Their impulsiveness means that they can't think methodically or strategically, or on a long-term basis. Their narcissism means that they can't consider multiple perspectives or options. Their self-delusion means that they misread situations and don't act effectively against crises. In terms of the chess analogy, they are like players who can only anticipate one or two moves in advance, who can only see small sections of the board at any one time, and who don't realise when their opponent has them under attack. As a result, although they frequently have some initial success, hyper-disconnected leaders always ultimately lead countries and businesses to ruin.

It's also important to remember that there is no correlation between intelligence or competence and desire for power. Most modern politicians aren't in their roles because they are more competent and qualified than others, but simply because they crave power and are tenacious in their pursuit of it. It's true that pathocratic leaders often have a wily intelligence, which enables them to manipulate others and outmanoeuvre their rivals. But this is completely different to the lucid, strategic intelligence that allows businesses or nations to thrive.

Hatred of Democracy

A final trait of hyper-disconnected leaders that's worth emphasising is their hatred of democracy, and their determination to undermine it.

Democracy is a way of protecting the majority of people from hyper-disconnected people in power. In this way, it is one of the most positive developments in history, particularly in its earliest forms, as practised by the earliest hunter-gatherer societies and other indigenous groups such as the Native Americans. This also applies to the direct democracies of Ancient Greece, where citizens would collectively decide laws and policies. (We will explore these early forms of democracy in more detail later.) In the modern world, elective or representative democracy has taken over from direct democracy. This is less ideal, but still effective to some degree.

We've repeatedly seen that pathocracies arise in the absence of democratic systems, such as in post-colonial Africa and the Middle East. Democracy doesn't necessarily prevent pathocracies taking hold, as the recent experiences of the US and the UK show. But it does make them less likely, whereas a lack of democracy makes them inevitable. In addition, the pathocratic regimes that do take hold in democracies are less severe than in non-democratic societies, such as post-revolutionary Russia or China, or Saddam Hussein's Iraq. This is because democratic processes and institutions constrain the power of pathocratic regimes. They act as checks on the power of potential tyrants, limiting their authority, and ensuring that power is separated and shared. This was the central idea of the American Constitution and the Bill of Rights. Aware of the corrupting influence of power, the founding fathers divided federal government into three different areas, the legislative, executive and judicial, with checks and balances between them.

Pathocrats despise democracy in the same way that criminals despise laws, or teenagers hate their parents' rules – because it constrains their behaviour. It stands in the way of everything they crave for. Like a defensive wall around a wealthy city, it denies them access to unlimited power, wealth and admiration. Moreover, pathocrats are unable to *comprehend* the concept of democracy. Since they see themselves as superior to others, and believe that their judgement is always sound, it makes no sense to them to share decisions or take other people's opinions into account. Pathocrats see themselves as Nietzschean supermen, to whom the normal rules of morality don't apply. (This was one of the reasons why Nazis were attracted to the philosopher Nietzsche, alongside his denigration of compassion as a corrupt Christian virtue which allowed mediocrity and weakness to flourish.)[9]

More broadly, hyper-disconnected people don't understand democracy because – as noted earlier – they see life as a competitive struggle in which the most ruthless deserve to dominate others. For them, hierarchy and inequality are the natural order of things. If people are powerful, it's because they've earned their power through their strength. If people are wealthy, it's because they've earned their wealth through their ingenuity. If people are stuck at the bottom of the social hierarchy, it's because they are weak and stupid.

It's therefore inevitable that democratically elected pathocrats (such as Donald Trump or Boris Johnson) attempt to undermine and undo democratic systems. Democracy is constantly under attack by hyper-disconnected politicians. In the last chapter of this book, I'll argue that present-day democracies don't do enough to protect us from pathocracy and will suggest some ways in which democracy can be enhanced. Nevertheless, we should be thankful that democracy has given us some protection from hyper-disconnected people. It's difficult to imagine, but the chaos and brutality of the last 150 years of history could have been even more extreme.

Chapter 8

Spiritual Pathocracy: Extremists, Gurus and Cult Leaders

After crime, business and politics, there is a fourth, perhaps less popular area that hyper-disconnected people gravitate towards: religion and spirituality.

Although all religions teach morality and altruism, it isn't hard to find examples of religious leaders with dark triad traits, who have behaved as appallingly as criminals and dictators. For example, many of the popes of the Middle Ages were as corrupt and malevolent as the Roman Emperors they effectively took over from. A good example was Pope Alexander VI, elected in 1492, who amassed vast wealth and scandalised his contemporaries with open air orgies and numerous illegitimate children. He routinely sold church offices and was notorious for his nepotism, making his friends and relatives cardinals. A more modern example is the Irish Catholic nuns who ran "mother and baby homes", persecuting unmarried mothers and treating their babies as if they were an "inferior sub-species" (in the words of the Irish Taoiseach, Enda Kenny). Infant mortality rates at the homes were unusually high, and many babies were secretly buried in mass graves, some in structures used for sewage. Another example from the Catholic Church is the thousands of priests around the world who used their positions to sexually abuse children.

Of course, it's likely that many of these people weren't genuinely religious. For example, most paedophile priests are probably just opportunists who see the role as an ideal place to secretly practise sexual abuse. However, genuine religion certainly isn't a safeguard against the abuse and cruelty of hyper-disconnection. In fact, in many ways religion encourages disconnection, and the most intensely religious people – such as fundamentalists and extremists – tend to be highly disconnected.

Religious Extremism

To some extent, this depends on how we define religion, and whether we distinguish it from spirituality. My view is that religion and spirituality are two distinct areas. Religion is about belief and identity. It's about adopting a specific belief system which explains the world and the purpose of life. It provides guidelines to live by, with conventions and practices to follow. Religion is also about identifying with a specific group and becoming a member of a community. It usually means believing that your group possesses "the truth" and that other belief systems are inferior and false. In this way, religion provides a sense of security and certainty that strengthens identity.

However, adopting a belief system also brings disconnection. Especially if the belief system is rigid and dogmatic, it means disconnecting from people with different beliefs, and withdrawing empathy from them. As we saw in Chapter 2, in extreme cases, this may lead to terrorism, when members of other groups are dehumanised to the extent that they become legitimate targets of violence.

Adopting an ideology also often means disconnecting from *reality itself*. Rigid and dogmatic belief systems act as conceptual filters, limiting and distorting our experience of the world. The events of our lives are interpreted through the prism of beliefs, and any evidence which doesn't correspond with them is ignored. In this way, rigid and dogmatic belief systems increase our separation from the world, enclosing us inside abstract mental space.

This helps to explain why so many barbaric and murderous acts have been committed in the name of God. In the Middle Ages, millions of innocent European women – often those seen as dangerous because they were unusually intelligent or independent – were murdered as "witches" at the behest of God-fearing clergymen. During the Spanish Inquisition – which lasted for more than 200 years – hundreds of thousands of "heretics" were tortured and executed, many burnt at the stake. We could also mention the horrors perpetrated by colonists of the New World who believed they were fulfilling God's work by conquering and killing indigenous peoples, together with the acts of religious terrorism we examined in Chapter 2.

Fundamentalism and Extremism

The link between religion and disconnection helps to explain religious fundamentalism and extremism. Fundamentalist or extremist groups and their ideologies are embodiments of disconnection, created and sustained by highly disconnected people. Such groups are effectively small-scale pathocracies, rigidly hierarchical and patriarchal and led by authoritarian and charismatic figures. Their ideology is an expression of their hyper-disconnected traits. For example, the hyper-disconnection of fundamentalist Christian groups manifests itself in homophobia, sexual repression (with taboos against premarital sex), strict codes of conduct (with severe punishments for any transgressions), and a powerful empire-building instinct to convert others to their beliefs.

At an even higher level of disconnection, there is the extreme form of Islam espoused by groups such as Al-Qaeda and the Taliban. Such ideologies are permeated with the sadism and malevolence that is characteristic of the most disconnected personalities. There is an antipathy towards all healthy and pleasurable aspects of life, such as sex, love, music and dancing. There is an antipathy to the human body itself, which is seen as a mere vehicle for the soul and is full of "unclean" desires and processes which should be repressed. There is antipathy to women, who give rise to unclean desires and manifest unclean biological processes, such as menstruation and pregnancy. There is even an antipathy to life itself. Our present life is seen as a brief and insignificant sojourn, to be endured and conducted in the proper way, before our *real* life begins in the afterworld. Such severe and malevolent ideologies are pervaded with what Erich Fromm called necrophilia – a worship of death, exemplified by the mass murders of terrorists and the self-destruction of suicide bombers.

These forms of religion can only arise from an intensely disconnected state. Indeed, disconnection permeates every aspect of fundamentalist religion – disconnection between the body and the soul, between the world and paradise, between God and the world, between man and woman, and so on. Such ideologies are a manifestation of the fragmented, degraded and discordant world experienced by hyper-disconnected minds – a world completely devoid of beauty, harmony and love.

The Spiritual Continuum of Connection

In its true sense, spirituality differs from religion because it's not about belief, but *experience*. If anything, spirituality is about letting go of beliefs and concepts, and opening up to a wider and more mysterious reality. Spiritual development (or spiritual awakening) refers to an intensification and an expansion of awareness, in which the world becomes more vivid and beautiful, in which we feel more empathic and compassionate towards other people, and have a wider, more global outlook. In this sense, spirituality is all about *connection*. Truly spiritual people are empathic, altruistic and tolerant. They have a sense of inner security and well-being, and so feel little or no impulse to accumulate power or wealth. They feel a healthy sense of integration with their own bodies, and a respect and appreciation for the world itself. They have little or no sense of group identity, nor any need to defend or propagate an ideology. In this sense, truly spiritual people have no need for religion. (We'll examine the characteristics of spiritually awakened people in more detail in Chapter 13, which specifically deals with spirituality.)

Having said this, religion and spirituality do sometimes overlap. Some religious people are genuinely spiritual and use their religion as a framework for spiritual growth. They aren't dogmatic and exclusivist but tolerant and liberal. They embody the altruistic principles of their faith, not just to other Christians or Muslims but to all human beings. Rather than seeing their religion as the truth, they respect all other faiths, viewing them as variations or interpretations of the same essential spiritual truths, or different paths to the same goal. This applies to some of the most ecumenical Christian groups, such as the Quakers and the Unitarians.

One way of illustrating the difference (and the relationship) between religion and spirituality is to think in terms of a "Spiritual Continuum of Connection". The spiritual continuum of connection (illustrated in Appendix 3) begins with extremely disconnected forms of religion such as fundamentalism, alongside extremely disconnected religious people such as extremists and religious terrorists. In the middle of the continuum, we move towards connected forms of religion, which are tolerant, ecumenical and liberal, alongside genuinely spiritual people who align themselves with a religion. On the right side of the continuum, we move away from religion in its conventional sense towards pure spirituality, which involves deeper and deeper degrees of connection, without specific beliefs or ideologies. This is also where what I call "awakening experiences" are situated – experiences of a more intense reality, in which we feel a sense of harmony and meaning, an awareness of the interconnection of all things and a sense of our own oneness with the world.

Spiritual Disconnection

However, even spirituality itself isn't free of disconnection. Or to put it more specifically, spirituality is often hijacked by hyper-disconnected individuals, who masquerade as spiritually awakened people. They adopt the role of spiritual teacher – or guru – as a way of expressing their desire for dominance and their malevolent impulses.

The guru tradition has been a part of Indian culture since time immemorial, as a way of transmitting spiritual teachings and supporting aspirants along the spiritual path. According to Indian tradition, the guru can also transmit his spiritual radiance to his followers, providing them with spiritual sustenance. In addition, the disciple's devotion to the guru is a form of spiritual practice, which helps them to transcend self-centredness. However, when the guru tradition is transplanted into Western culture, it often becomes problematic, mainly because it is exploited by hyper-disconnected people. (I'm sure it is sometimes problematic in Indian culture too, but probably to a lesser extent.)

Many people feel an impulse to develop spiritually and seek teachers to guide them. This is understandable because, particularly in Western cultures, the landscape of spiritual experience is unfamiliar territory – if not complete *terra incognita* – and fraught with possible dangers. So naturally, we look to people who are more familiar with the territory to give us direction. Unfortunately, however, many of the people who volunteer themselves as teachers create more difficulty than they alleviate.

Here we could return to the careers advisor we first met at the beginning of Chapter 2. As we saw in earlier chapters, he or she would probably advise a hyper-disconnected person to follow a career as a CEO or a politician. But another possible career avenue would be a spiritual teacher. After all, what could be a better place for someone with a strong need for power and admiration than at the head of their own cult or spiritual community? What better way to ensure a constant flow of attention and adoration than to surround themselves with fawning followers, who worship them as a deity and unquestioningly follow their commands? What better way for them to express their grandiosity by presenting themselves as an omnipotent and infallible being?

For a hyper-disconnected person with prevalent narcissistic traits, this is an even better option than politics, particularly in democratic societies. As we saw at the end of the last chapter, democracy constrains the power of pathocrats. It also allows for opposition and criticism. But if you become a spiritual teacher and set up your own self-sufficient spiritual community in isolation from the outside world, then you can remove any limits to your power. You can have what every dictator dreams of: complete authority and unlimited attention and adoration. You can dispense with all the laws and conventions that regulate human behaviour in normal society and convince your followers (and yourself) that you are a superior being who is entitled to live by his own principles.

Hyper-Disconnected Gurus

In the 1960s and 70s, there was a massive upsurge of interest in Eastern spirituality in the United States and Europe. In response, large numbers of Western spiritual seekers travelled to India, in search of gurus. There was movement in the opposite direction too. A large number of enterprising spiritual practitioners travelled to the West to share their wisdom and their traditions.

Roughly speaking, there were three types of new spiritual teachers. The first type were genuinely spiritually developed people who offered real wisdom and guidance to their followers. Even if they moved to the US or Europe, they remained relatively grounded, retaining their integrity and morality. In my view, examples of such teachers include Sri Aurobindo and Nisargadatta Maharaj (both of whom remained in India) and Vivekananda and Thich Nhat Hanh (both of whom travelled to the West).

Spiritual Pathocracy: Extremists, Gurus and Cult Leaders

The second type were teachers who began with some degree of spiritual knowledge and insight (perhaps even a degree of spiritual awakening) but were corrupted by the fawning attitude of their followers and by the temptations of the guru role. In other words, they fell victim to the "leadership trap", usually in a very dramatic and extreme way. (We will look at some examples in a moment.)

The third type of teachers had no real spiritual insight or development (except perhaps in an intellectual sense). They were simply narcissistic, manipulative or deluded figures who exploited the psychological and spiritual needs of Western seekers. They were simply hyper-disconnected people who saw spirituality as an opportunity to gain power, admiration and wealth. In their self-deluded grandiosity, some may have believed they were spiritually awakened, when in fact they were at the opposite end of the continuum of connection, as far away from enlightenment as it's possible to be.

A good example of the latter type of teacher is the yoga entrepreneur Bikram Choudhary. After learning a variation of traditional Indian yoga from his own teacher, Choudhary travelled to the United States in the 1970s. Promoting himself as a "two times Yoga champion of India" (although no such competition ever existed), he marketed his teacher's yoga method as his own creation and showed an amazing talent for self-promotion. This was mainly due to the sheer audacity of his claims. For example, he claimed to have taught yoga to President Nixon, Elvis Presley and Frank Sinatra. He quickly became wealthy, mainly through selling franchises of his yoga method and running 9-week training courses for teachers, attended by up to 500 people at a time. Choudhary enjoyed gratuitously displaying his wealth, buying fleets of expensive cars and wearing garish designer clothes, at the same time as proclaiming himself a "spiritually pure" person.

However, Choudhary's claims of spirituality were most

133

seriously undermined by multiple claims of sexual assault, as well as multiple allegations of verbal abuse and threatening behaviour. In 2018, a Californian court upheld allegations of abuse and he was ordered to pay $7 million damages. Instead, he fled the US, and effectively became an international fugitive. However, like all severe narcissists, he was unable to live anonymously, due to his need for attention and admiration. He has continued to run his famous 9-week yoga training courses in countries such as Mexico and Spain.

The Guru Syndrome

A case such as Choudhary's is fairly easy to understand. We can see him as a hyper-disconnected person who craved dominance and was malevolent in his use of power. He could easily have chosen to become a politician or a business magnate (which in a way he was, in an unconventional sense).

The second type of leader I described above is more complex: those who begin with a degree of spiritual insight (and perhaps even some integrity and positive intentions) but are soon corrupted by the role, becoming increasingly disconnected. A good example was Bhagwan Rajneesh, also known as Osho.

Rajneesh clearly had a high degree of spiritual understanding and insight. If you peruse any of his books, you'll be struck by the clarity of his thinking. In fact, Rajneesh was an intelligent and academically gifted man. He had a master's degree in philosophy and worked as a university lecturer for several years. However, Rajneesh also had classic dark triad traits. He had a troubled and unstable childhood – his parents abandoned him soon after his birth and he was brought up by his grandparents. Although a bright student, he was rebellious and disruptive at both school and university. He was expelled from his first college after conflict with a tutor, then banned from attending lectures at his next college for repeatedly arguing with lecturers. He behaved the same way outside university, while exploring his wider political, intellectual and spiritual interests. He joined many groups but never remained for long, due to his restlessness and disruptive impulses.

Rajneesh was the kind of person who could not belong to any organisation, and so had to form his own. His brand of tantric spirituality was especially attractive to Westerners, and he became one of the most popular spiritual teachers of the 20th century. He was an articulate exponent of spiritual knowledge and some of his techniques (such as his body-centred meditation methods) were original and effective. However, there is also no doubt that Rajneesh generated a massive amount of conflict, chaos and confusion. There is evidence from multiple reports that he was addicted to nitrous oxide, was obsessed with pornography and had sex with hundreds of his female followers. Perhaps most famously, he had a collection of 93 Rolls-Royces. In an unusual variant of the Indian tradition of *darshan* (when gurus sit with their followers), once a week Rajneesh would slowly drive by endless lines of his followers, waving regally from a Rolls-Royce as they prostrated themselves and proclaimed their devotion.

One member of Rajneesh's inner circle – who spoke to me on condition of anonymity – reported that during talks Rajneesh's bodyguards would wander through the audience looking for pretty young women with large breasts. The girls would be invited for a private audience with Rajneesh, who would ask them if they wanted to practise tantric rites – which of course meant sex. He liked to use "poppers" (amyl nitrate) before and during sex, but reportedly wasn't a very satisfactory lover. He would ejaculate quickly, giving his partners little opportunity for pleasure. This member of his inner circle also reported that Rajneesh spent most of his time in seclusion watching pornographic films on a cinema screen, while inhaling nitrous oxide, like a debauched rock star.

Over the years, Rajneesh became more reclusive, leaving the day-to-day running of his spiritual community to manipulative, power-hungry people who clearly had dark triad traits themselves. This led to conflict and violence, including attempted murders, poisonings, and even a biological attack in which several hundred people were poisoned with salmonella. Rajneesh died at the age of 58, officially due to a heart attack, although there were reports that he was suffering from AIDS.

Another sad example of a teacher who seems to have been corrupted by his role was the Tibetan teacher Chogyam Trungpa Rinpoche. Trungpa had an important role in transmitting his Buddhist tradition to the West, at a time when it was threatened by the Chinese invasion of Tibet. He also published some insightful writings. For example, his book *Cutting Through Spiritual Materialism* is an excellent overview of the different ways that the spiritual impulse can be hijacked by the ego. Trungpa described how the ego's acquisitive impulses can be smuggled into the spiritual area, manifesting as an egoic desire to gain enlightenment. Enlightenment becomes something that is *added* to the self, like status or achievement, when it's really about letting go.

It is sad that Trungpa was unable to avoid such pitfalls himself. He was a heavy smoker and drinker, who sexually exploited his female disciples. According to some reports, he would start the day with large glasses of gin, and sometimes have to be carried around because he was too drunk to walk. A memoir by his student John Steinbeck (son of the famous novelist) reported that Trungpa regularly took cocaine, from which he also used sedatives to come down. In a stark illustration of the parallels between dictators and corrupt gurus, he had his personal militia, the *Varja Guard*. (In a similar way, Rajneesh had his own armed security men.) In an infamous incident, two visitors to his institute – the poet William Merwin and his wife – were dragged out of their rooms by members of *Varja Guard* and forcibly stripped naked in front of an audience.

Trungpa's alcoholism led to severe health problems, and to

his death at the age of 48. However, his destructive impulses also expressed themselves in his choice of his "dharma heir" (Tibetan Buddhism operates through a lineage of teachers, who are trained and inherit the teachings). He chose his student Osen Tendzin (originally an American man named Thomas Rich) who proved to be even more exploitative and degenerate than Trungpa himself. Tendzin had already contracted AIDS by the time he inherited the dharma. But the news of his diagnosis was kept secret, and he continued to have sex with both male and female students for almost three years, infecting some of them with the virus.

Rajneesh and Trungpa are clearly examples of the leadership trap. They probably had some dark triad traits to begin with, which were exacerbated by their teaching role. As Lord Acton said, "Absolute power corrupts absolutely," and there is no power more absolute than that of a guru over his followers. A guru's narcissism is inflated by the endless flow of devotion from his followers. In the enclosed environment of the spiritual community, he loses his sense of perspective and moral principles. Even when he behaves cruelly and exploitatively, his followers accept it, often extolling the abuse as a test or form of "divine play". Even if the guru did begin with some altruistic intentions, even with some degree of spiritual awakening, this is quickly subsumed by increasing narcissism.

The word "degenerate" (which I used for Ozen Tendzin) is very apt to describe the effect of power and adoration on gurus (and hyper-disconnected political leaders too). Power corrupts by causing a degeneration of personality towards a less empathic, moral and responsible state – in other words, a less *connected* state. Personal or spiritual development means moving further forward along the continuum of connection. But power often has the opposite effect, moving us further back along the continuum – which is essentially what degeneracy means.

Home-grown Gurus

The upsurge of interest in spirituality in the 1960s and 1970s also offered an opportunity for home-grown spiritual practitioners to establish themselves as gurus. There have certainly been some genuinely awakened American and European spiritual teachers, with a genuinely altruistic impulse to spread wisdom and alleviate psychological suffering. (I would suggest the examples of Eckhart Tolle and the late Ram Dass, who retained their integrity and morality whilst becoming famous and revered.) However, it was all too easy for hyper-disconnected people to establish themselves as spiritual teachers. There was, you might say, a new context for them to satiate their need for power and admiration. They didn't have to become criminals or politicians or join corporations – they could become spiritual teachers or form their own religion. They could proclaim themselves as an avatar or messiah, in the knowledge that they would quickly attract followers. At the same time, it was all too easy for spiritual teachers with initial good intentions and some degree of spiritual insight to become corrupted.

The American teacher Adi Da (also known as Da Free John, amongst other names) is perhaps the archetypal example of a home-grown guru. As a young man, he was a spiritual seeker who had powerful awakening experiences which provided him with insight. Even more so than Rajneesh, if you read any of Adi Da's books, you'll find an acute intellectual understanding of spiritual issues. However, these insights weren't sufficient to offset his narcissistic tendencies. Perhaps they even inflated his narcissism, encouraging him to perceive himself as a superior enlightened being.

At any rate, once Adi Da attracted a large number of followers as a spiritual teacher, his narcissism increased to the point of megalomania. He proclaimed himself as the sole saviour of the human race, stating that the only way to become awakened was to follow him. He also routinely humiliated and abused his followers. Like many corrupt gurus, he justified his behaviour by claiming that he was overhauling conventional morality to give his students insight into their habitual reactions and emotional attachments.

Commenting on Adi Da's case, another American guru, Andrew Cohen, described his disappointment at such appalling behaviour from spiritual teachers:

> How could a spiritual genius and profoundly Awakened man like Da Free John [Adi Da], who makes such a mockery of his own genius through his painfully obvious megalomaniacal rantings, leave so many lost and confused? And how is it that his teacher, the Guru of gurus, the extraordinarily powerful Swami Muktananda, who literally jolted so many thousands far beyond what they imagined possible, could leave behind him so much skepticism and doubt as to the actual depth and degree of his attainment? How is all this possible?[1]

Unfortunately, Cohen's own name could be added to this list. Cohen was one of the many Americans who travelled to India in search of enlightenment in the 1970s and 80s, and a powerful awakening experience in the presence of his guru convinced him that he had found it. He felt compelled to return to the US and begin a new life as a spiritual teacher. He quickly attracted followers and eventually established his own spiritual community in Massachusetts, which grew to several thousand members.

However, several years later, allegations began to surface about Cohen's misconduct. In 2009, some of his former students published a book called *American Guru*, which reads like a textbook description of a hyper-disconnected personality. It described how Cohen became increasingly authoritarian, demanding complete obedience and devotion. He put his students under intense psychological pressure, verbally abusing them and even using physical force when angry and frustrated. He demanded ever-increasing amounts of money, threatening his followers with expulsion if they didn't comply. In 2013, because of these accusations, Cohen stepped down as a spiritual teacher, admitting that "in spite of the depth of my awakening, my ego is still alive and well."[2] In 2015, he wrote a public letter to his former students, apologising for his harsh teaching methods and the distress he had caused.

However, as we've seen many times already in this book, people with severe narcissistic traits never slip quietly into anonymity. They need attention and admiration in the same way that addicts need drugs. So it wasn't surprising when, in 2016, Cohen announced his comeback as a spiritual teacher. He even rolled back on his previous apology, claiming that, despite the hurt his teaching methods caused, his former students should be grateful for the spiritual benefits he had given them. Upon hearing the news of his return, over 270 of his former students signed an online petition entitled "Stop Andrew Cohen teaching again".

Understanding the Guru Syndrome

These summaries of corrupt spiritual teachers could be extended almost indefinitely. Sometimes it seems hard to find examples of spiritual teachers who are *not* corrupt. Or using the terminology of this book, it seems easier to find disconnected spiritual teachers rather than connected teachers who are altruistically guiding others to enlightenment.

I'm certainly not disputing that there are some genuinely awakened teachers – I have met some of them myself. However, because the role of spiritual teacher is completely unregulated, and because it's so attractive to hyper-disconnected people, it's almost inevitable that a high proportion of teachers stem from the wrong side of the continuum of connection. This trend has become especially pronounced in recent years, now that social media allows anyone to proclaim themselves as "enlightened" and to attract attention with videos and other posts. Due to their need for attention and admiration, such teachers are very forceful in their attempts to attract followers, and ruthless in their exploitation of their follower's psychological needs. The situation is even more complex when grandiosity and self-delusion convinces hyper-disconnected gurus that they actually *are* spiritually awakened.

In this regard, it's important to note that understanding and even insight aren't equivalent to spiritual awakening. As in the cases of Trungpa, Rajneesh or Adi Da, any intelligent person can understand spiritual teachings *conceptually*. They may even gain some insights about the nature of reality or about human psychology. They can use this understanding to present a simulation of spiritual awakening and attract followers. They may end up believing in the simulation themselves, like actors who play a role for so long that it takes them over.

It's also important to bear in mind that there is a difference between awakening experiences – or spiritual experiences – and wakefulness as an *ongoing* state. For example, both Adi Da and Andrew Cohen appear to have had powerful spiritual experiences, but it's doubtful that they experienced *ongoing* wakefulness. This is like visiting a beautiful country on vacation, as opposed to actually *living* in the country. In most cases, temporary awakening experiences are beneficial. They give people a new sense of optimism and trust, and an awareness that the world is more complex and beautiful than they had imagined. Such experiences encourage people to investigate spiritual practices, as a way of recapturing them.

However, in disconnected people, awakening experiences can be dangerous, encouraging narcissism and grandiosity. A temporary experience may be interpreted as a permanent shift. A brief glimpse of illumination convinces them that they are permanently and completely enlightened. In my view, this is probably what happened to figures such as Adi Da and Andrew

Cohen. And of course, once such people establish themselves as spiritual teachers – and especially once they establish their own isolated spiritual communities – their dark triad traits grow more severe.

But perhaps the situation isn't as clear-cut as this? Is it possible that corrupt gurus could be spiritually awakened, despite their appalling behaviour? Do spiritually awakened people *have to* be benevolent?

The American spiritual author Ken Wilber was a great admirer of Adi Da. Even when Adi Da's megalomania became obvious, Wilber commented that "he is one of the greatest spiritual Realizers of all time... yet other aspects of his personality lag far behind those extraordinary heights. By all means, look to him for utterly profound revelations, unequaled in many ways; yet step into his community at your own risk."[3] Andrew Cohen makes a similar point above, suggesting that his own corrupt behaviour occurred in spite of his wakefulness.

However, I don't believe that wakefulness is independent of other aspects of our personality. I don't believe that it's possible to be awakened and to behave as appallingly as Cohen or Adi Da. When a person undergoes spiritual development, it informs every aspect of their personality and behaviour. It inevitably makes them less narcissistic, and more empathic and altruistic. This makes abuse and exploitation impossible. As we saw earlier, spiritual awakening is about connection, while narcissism and exploitation are linked to disconnection. You can't be both connected and disconnected at the same time. Returning to the beginning of this book, you can't be both Gandhi and Hitler at the same time. You could *begin* as Gandhi and end up as Hitler, after a long process of degeneration, but you can't be a psychopath and a saint simultaneously.

The mistake Wilber makes is the same one that many hyper-disconnected spiritual teachers themselves make, including Andrew Cohen: they confuse the revelations and insights of temporary awakening experiences with a state of permanent wakefulness.

Hyper-Disconnected Cult Leaders

A similar area where we can find many examples of hyper-disconnected personalities is religious cults (or "new religious movements", as academics prefer to call them). Here I'm referring to groups such as the Unification Church (or "Moonies"), Heaven's Gate, and the Children of God. I'm referring to cult leaders such as Jim Jones, David Koresh or L. Ron Hubbard (the founder of Scientology). Perhaps the only real difference between cult leaders and gurus is that almost all cult leaders belong squarely to the third category I mentioned above. In other words, they rarely begin with real spiritual insights and altruistic intentions before becoming corrupted by their role. Rather, they tend to be deeply malevolent people right from the start, motivated purely by a desire for dominance and admiration.

As we would expect, cult leaders almost always emerge from abusive and traumatic childhoods. For example, David Koresh – who led the Branch Davidians sect and was killed with around 80 of his followers after a siege in 1993 – was abandoned by his father before his birth. Shortly after his birth, his mother started a relationship with a violent alcoholic, before also abandoning him when he was four, leaving him to be brought up by his grandmother. Jim Jones – whose followers committed mass suicide at his Jonestown commune in 1978 – also had a severely emotionally deprived upbringing. His father was too ill to work and often in hospital, while his mother was psychologically unstable, and had no emotional attachment to him. He was left to wander the streets of his town alone, and neighbours would sometimes find him walking around naked. As with pathocratic leaders such as Mussolini and Franco, the disconnective effects of this upbringing expressed themselves during Jones's childhood. According to childhood friends, he would torture and kill animals, and became obsessed with religion and death.

The standard cult scenario is as follows: a hyper-disconnected man (again, it's almost always men) with a strong desire for power and admiration proclaims himself a messiah or messenger of God. He attracts followers through his Machiavellianism and charisma, then establishes a community or organisation where he can exercise power and receive the admiration he craves. In order to gain complete control over his followers, the leader orders them to break with their previous lives, including their families. To reinforce the break, the followers are often given new names.

The leader controls every aspect of his followers' lives, including their leisure activities, diet, medicines, sex life and (of course) their thoughts. At his Jonestown commune in Guyana, Jim Jones had strict rules on hairstyles and used a team of barbers to enforce the rules. (This recalls Kim Jong-un of North Korea, who has offered his people a choice of officially approved hairstyles.) In many cases, the leader even gains control over life and death. He is able to instruct his followers to kill others, to even to kill themselves. In Jim Jones's case, this led to the suicide of over 900 people.

As time goes by, the cult leader becomes increasingly authoritarian. He establishes ever more strict codes of behaviour and punishes transgressions more severely. His grandiosity and self-delusion increase. He becomes more suspicious of outsiders and more hostile to the outside world. Away from the constraints of normal society, his bizarre and abusive behaviour is normalised, and grows more extreme.

At the same time, the leader feels growing frustration, because the limited cult environment can't provide the ever-increasing adulation he craves. Power and worship are affected by the law of diminishing returns, so a leader has to keep increasing the amounts he receives, like a drug addict who keeps increasing his dose. A cult leader can't do this indefinitely, which leads to frustration and destruction. This helps to explain why the lifespan of cults is usually very short. The leader's destructive impulses lead him to proclaim that the end of the world is approaching, and that his followers will be the only survivors. Eventually, his growing frustration and malevolence erupts into a frenzy of destruction, typified by the siege and the killings at David Koresh's community in 1993, and by the mass suicides at Jonestown.

Cult Leaders as Dictators

The behaviour of cult leaders is a microcosmic version of the behaviour of dictators. There is the same authoritarianism and intolerance of dissent; the same mistrust and paranoia towards the outside world; the same malevolence to the followers they purport to love. There may even be (as we saw in the cases of Trungpa and Rajneesh) the same militaristic impulses – the same love of uniforms and weapons, and the same threats of violence. Like dictators, cult leaders only love their followers if they can provide them with their adulation they require. If their adulation fades or seems insufficient, they are willing to let them die.

These similarities aren't surprising, since dictators and cult leaders share the same hyper-disconnected personality. In a different environment – if they hadn't been attracted to religious fundamentalism as a way of expressing their hyper-disconnected traits – Koresh and Jones might easily have become pathocrats or serial killers. In some ways, cult leaders are more successful than dictators. Since their communities are smaller and more compliant, it's easy for them to establish complete control and receive unceasing adoration.

At the same time – as mentioned above – the limited nature of cult communities causes a problem, since it limits the leader's power. In a nation of millions of people, there are endless ways for a dictator to satiate his pathological needs – such as invading other countries, finding more (imaginary) enemies to persecute or kill, or new ways to glorify themselves. But cult leaders are much more restricted, even if they keep attracting new followers or expanding their organisations.

The link between hyper-disconnection and spirituality and religion is sadly ironic. As we saw at the beginning of this chapter, genuine spirituality is all about connection. It involves compassion, altruism, equality, tolerance and peace – qualities that are polar opposite to the malevolence of the gurus and cult leaders we've discussed. And yet these hyper-disconnected figures masqueraded as highly *connected* people. Somehow, they managed to convince legions of followers – and in many cases, even convince *themselves* – that they were genuinely spiritually awakened, when they were as disconnected as fascist dictators.

This relates to the next chapter, when we'll consider why hyper-disconnected people – in their various guises – are often appealing to ordinary people and find it easy to attract followers.

Chapter 9

The Abdication Syndrome: The Appeal of Hyper-Disconnected People

I hate to say it, but so far in this book I've been slightly unfair to hyper-disconnected dictators, gurus and cult leaders. This is because the abuse and destruction they cause isn't entirely their fault.

In the case of gurus and cult leaders, it isn't just a matter of hyper-disconnected people brainwashing their followers and using nefarious means to maintain their hold. It's a two-way process. Just as important is people's *psychological need* to follow gurus and cult leaders. Rajneesh or Adi Da didn't force people to become their disciples – they came of their own free will. The disciples' worship of their guru, and their subservience to him, fulfilled deep psychological needs.

In the same way, pathocratic leaders don't just gain power by imposing their authority on people against their will. In most cases, they initially have the support of a large proportion of the population. This support is partly the result of propaganda and the suppression of alternative perspectives, but it also stems simply from their *appeal* to ordinary people. As mentioned previously, many people find pathocrats attractive as personalities, and even develop the kind of deep attachment that disciples feel to their gurus.

In fact, some pathocrats effectively *do* become cult leaders, although on a much larger scale. Hitler held the same kind of hypnotic power over many German people as Jim Jones did over his followers. Like all cult leaders, Hitler was worshipped as a messianic figure who was incapable of making errors and destined to lead his people to greatness. President Trump had (and still has even now) the same kind of cult-like appeal to a sizeable section of the American population. He behaved exactly like a narcissistic guru who craved the adoration of his disciples. With his self-deluded sense of importance and infallibility, he projected an illusion of strength and competence that his followers were more than happy to believe. Some Americans even professed their willingness to die for him, like Jim Jones's followers.

So why do many ordinary people find hyper-disconnected people appealing? Lobaczewski mentioned some important aspects in his studies of pathocracy. He mentioned that ordinary people find psychopaths appealing because of their charisma and charm, and their ability to act decisively and quickly. For normal people who are often cautious and indecisive, the thoughtless impulsiveness of psychopaths seems intoxicating. Particularly in times of economic hardship or political deadlock, psychopathic leaders seem to be the right people to shake up the status quo and "get things done". They appear to be strong, confident figures who can take tough decisions and restore national pride and strength. As Lobaczewski also highlighted, once pathocrats start to carry out a nationalist agenda, acting aggressively towards other nations and persecuting unwanted groups, this creates an exhilarating sense of national unity, which helps to spread psychopathy to the general population.

Of course, all of this is based on an illusion – or more accurately, a misinterpretation. A helpful concept here is the "pre/trans fallacy" developed by Ken Wilber (who I mentioned briefly in the last chapter in connection with Adi Da). This concept describes the common tendency to confuse pre-egoic states of consciousness with trans-egoic states, and vice-versa – or more simply put, to confuse higher traits with lower ones. Wilber gives the example of Freud, who tried to explain spiritual experiences of oneness (which are higher states of consciousness, or trans-egoic states) as a regression to an early childhood state of oneness with the mother (which is a pre-egoic state). According to Wilber, Freud's contemporary (and early follower) Carl Jung made the reverse mistake, by interpreting encounters with the collective unconscious (which according to Wilber are magical and mythical experiences of a pre-egoic state) as higher states of consciousness, equivalent to mystical experiences.[1] In my view, a similar type of misinterpretation occurs with hyper-disconnected leaders. Traits that are essentially negative, and belong to a lower level of human development, are misinterpreted as positive traits of a higher level of human development. Their obsession with power is misinterpreted as selfless dedication. Their ruthlessness and cruelty are misinterpreted as resolution. Their recklessness is mistaken for fearlessness. Their impulsiveness is mistaken for decisiveness. Their lack of emotion and empathy is interpreted as a sign of strength, when in reality it is a massive flaw.

The Abdication Syndrome

However, in my view there is a more fundamental reason for the appeal of hyper-disconnected people. I call this "the abdication syndrome".

One reason I remember my early childhood with affection is because I had the feeling that my parents were in complete control of my world. I felt that they could protect me, provide for me, and take responsibility for my life. If there were any problems, they would work them out. If there was anything I didn't understand, they would tell me the answer. I didn't have to worry about anything. I could go to school, play with my toys, have fun with my friends, and they would take care of the rest.

When I was little older, perhaps 11 or 12, I became aware that my parents weren't omnipotent and omniscient after all. I remember asking my father a question about my school homework and feeling disappointed when he couldn't help me. I began to realise that my dad was a very anxious person who worried constantly about the smallest things and didn't have much knowledge about life or the world. However, by that point I was becoming independent, so no longer had the same strong need for protection.

For many people, this phase of early childhood is an ideal that they long to return to. Unconsciously, they long to worship powerful parental figures who can take responsibility for their lives, protect them from the world, and provide answers to all their questions. This is why they feel drawn to cult leaders and gurus, and hyper-disconnected leaders. They abdicate responsibility for their own lives, handing it over to the guru or leader, in an attempt to rekindle that childhood state of unconditional devotion and irresponsibility. There's no need for them to think for themselves, because the leader knows all the answers. There's no need for them to worry about anything, because the guru will provide everything they need. They don't feel insecure or incomplete or confused anymore. They just bask in the love and protection of the guru, as they used to with their parents.

When we say that a person has been "brainwashed", it means that they have fallen prey to the abdication syndrome. As a result, they're unable to think critically or independently, and are incredibly easy to manipulate. They're ready to believe anything their leader tells them, or to do anything he instructs them to. Again, this is very similar to the state of early childhood, when children are completely open to the influence of their parents.

This helps to explain why, once people abdicate their lives to a leader, they find it impossible to believe anything negative about him. Over the years, in my interactions with followers of hyper-disconnected gurus, I've received some amazingly contorted and ingenious explanations of their terrible behaviour. When gurus get drunk, hold orgies or insult their followers, it's because they are exponents of "crazy wisdom", or demonstrating "divine play" or obscure Tantric practices. When they have sex with their female followers, they are trying to "raise their kundalini". When they are cruel and abusive, they are testing the loyalty and resilience of their disciples. When they smoke cigarettes, eat junk food or watch pornographic movies, they're attempting to break down their followers' unhealthy illusions about them. No matter how appallingly they have behaved, there is always some rational reason or spiritual purpose.

Once I asked an ex-follower of Rajneesh about his 93 Rolls-Royces, and she told me that he built up the collection "to make a satirical point about Western consumerism." An admirer of Chogyam Trungpa told me that although he sometimes behaved badly, it didn't matter because he had reached a level of awareness that transcended conventional notions of morality. Similarly, although he drank a lot, Trungpa's level of awareness was so high that he could never be drunk – and if he appeared to be, he was only pretending; it was to make a point about his own fallibility. A follower of a contemporary guru who is renowned for his affairs with young female disciples told me, "For them, it's a divine encounter. It's a blessing, to share his spiritual power with them. Of course, they get upset when he transfers his affection to another girl, but they know what he's like."

This is the same as when young children find it impossible to believe anything negative about their parents. Like young children, disciples refuse to accept that the guru is imperfect because they don't want to give up the sense of protection and safety that he provides. They don't want to face reality, and take responsibility for their own lives.

It's very telling that cult groups often use family terminology. The leader is often referred to as "father", while the community is often referred to as a "family". The cult led by Jim Baker – which formed in Los Angeles in the late 1960s – explicitly called itself "The Source Family", while Baker took on the name "Father Yod". At roughly the same time in the same city, Charles Manson's group referred to themselves as "the family". In retrospect, many ex-followers of gurus and cults have recognised that they were attracted by these familial aspects. In many cases, they were young people from unstable backgrounds, who lacked father figures and relished both the worship of a father figure and the kinship of the cult community.

In some cases, disciples do wake up to the leader's failings and shake themselves free of the abdication syndrome. As we saw in the last chapter, some of Andrew Cohen's followers courageously stood up to his abusive practices. Unfortunately, though, this is quite rare. The abdication syndrome has an almost uncanny power over the human mind. Once we slip into it, and effectively become young children again, it's difficult to extricate ourselves.

However, I certainly don't want to imply that *all* spiritual seekers fall victim to the abdication syndrome. Many people follow gurus out of a genuine impulse for spiritual development. And as I emphasised in the last chapter, there *are* many genuine spiritual teachers who have no desire for power and admiration and do carefully nurture the development of their followers. In fact, it's perfectly possible to be a spiritual teacher without being a guru – that is, without having a community of disciples around you, offering you unconditional devotion. In fact, the best thing a spiritual teacher can do is to avoid guru worship. And the best thing a spiritual seeker can do is to avoid gurus.

The Abdication Syndrome in Politics

The abdication syndrome can be applied to politics too, where it helps to explain the popularity of pathocrats such as Hitler, Stalin, Mao Zedong and Mussolini. A large part of the appeal of such figures is the "paternal" authority they project. As authoritarian strongmen with a grandiose sense of infallibility, they offer the same sense of protection and certainty as gurus. They appeal to the same desire to return to a childhood state of irresponsibility and innocence.

Every authoritarian leader (and his cohorts) is instinctively aware of the abdication syndrome and exploits it. They do this by creating personality cults, promoting the leader as an omnipotent figure who controls the country's destiny and constantly watches over his people. As with religious cults, there is a direct appeal to the abdication instinct by referring to the leader as a "father". Soviet propagandists referred to Stalin as "Father of Nations" or "Dear Father", portraying him as a caring but strict father who was looking after the well-being of his children, the people of Russia. The North Korean dictator Kim Jong-il (father of Kim Jong-un) also used the title of Dear Father, as well as Dear Leader. The "father" may act as appallingly and abusively as a corrupt guru, and show himself to be incompetent and ignorant, but once people have attached themselves to him, they are reluctant to give up their allegiance. As with gurus, their followers go to great lengths to explain away their faults and mistakes.

This helps to explain the enduring appeal of Donald Trump to millions of Americans. It didn't matter how incompetently Trump acted, even when he disastrously mishandled the coronavirus epidemic, or suggested injecting bleach as a cure for the virus. It didn't matter how immorally he acted, even when he pressurised state electoral officials to change election results, then encouraged his followers to march on the Capitol, leading to violence and death. Like the disciples of corrupt gurus, his followers denied or explained away his behaviour, in order to preserve their image of him as an infallible father figure.

In the same way that children cling more tightly to their parents when they feel insecure, adults are more vulnerable to the abdication syndrome in times of turmoil and insecurity. Research has shown that people are more attracted to cults during times of upheaval in their lives – for example, after a bereavement or divorce, or during a struggle with addiction or depression. Similarly, populations are more vulnerable to the paternal appeal of dictators in times of economic insecurity and global instability. As well as helping to explain the popularity of Trump, this explains the popularity of Hitler and Mussolini in the 1930s, and Berlusconi in the 2000s in Italy.

However, dictators are never able to hold the same power over their nations as cult leaders over their communities. This is the positive side of the restricted cult environment: cult leaders and gurus can command complete and unconditional adoration. But dictators can't control the minds of millions of people in the same way. Despite their control of the media and their secret police forces, a certain proportion of the population – perhaps because they don't experience the same psychological need for a paternal figure – will never fall victim to the abdication syndrome. They will always be able to see pathocrats for the incompetent and malevolent charlatans they really are.

An Abdicated State of Consciousness

The abdication syndrome can be so powerful that it gives rise to a specific altered state of consciousness – or as we could call it, an abdicated state of consciousness.

In 1999, I went to a talk by Andrew Cohen in Manchester, England. Arriving early, I wandered around the venue, perusing the books and other merchandise. I chatted with one of Cohen's followers, who slightly unnerved me with his vacant stare and childlike admiration of his guru. "Andrew is the guy!" he told me with wide-eyed enthusiasm. "He's everything I've been looking for. Everything's been going so well in my life since I've been following him."

I remembered that I had seen that vacant look before. A few years earlier, an acquaintance invited me and my girlfriend to attend a workshop of her spiritual group. I realised straight away that it wasn't for me. I was put off by the massive reverence they showed to their teacher (who wasn't actually present).

Every time they mentioned his name, a giant smile broke across their faces, like teenagers in love. I was also bemused by the poor quality of the teachings, which were mostly incoherent psychobabble, full of cliches and platitudes. But what disturbed me most was the strange, absent look of most members of the group. They shared the same vacant stare, as if they had been collectively hypnotised.

Anyone whose friends or relatives have joined a cult will recognise this trance-like stare. As a former follower of the Unification Church noted of the group's members, "They all had glassy eyes, like two eggs sunny-side up, open so wide that the pupils seemed to bulge out of their faces."[2] In fact, this "glassy-eyed" stare has been investigated by researchers. The sociologist Benjamin Zablocki described this "glazed, withdrawn look" – along with an eerie, frozen smile – as a classic sign of brainwashing, or "extreme cognitive submissiveness."[3] Another sociologist, Marc Galanter, believed that the "glassy stare" has an insulating effect, establishing the boundaries of the group and pushing outsiders away.[4]

From my point of view though, the glassy-eyed stare is a sure sign of the abdication syndrome. It's the look of people who have given up responsibility for their lives and returned to a childlike state of devotion to a paternal figure. This abdicated state of consciousness is similar to hypnosis. After all, the essential feature of hypnosis is that a person gives up their will, and allows the hypnotist to take over the "executive functions" of the mind, which manage our behaviour and control our decisions and emotions.

However, I'm a little reluctant to use the terms "brainwashed" or "brainwashing" in this context. The terms imply that cult members are innocent victims of malevolent leaders, which is too simplistic. As with hypnosis – when a subject allows the hypnotist to take over their will – the abdication syndrome is (at least initially) an agreement between the follower and leader.

The follower has a psychological need to worship someone, and the leader has a psychological need to be worshipped. It's an agreement between a person who wants to take the role of child and a person who wants to take the role of parent.

The abdication syndrome never has a good outcome. Like all toxic relationships, the relationship between authoritarian leaders and their submissive followers is doomed from the start. After all, the relationship is based on pathology, on both sides: the hyper-disconnection of the leaders, and the insecurity and psychological immaturity of their followers. It's also a highly unstable relationship, due to the giant gulf between the leader (with his acolytes) and his submissive followers. Every pathocracy – in the form of a cult or a government – leads inevitably towards conflict, chaos and self-destruction.

Chapter 10

Disconnected Societies

At this point, we're going to take a detour from individual psychology and examine disconnection from a social perspective. This will also involve a detour in historical terms. So far we've mainly been looking at recent human history, but now we're going to travel much further back – in fact, further back than history as we normally understand it, into *pre*history. We're going to survey the entire span of the human race's existence, including the tens of thousands of years we spent as hunter-gatherers, before the advent of farming several millennia ago. At the same time, we're going to take a global perspective, examining present-day societies around the world in terms of connection and disconnection.

Like individual human beings, human societies can be evaluated in terms of their degree of connection. Here we can refer to the social continuum of connection (which you can see at the back of the book, as Appendix 2). As with individual human development, social progress can be measured by moving along the continuum, from left to right. The most disconnected societies are equivalent to dark triad personalities, who are immoral and brutal and devoid of empathy and conscience. These are "psychopathic" societies with high levels of violence, hierarchy and patriarchy. Just as psychopaths have a chronic lack of empathy and conscience, psychopathic societies have a chronic lack of equality and justice. Just as psychopaths are characterised by their manipulation and abuse of other people, psychopathic societies are characterised by brutality and oppression. Psychopathic societies usually have slavery, highly stratified classes or castes, with an elite of authoritarian leaders. Children are usually brought up harshly, with strict discipline and little affection. Women have low status, and there is a high level of domestic violence.

Such societies also have very clear distinctions between gender roles. The male domain is the "outdoor" world of work and society, whereas the female domain is the "indoor" world of child-raising and housework. There is a great deal of sexual repression, with premarital sex and adultery viewed as serious offences (particularly for women). Criminals are brutally punished, and animals are treated cruelly. Disconnected societies also tend to be highly religious, with rigid, strictly enforced beliefs and practices. It is a crime to be an atheist, or to follow any religion besides the state-sanctioned one. There is very little (if any) democracy or freedom of speech, and dissent is a criminal offence, also with harsh punishments.

Connected societies are the equivalent of compassionate and altruistic individuals. They have low levels of violence and brutality, and little hierarchy and oppression. Women have high status, and there is a good deal of overlap between gender roles, with men and women sharing both the outdoor and indoor worlds. There is a high level of equality and democracy, with similar opportunities and rights for all. The power of leaders is limited, and decision-making is shared. Criminals are treated humanely, with an emphasis on rehabilitation rather than punishment. Connected societies are also sexually open, with an acceptance of premarital sex and homosexuality. Children are usually brought up in an affectionate, liberal way, without physical punishment.[1]

There is a symbiotic, mutually reinforcing relationship between disconnected societies and disconnected individuals, or between connected societies and connected individuals. Put simply, disconnected societies tend to produce disconnected people, while connected societies produce connected people. Disconnective social traits of patriarchy, hierarchy and sexual repression create an atmosphere of aggression and malevolence that encourages individual brutality and discourages empathy and benevolence. In the terminology of the Norwegian sociologist Johan Galtung, the "structural violence" (or indirect violence) of disconnected societies leads to direct, individual violence.[2] One example is that disconnected societies with low female status also have high levels of domestic violence and sexual assault. On the other hand, connective social traits of equality, democracy and sexual openness create an atmosphere of social harmony that encourages individual empathy and kindness. There is a lack of structural violence and so a relative lack of direct violence. Connected people are encouraged to express their innate compassion and kindness.

In disconnected societies, it's difficult for highly connected people to thrive. They may face ridicule and hostility, and become social outcasts, or enemies of the state. They may even repress their natural empathy and kindness, because these qualities are so socially unacceptable. Similarly, it isn't easy for disconnected people to thrive in connected societies. They are constrained by democratic processes, by the absence of hierarchical structures for them to climb, and by prevailing social attitudes which disapprove of narcissism and greed.

Present-Day Societies

Let's assess some present-day societies around the world in terms of their level of connection.

Some of the most disconnected societies in the world are in the Middle East, with very low female status, a high level of sexual repression and a lack of democracy. Such societies are highly religious and ruled by pathocratic elites of hereditary rulers (with high levels of environmental narcissism) or religious zealots. In Saudi Arabia, many women effectively live as prisoners, confined to the indoor domain of housework and childcare. A woman may be stoned to death for adultery, while a man can marry multiple times. Homosexuality is illegal, and sodomy is punishable by death. Punishments for other crimes include public beheading, amputation and lashing. And as the 2018 case of the journalist Jamal Khashoggi showed, political dissidents are liable to be tortured and murdered.

In contrast, in other parts of the world there has been a trend towards social connection. At present, the most connected parts of the world are Scandinavia and some other northern European countries such as Holland and Germany. These countries have high levels of equality, social support, female status, democracy, and sexual openness, together with humane treatment of criminals. They also favour international cooperation over conflict. They are largely secular rather than religious. (Significantly, Scandinavian countries are always near the top of surveys of global well-being.)

Other countries lie somewhere between these extremes. The US and the UK possess a medium to high level of social connection, with reasonably high degrees of democracy, female status and sexual openness. At the same time, they possess significant levels of inequality. The UK still has a strong class system, in which elite private schools and universities act as feeder systems for leadership positions. The US is a highly competitive and individualistic society, with little social support and a wide disparity of opportunity and status between whites and other ethnic groups.

Other countries are highly disconnected because they are pathocracies. In the cases of Russia and China, for instance, there are some *cultural* signs of connection amongst the general population, such as reasonably high female status and sexual openness. However, the pathocracy of the governments ensures a high level of disconnective traits, including a severe lack of democracy and freedom of speech, with harsh punishments for dissenters. At the same time, these countries have aggressive, expansionist foreign policies, and a distrust of international agreements or alliances.

We can also assess societies throughout human history in terms of their level of connection. This is where the story becomes more complex, and even surprising. Because a careful look at the earliest human societies reveals that they possessed a high level of connection. In fact, it appears that for the vast majority of the time that our species has lived on this planet, our societies have been highly connected – and only became disconnected fairly recently.

This is quite a large claim, so let me unpack it in some detail.

The Myth of Prehistoric Hardship

Imagine what life was like for early human beings, before the dawn of civilisation a few thousand years ago. You might picture dirty, hairy savages, carrying spears or clubs, grunting and shouting at one another. You might picture our ancestors half-starved and freezing, living in fear of attack by wild animals and other humans. You might assume that they lived in small tribes led by powerful chieftains and were constantly at war with neighbouring tribes.

In fact, prehistoric life was nothing like this caricature. One of the biggest myths about human history is that it has been a continual progression. According to this myth, human beings began as ignorant and violent savages, whose lives were a brutal struggle for survival. Since then, we have become gradually more peaceful and civilised, and life has become gradually easier and more harmonious.

However, archaeological and anthropological evidence suggests that this myth is a distortion, and that in many ways human history has been a *regression*. For example, it isn't true that early human beings had to struggle to survive. In fact, prehistoric groups had a fairly easy time. For most of human history – in fact, 95% of our time on this planet – our ancestors lived as hunter-gatherers, in small tribes which usually moved to a different site every few months. These groups survived by hunting animals and collecting fruits, vegetables, roots and nuts. Studies of hunter-gatherer groups who live in the same way as our ancestors have shown that they only spend around 2-3 hours a day (or 12-20 hours a week) searching for food. For example, in 1979, the anthropologist Richard B. Lee published a famous study of the !Kung people of Africa, describing how they only spent about 15 hours a week collecting food, and had an abundance of leisure time.[3]

In other words, our hunter-gatherer ancestors probably "worked" much less – and had much more leisure time – than we do. This makes sense when we consider that, in prehistoric times, human beings were very thinly spread over the surface of our planet. Back then, the world's population was tiny. According to some estimates, around 15,000 years ago, the population of Europe was only 29,000, and the population of the whole world was no more than half a million.[4] This means that resources would have been plentiful, and that no one would have needed to fight for survival, or even look very hard for food.

Early human beings' lives were easy in other ways too. Their diet was superior to most modern human beings', with no dairy products and a wide variety of fruits, vegetables, roots and nuts, all eaten raw, together with meat. Prehistoric humans were also less vulnerable to disease than later peoples. In fact, until the advances of modern medicine and hygiene of the 19th and 20th centuries, they may well have suffered less from disease than any other human beings in history. Many of the common diseases that afflict present-day human beings arose in the agricultural era (beginning around 10,000 years ago in the Middle East and spreading slowly around the rest of the world), passed on by the animals we domesticated. In a review of the relationship between agriculture and human disease, the United Nations' Food and Agriculture Organization found that almost three-quarters of human diseases originated in animals. Pigs and ducks passed the flu on to us, horses gave us colds, cows gave us the pox and dogs gave us the measles, and so on.[5]

The Myth of Prehistoric Warfare

Prehistoric life was free of struggle in a more overt way too: there was an absence of warfare. The idea that early human beings were savagely violent and warlike – and that over time we have become gradually peaceful – is one of most baseless (but most entrenched) myths of all. In 2005, when I published *The Fall*, the notion of "prehistoric peace" seemed controversial, and some reviewers suggested that I was perpetuating the myth of the noble savage. However, since then, I'm glad to say that much more evidence has become available, and now the notion of prehistoric peace is much more widely accepted. For example, in 2013 the anthropologists Jonathan Haas and Matthew Piscitelli surveyed descriptions of 2900 prehistoric human skeletons from scientific literature. Apart from a single massacre site in Sudan (in which two dozen people were killed), they found only four skeletons with signs of violence – and even these signs were consistent with homicide rather than warfare. This dearth of violence completely contrasted with later periods when signs of war were obvious in skeletal marks, weapons, artwork, defensive sites and architecture.[6] Also in 2013, the anthropologist Brian Ferguson carried out a detailed survey of archaeological findings from Neolithic Europe and the Near East, and found almost no evidence of warfare. Evidence suggested that warfare only became common in these areas around 3500 BC.[7]

In fact, when we consider the tiny populations of prehistoric times, a lack of warfare makes sense. Many anthropologists believe that warfare is the result of competition for territory and resources. And since population densities were so low during prehistory, such competition probably didn't exist. In a world without scarcity, why would people need to fight? As Haas and Piscitelli have put it, "For 190,000 years of human existence on the planet, low population densities obviated all the proposed biological or cultural reasons for warfare and intraspecific conflict."[8]

A lack of warfare also makes sense in terms of our ancestors' mobile way of life. This means that our prehistoric ancestors wouldn't have identified themselves with a specific territory and felt the need to protect and expand their living space. Why would they become attached to one specific area, knowing that they would only be there for a short while? Research has shown that even modern-day nomadic hunter-gatherers are generally not territorial – that is, they don't think in terms of owning a particular area of land, and don't aggressively resist anybody who encroaches on it. Rather than being in conflict, hunter-gatherer groups interact with each other a good deal. They regularly visit each other, make marriage alliances, and often switch membership.[9] In line with all this, a recent study of 21 contemporary hunter-gatherer groups by the anthropologists Fry and Soderberg showed a striking lack of evidence for inter-group conflict over the last hundred years. There was only one society (an Australian Aboriginal group called the Tiwi) who had a history of group killings.[10]

Simple and Complex Hunter-Gatherer Groups

But hold on, you might be thinking, what about the tribal peoples I've heard about who are fierce warriors, continually fighting against neighbouring tribes and murdering – and possibly even eating – strangers who wander into their territory? For example, you might have read Steven Pinker's book *The Better Angels of Our Nature*, which purports to provide statistical evidence of prehistoric warfare, based on a number of contemporary tribal peoples.

However, it's important to distinguish (as Pinker does not) between what anthropologists refer to as "simple" and "complex" hunter-gatherer groups. Simple hunter-gatherer groups live an "immediate return" way of life, immediately using any food or resources rather than storing them for later use. They live in small, egalitarian mobile groups with few possessions. There is often a lot of cooperation between different groups, and such groups are generally peaceful. And it is in such societies that human beings have lived for the vast majority of our time on this planet. As Brian Ferguson has put it, "Simple hunting and gathering characterized human societies during most of humanity's existence dating back more than 200,000 years."[11]

On the other hand, complex hunter-gatherer groups tend to stay in the same site and have larger populations. They tend to have authoritarian leaders and social ranking, ancestral privileges, and less democratic power structures. They are also warlike. These complex hunter-gatherer groups are a much more recent historical development. However, some authors – such as Pinker – misrepresent them as proof of the ubiquity of warfare in human history. (Pinker also chooses groups who are unrepresentative of prehistoric hunter-gatherers because their way of life has been severely disrupted by contact with European colonists.)

Prehistoric Connection

All the evidence suggests that simple hunter-gatherer groups were highly connected societies.

Over the last hundred years so, anthropologists have observed many groups who live the same simple hunter-gatherer lifestyle as our ancestors (although as time goes by, more and more groups have suffered cultural disruption due to colonisation and globalisation). They have consistently reported connective social traits. For example, most simple hunter-gatherer groups are democratic to a sophisticated and highly rational degree. Most societies do operate with a leader of some kind, but their power is usually very limited, and they can easily be deposed if the rest of the group are dissatisfied with them. Leaders don't have the right to make decisions on their own. In most tribal groups, decisions are reached by consensus.

Simple hunter-gatherer groups are also extremely egalitarian. They don't have hierarchies based on power and wealth. In fact, the notion of individual property or territory is completely foreign to them. The anthropologist James Woodburn has spoken of the "profound egalitarianism" of hunter-gatherer groups, describing how they "are not entitled to accumulate movable property beyond what they need for their immediate use. They are morally obliged to share it."[12] One example is the Hadza of Africa, who never own an "unnecessary" possession – such as a second axe or a second shirt – for more than a few days, and usually not more than a few hours. They feel a moral obligation to share possessions.

Simple hunter-gatherer groups are egalitarian in gender terms too. The anthropologist Bruce Knauft has spoken of their "extreme political and sexual egalitarianism."[13] In contrast to disconnected societies, men have no authority over women. Women usually choose their own marriage partners, decide what work they want to do and work whenever they choose to. If a marriage breaks down, women have custody rights over their children.[14]

It's perhaps significant here that, in economic terms, the role of women in hunter-gatherer groups is just as important as (and often more important than) the role of men. It's common for women to provide most of the group's food, through gathering. For example, studies of Australian Aboriginal communities have found that there are frequent periods where most of a group's food stems from roots, fruits and seeds foraged by women, rather than from meat hunted by men. In some circumstances, men provided less than 10% of a group's food.[15] (In this respect, it would be more accurate to call the groups "gatherer-hunters".)

Simple hunter-gatherer groups go to great lengths to preserve their egalitarianism. In the words of the anthropologist

Christopher Boehm, they "apply techniques of social control in suppressing both dominant leadership and undue competitiveness."[16] One way they do this is by sharing credit. For example, the !Kung of Africa swop arrows before hunting, and when an animal is killed, credit doesn't go to the person who fired the arrow, but to the person who brought it. At the same time, they denigrate and ridicule people who are arrogant and self-aggrandising. The groups also take great care to ensure that unsuitable people don't attain power. Any person who shows signs of a desire for power and wealth is usually barred from consideration as a leader. When power-hungry individuals (who we would refer to as disconnected) start to assert their drive for dominance, the groups practise what Christopher Boehm calls "egalitarian sanctioning." They gang up against the domineering person, ostracise him, desert him, or even – in extreme circumstances, when they feel that their own lives may be in danger due to his tyrannical behaviour – assassinate him. As Boehm has noted, "This egalitarian approach seems to be universal for foragers who live in small bands that remain nomadic, suggesting considerable antiquity for political egalitarianism."[17] (We will return to these measures later, when we look at what modern societies can do to protect ourselves from disconnected leaders.)

I've suggested that the best way of measuring progress (both individually and socially) is in terms of connection. In these terms, there is a massive amount of evidence that prehistoric societies were more advanced than later societies – and even many contemporary societies. They lacked disconnective social traits such as warfare, hierarchy, patriarchy and authoritarianism. Conversely, they possessed connective traits of egalitarianism, democracy, caring child-raising practices, sexual openness, a lack of distinctions between gender roles and so on. The fact that these connected societies existed for 95% of our time on this planet suggests that connection is natural to human beings, and that the highly disconnected societies of more recent times are an aberration.

The Shift to a Settled Lifestyle

If disconnected societies are an aberration, how did they come about? What brought a shift from social connection to disconnection?

About 10,000 years ago, some human groups began to give up the hunter-gatherer lifestyle and settle down. They began to live in small villages – probably of no more than 150 people – where they cultivated crops such as barley and wheat, and domesticated animals such as sheep and goats (dogs were already part of hunter-gatherer groups). Initially, they weren't really farmers so much as gardeners, or horticulturalists. By about 7000 BC, this settled lifestyle was well-established in parts of the Middle East and began to spread slowly around Europe and Asia. By 5000 BC it had spread to India, and it finally reached Britain and Scandinavia – and to the East, China – during the third millennium BC.

Some authors have linked the end of the hunter-gatherer era with the shift to hierarchical and warlike societies (or as we would say, disconnected societies). According to this theory, when our ancestors settled down, they started to be territorial, to accumulate wealth and property, and to covet the territory and wealth of other groups. However, there isn't a straightforward link between the end of the hunter-gatherer lifestyle and the advent of social disconnection. The first settled communities had very similar social characteristics to hunter-gatherers. There is certainly the same lack of evidence for violent conflict. Brian Ferguson found no evidence of warfare in the Levant – an area which includes present-day Jordan, Syria, Israel and Palestine – until 3500 BC, even though the area was densely populated and farmed from 9000 BC.[18] In addition, evidence from the burial practices of horticultural societies suggests a lack of status differences and powerful individual leaders. Women still had high status, with important social roles. In fact, it was mainly women's responsibility to cultivate the crops, while the men cleared land for new gardens or continued to hunt. The same patterns are true of many contemporary groups who live a horticultural lifestyle. According to Christopher Boehm, horticulturist groups are similar to hunter-gatherers in that they "lack strong leadership and domination among adult males, they make group decisions by consensus, and they too exhibit an egalitarian ideology."[19]

In other words, these early settled peoples continued to live in social connection for thousands of years after giving up the hunter-gatherer lifestyle.

The Fall into Disconnection

However, around 6000 years ago, a shift began. Highly disconnected societies started to supplant connected groups. Beginning in the Middle East and Central Asia, groups started to show signs of hierarchy, warfare and patriarchy. Whereas earlier peoples were usually buried communally, now individual burial became the norm. People were buried with signs of identity and property, and important people – such as chieftains – were buried with a great deal of wealth, including horses, weapons and even wives. Now artwork was full of battle scenes and images of weapons. Numerous battle sites show that the long period of prehistoric peace gave way to a new phase of chronic, savage warfare. In economic terms, the simple horticultural lifestyle of early settled groups gave way to a heavier type of agriculture, more akin to modern farming, including ploughs and the domestication of animals such as cows and horses.

Over the following centuries, these new disconnected groups migrated across Asia and Europe. All over the two continents, there are signs of disruption and destruction, as the groups conquered the old connected societies they came across. By around 2500 BC, most of Europe, the Middle East and Asia were occupied by disconnected societies. In some isolated places, connected societies survived for longer. For example, on the island of Crete, a highly connected society flourished until about 1500 BC. This was the Minoan culture, where women had high status, and there were no signs of warfare. Minoan artwork depicts women as priestesses, goddesses, and dancing and talking at social occasions. Minoan artwork shows a deep reverence of nature, with colourful and vibrant images of flowers, birds, fish and other animals, together with beautiful symbols and patterns. The whole culture seemed to have an atmosphere of joy and lightness, a lack of oppression and fear. However, eventually the island was invaded by warriors from mainland Greece, who brought their new disconnective traits. Now there were signs of warfare and low female status, and artwork was dominated by images of warfare and anthropomorphic gods.

The fall into disconnection was drastic. All over the Eurasian landmass, women's status fell to the point where they were treated as mere property. In ancient India and China, once a husband died, his wife was expected to kill herself (or be killed) shortly afterwards, as if her life had no value without him. In some cultures, women could be confiscated by money lenders or tax collectors to help settle debts. In many societies, women were expected to cover their whole bodies and heads, so that as "property" they wouldn't be coveted by other men.

Whereas prehistoric societies were egalitarian, the new disconnected societies included large numbers of slaves, together with elite groups who lived lives of wealth and privilege while peasants and serfs lived close to starvation. Whereas prehistoric societies appear to have had a healthy, open attitude to sex and the human body, the new disconnected societies treated premarital and extramarital sex as crimes, sometimes punishable by death. Another change was that children started to be treated more harshly. People began to believe that harsh treatment was actually *beneficial* for children. Even physical abuse (such as beating or smacking) was advocated as a way of teaching children discipline and making them more resilient.

The shift was evident in religion too. The "religion" – if that's the right term – of prehistoric peoples wasn't theistic. It was based on the twin concepts of individual spirits (that filled the air and could inhabit natural phenomena) and a more fundamental spiritual force which pervaded all things, giving them life and sentience. However, the new disconnected cultures conceived of personal Gods who were separate from the world, and overlooked it from a distance, with the power to intervene in its affairs. Originally, disconnected peoples conceived of different gods who controlled different aspects of human life, like ministers who manage different parts of government. Later, some groups developed the concept of a single all-powerful God who was responsible for every aspect of life, like an absolute ruler. In other words, there was a shift from polytheism to monotheism, which eventually became dominant throughout the Middle East and Europe.

Psychopathic Civilisations

The so-called "great" civilisations and cultures of the ancient world were so disconnected that they could be classed as psychopathic societies. The advent of civilisation may have brought some technological and cultural advances, but in every other respect it wasn't a progression but a massive regression. Ancient Egypt and Sumer – usually seen as the first civilisations – were highly warlike, patriarchal and hierarchical, ruled by tyrannical warrior-leaders and aristocratic elites. In the words of one archaeologist, Sumerian culture was characterised by an "obsessive drive for wealth and possession" which led to massive social inequality.[20] The Sumerians were also incredibly brutal, even to their own families, with an "ever-growing ferocity... of the punishments to be inflicted on adulterous wives or disobedient children."[21] In ancient Egypt, all land was owned by a small group of nobles which the rest of the population worked on as serfs. The serfs could be called away from their fields at any time to do other work for the nobles – work which included building the pyramids.

The later civilisations of Ancient Greece and Rome were more connected in that they understood the importance of democracy and power-sharing, but they were also extremely warlike, with slavery and very low status for women. In Ancient Greece, women couldn't own property and had no political rights, and weren't allowed to have contact with men beyond their own family or to leave their homes after dark. (Paradoxically, the Ancient Athenians developed highly sophisticated and enlightened political systems, which we will examine in detail in Chapter 14.) Ancient Rome was effectively a slave society, where slaves made up between 20-30% of the population and performed many essential jobs. The Roman Empire was a massive project of conquest, enslavement and murder that appropriately was the inspiration for the Nazi Third Reich.

These ancient societies set the mould for centuries of so-called "civilisation" throughout Europe, the Middle East and Asia. Until modern times, the standard social model around the world was a feudal hierarchy in which a small minority of chieftains, nobles or aristocrats dominated a vast majority of underlings, serfs or peasants. The gulf between the two classes was so wide that nobles often saw themselves as a different species to peasants. There are legal documents from medieval English estates where peasants' children are referred to as their "brood" or "litter". Other nobles listed their peasants under the category of "livestock".

Warfare was so endemic to these societies that they viewed attacking and killing other humans as a natural and even honourable activity. Until the nineteenth century, European countries were at war with one or more of their neighbours for an average of nearly every second year. In other words, there was one year of war for every year of peace. Naturally, these pre-modern societies were highly patriarchal too. Even at the highest echelons of society, women had little or no rights, no influence over the political or cultural lives of their communities and were seen as intellectually inferior to men.

Later, beginning about five hundred years ago, groups of people from highly disconnected societies carried their disconnectve traits to other continents, spreading across North and South America, Africa and Australasia. (This is the colonial pathocracy described in Chapter 5.) Disconnected societies have continued to dominate the world to the present day, despite a trend towards increasing connection (which we will examine in a moment).

From Psychological to Social Disconnection

How should we explain the fall into social disconnection which began around six thousand years ago?

In *The Fall*, I suggested that this shift was essentially psychological. Some human groups began to experience an intensified sense of individuality, which generated a new sense of separation. People began to feel that they were separate individuals, living inside their own mental space, with the rest of the world and all other people "out there" on the other side. Prehistoric peoples certainly had a sense of individual identity too, but now people's identity became more defined and circumscribed. People began to feel not only separate to the world around them, but also to their own communities, and even to their own bodies. The world "I" became much more important than before. People became more concerned with their personal desires and ambitions, and their personal stories of achievement and status. And this psychological disconnection gave rise to social disconnection. The new disconnected societies were a manifestation of individual disconnected minds.

The question of why the fall into social disconnection occurred is therefore a question of why the members of certain groups experienced a psychological shift. It's obviously difficult to establish causes of an event that happened thousands of years ago, but in *The Fall*, I suggest that it may have been due to environmental factors. About 6000 years ago, large areas of the Middle East, Central Asia and North Africa began to dry up. The areas had previously been fertile and supported many animal and human groups. But now rainfall decreased, rivers and lakes dried up, vegetation disappeared, and famine and drought took hold. This environmental change is significant because it coincided – at the same time and in the same area – with the emergence of new signs of psychological and social disconnection.

In *The Fall*, my theory is that these new environmental pressures brought a need for ingenuity and technological innovation which necessitated a new kind of abstract, egoic intelligence. At the same time, the hardship of life must have encouraged a new spirit of selfishness and competition. As a result, people developed a stronger sense of individual identity. They began to be "separated off" from the world, living inside themselves. They became disconnected from each other and from their own bodies. Their new abstract intelligence also brought new technologies and practical skills which enabled them to easily conquer the old connected cultures and to spread their new disconnected culture around the world.

Socially disconnective traits such as warfare, hierarchy and patriarchy are the collective results of groups of disconnected minds. In Chapter 1, I described how highly disconnected people feel a strong desire for wealth and power because they feel a powerful sense of lack and vulnerability, which creates an impulse to accumulate. Warfare – which means attacking and conquering other groups and stealing their territory and property – is a collective manifestation of this impulse. The same urge to accumulate impelled disconnected people to compete for wealth and status within their own societies, which gave rise to hierarchy and inequality. The same urge impelled them to dominate women, and to oppress other social classes and ethnic groups. The new sense of separation between mind and body led to a sense of otherness and hostility towards physical urges and processes, which resulted in sexual repression. Another result of collective disconnection was theistic religion. The notion that all-powerful deities were watching over the world and controlling the events of people's lives was an attempt to offset the separate ego's new sense of insignificance and vulnerability.

From this point on, disconnection was normal to members of these groups. Obviously, there were different degrees of individual disconnection. As with modern humans, many members of the groups probably only experienced a mild degree of disconnection and were still capable of some degree of empathy and altruism. But like modern societies, the groups would be dominated by the most intensely disconnected people. And the general level of disconnection of groups probably increased over time, as disconnective social structures and traits became more established.

It's important to remember that there is a symbiotic relationship between individual and social disconnection, as described earlier in this chapter. This helps us to understand why psychological disconnection has maintained itself for thousands of years. Since disconnection has only existed for a small proportion of human history, and is so contrary to previous human behaviour, we can hardly say that it is innate to human beings. If anything, the opposite is likely to be the case. Since we've lived in a state of connection – both individually and socially – for 95% of our time on this planet, surely connection is innate to us.

However, once a society becomes disconnected, it perpetuates individual disconnection. A pervasive lack of fairness and justice encourages cruelty and oppression. Disconnective traits of wealth-accumulation and status-seeking become established as socially desirable. Individual aggression and ruthlessness are encouraged, while empathy and emotion are discouraged. If children or young people did show signs of empathy and emotion, they would quickly learn that these were socially unacceptable and start to repress them.

Perhaps even more importantly, social disconnection perpetuates individual disconnection through child-raising practices. I suggested in Chapter 1 that childhood emotional deprivation and trauma are the main cause of hyper-disconnection. So once disconnected societies established austere and affectionless child-raising practices – usually including physical punishments and other forms of harsh discipline – it's inevitable that adults developed a certain degree of psychological disconnection. Many members of such societies would learn to "switch off" their natural empathy.

At the same time, disconnection is perpetuated by hardship. Psychological disconnection began with a struggle to survive, and for most people around the world, this struggle continued for thousands of years (and is still continuing now for many people). Initially the struggle was mainly environmental, a straightforward battle against hunger and hardship. But once disconnected societies became established, ordinary people faced many other issues: warfare, oppression, slavery, lack of freedom and opportunity, more disease, and so on. These social conditions encouraged the same egoic intelligence and selfishness which caused the fall in the first place, and so perpetuated disconnection.

A Movement towards Connection

For the last few thousand years – and even more so, over the past few centuries, since colonisation spread social disconnection all over the world – human life has largely been filled with brutality, conflict and suffering, caused by disconnected individuals and the disconnected societies they established. It's no wonder that many people consoled themselves with belief in an idyllic afterlife. Understandably, they couldn't accept that life could be so full of injustice and hardship without some compensation at the end.

However, over the last 250 years or so, a significant change has taken place. In large parts of the world, a movement towards connection has begun.

If modern Europeans or Americans could travel back to, say, the 17th century, they would be astonished at the brutality that filled their ancestors' lives. In countries like Britain and France, there was massive cruelty to children and animals. Unwanted babies were routinely abandoned, while poor parents sometimes trained their children to be thieves or prostitutes. The streets thronged with homeless children, who were often arrested for vagrancy and sent to prison. The most popular sports were forms of animal torture, like cat-dropping (when cats were dropped from high windows and people would bet on which hit the ground first) or ratting (when people bet on how many rats a dog could kill). The punishment of criminals was as barbaric as modern-day Saudi Arabia or the Taliban. People were hung for trivial offences like theft or burglary, and another popular form of entertainment was the stocks, when members of the public threw rotten fruit and stones at petty criminals, who would sometimes die from their injuries.

In fact, in many ways life in most European countries before the 18th century was similar to modern hyper-disconnected societies such as Saudi Arabia. Women had very low status, with little or no access to education or professions. Societies were ruled by hereditary elites who lived lives of enormous privilege and wealth while peasants struggled to survive. Such societies were highly religious, and prone to civil wars between different religious denominations, and to religious wars with neighbouring countries.

However, in the second half of the 18th century, a shift began. A new wave of empathy and compassion emerged, together with a new awareness of the importance of justice and rights. This led to the emergence of the women's rights movement, the anti-slavery movement, the animal rights movement, the development of concepts of democracy and egalitarianism, and so on. It was as if human beings had a new ability to connect with one another, as if now they were able to see the world from each other's perspective and could sense each other's suffering.

This new awareness of injustice and human rights gave rise to the French Revolution and the American Constitution. Both challenged the old social order by insisting that all human beings were born equal and entitled to the same opportunities and rights. The new awareness manifested itself culturally, in the Romantic movement. The Romantic poets, painters and composers of the late 18th and early 19th centuries were inspired by the new social ideals of justice and democracy. In addition, their work was inspired by a new sense of the beauty and grandeur of nature. It was almost as if a boundary had dissolved away and human beings were able to participate in the world again, rather than observing it from a distance. At the same time, it was as if the Romantics were more connected to their own inner being, particularly to their emotions. In a sense, the Romantic movement was a giant outpouring of emotion, like water flooding over a dam of cold rational disconnection.

The trend towards connection continued through the 19th and 20th centuries. Democracy spread to other countries. Women's status continued to rise, along with increasing openness to sex and the body. Class divisions eroded away, as large sections of the population (including women) gained access to education, health care, sanitation and an improved diet. (Although as we saw earlier in this book, one devastating side effect of the dissolution of the old social structures was that it allowed hyper-disconnected people to rise up and seize power, as in Soviet Russia and Nazi Germany.)

In the 20th century, an increasing sense of connection to nature gave rise to the environmental movement. Growing empathy for animals led to increasing vegetarianism and veganism. Gender roles have become less defined, with men and women sharing both the outdoor and indoor worlds. Since the end of the Second World War, there has been a trend towards peace and reconciliation, particularly in Europe. Nations that were constantly at war with each other – such as France, Spain, Britain, Germany and others – have been at peace for almost eight decades. Another significant trend over recent decades has been the ever-growing number of people following spiritual paths and practices – and in so doing, exploring their own being and expanding their awareness. (This is especially significant because – as I will explain in more detail in Chapter 13 – spiritual development is essentially a movement towards increased connection.)

Culture Wars

One of the most significant cultural issues of our time is a conflict between old disconnective traits and emerging new connective traits. More specifically, this is a conflict between people who uphold and defend traditional values such as patriarchy, materialism, nationalism and monotheistic religion, and people who embody new values such as equality, environmentalism, transnationalism and spirituality. The traditional "disconnectives" feel threatened by the rising "connectives" and are trying to assert their values more forcefully, in the same way that a person who is falling tries to strengthen his grip. People with a patriarchal and ethnocentric mindset feel threatened by growing demands for gender and racial equality. Traditionally religious people feel threatened by the rising tide of non-denominational spirituality, and so have become more rigid in their beliefs. The assertion of disconnective values has also expressed itself in a recent resurgence of right-wing nationalism, as shown by the UK's exit from the European Union, the increasing extremism of the US Republican Party, and the election of hard right rulers such as President Modi of India.

These are the "culture wars" that are so characteristic of our time. More accurately, they can be seen as "connection wars" – the struggle of disconnected societies to maintain their structures in the face of a rising wave of connected values and traits. After thousands of years, the disconnective traits are deep-rooted and rigid, and difficult to dislodge. But the connective traits have vitality and momentum, and appear to be growing stronger year by year.

The values that are sometimes referred to as "woke" are fundamentally connective values. It's true that "wokeness" can be applied too heavy-handedly and may sometimes become a rigid ideology that creates identity and otherness (and therefore engenders disconnection). However, "woke" values are rooted in empathy and compassion. They're about challenging injustice and inequality, respecting other people's rights and being sensitive to their needs. In this way, "wokeness" is another expression of the movement towards social connection. It's therefore not surprising that disconnected people are so disparaging to "woke" values. When they accuse people of being oversensitive "snowflakes", they're behaving in the same way as the disconnected people who disparage emotion and empathy as weakness.

The Struggle Between Left and Right

Broadly speaking, in political terms, connective and disconnective traits manifest themselves in terms of the left and right. This is a complex issue, because – as with woke values – left-wing ideals can easily be hijacked by disconnected people. As we saw earlier, some of the most severely disconnected people in history have adopted left-wing ideologies, such as Mao Zedong, Stalin and countless other communist leaders. In fact, as a political ideology, communism is perfectly suited to pathocratic leaders. Communism is so contrary to human psychological needs that it can only survive through suppression and domination. It involves the repression of individual identity and volition, and the denial of human needs such as personal achievement and ownership. It therefore inevitably takes the form of a pathocracy.

However, communism is a perverted form of left-wing politics. The fundamental principles of left-wing politics – or socialism – are connective, while the general principles of right-wing politics are disconnective. In its true sense, left-wing politics is an empathic response to social injustice, which aims to increase equality and fairness, and to extend the same rights and opportunities to every citizen. It aims to dismantle the hierarchical social structures that concentrate power and wealth in the hands of a minority of privileged people.

On the other hand, right-wing politics defends traditional disconnective social structures. It emphasises competition and individualism, and maintains hierarchy and inequality. Right-wing politicians may voice a desire to help their citizens and to reduce poverty, injustice and privilege, but in practice their polices always increase inequality. Their emphasis on competition and the free market means that they are reluctant to take any action to limit the power of the privileged and wealthy. Their emphasis on individual responsibility makes them reluctant to provide social support and opportunity for underprivileged people, which maintains poverty. In addition, the ideology of capitalism is based on the disconnective need to *accumulate* – that is, the psychological need to accumulate possessions, wealth, status and power to strengthen the separate ego. In this sense, capitalism is a direct expression of disconnection.

Connection and Evolution

Why has there been a movement towards connection since the 19th century? We saw earlier that disconnection is linked to hardship, so one possibility might be that this movement is simply the result of improved living standards in recent times.

However, most people's living conditions didn't improve significantly until well after the movement towards connection began. For most ordinary European and American people, life continued to be hard until the 20th century. During the 19th century, living conditions actually grew worse for many ordinary people, because of the Industrial Revolution. In fact, we can probably reverse the causal link between connection and living conditions: it was a movement towards connection which brought about an improvement in working class people's living conditions, when middle- and upper-class people (such as politicians and factory owners) began to empathise with their plight and took measures to improve living and working conditions.

In *The Fall*, I suggested that the movement towards connection is essentially an *evolutionary* phenomenon. On a physical level, evolution is a process of variation and complexification in life forms. But evolution is also an inner, mental aspect. As living beings become more complex physically, they also become more sentient and conscious. They become more aware of the world around them, of other living beings and of their own inner lives. From this point of view, evolution itself is a movement towards connection. As living beings become more conscious, they become more connected to the world, to each other, and to their own inner beings. So in my view, the increasing social connection over the last 250 years was an expression of this evolutionary movement. Essentially, it represented – and was due to – a collective expansion of awareness. (In Chapter 13, we'll see that this also applies to individual spiritual development, which involves an individual expansion of awareness, and is also a process of increasing connection.)

All of this begs the question: why would such an evolutionary movement be taking place now? Why would it have begun about 250 years ago, and have increased in intensity over the last few decades?

Perhaps there's no particular reason why it's happening. Evolutionary developments may simply occur spontaneously from time to time. As anyone who has read my previous books will know, I don't subscribe to the Neo-Darwinist view that evolution is an accidental and random process. As discussed in my book *Spiritual Science*, Neo-Darwinism is being questioned by more and more biologists, who believe that the staggering creativity of the evolutionary process can't be explained in terms of random mutations and natural selection. The kind of random mutations that confer a survival advantage happen too infrequently to account for the full diversity of life on Earth.

I believe there is a creativity *inherent* within the evolutionary process, an impetus that moves life forms towards increasing physical complexity and subjective awareness. As the palaeontologist Simon Conway Morris has written, evolution has an "uncanny ability... to navigate to the appropriate solution."[22] One manifestation of this is the phenomenon of "adaptive mutation" (or non-random mutation) which suggests that beneficial mutations can occur spontaneously, when they are needed to help life forms survive. For example, when bacteria that are unable to process lactose are placed in a lactose-rich medium, 20% of their cells quickly mutate into a Lac+ form, so that they can process lactose. These mutations become part of the bacteria's genome and are inherited by future generations.

You could compare the process of evolution to the process of biological development that human beings undergo from conception to adulthood. There is a similar process of inevitable growth – both in terms of physical complexity and consciousness – on a massively extended scale, from the first single-celled life forms through to animals and human beings and beyond. In these terms, perhaps the changes of the last 250 years or so are similar to the growth spurts which children undergo from time to time.

Ecopsychopathology – A Threat to Survival

On the other hand, the growth spurt could be occurring because it is needed, in the same way that adaptive mutations occur when they're necessary for a life form's survival. Perhaps it's happening because of the potential ecological catastrophe that is threatening our survival as a species.

This potential ecological catastrophe is the most serious consequence of the fall into disconnection. With the fall, human beings developed a sense of separation to nature. Prehistoric humans were deeply connected to nature, as if they were *inside* it, living in participation. Judging by contemporary indigenous peoples, our ancestors felt an intimate bond with their land, as if they shared their being with it. They felt that natural phenomena were sentient and sacred, imbued with a spiritual essence. However, the fall broke our connection to nature. We were now *outside* nature, observing it from a distance, in a state of duality. Nature became disenchanted. It became *other* to us, an enemy to fight against and a supply of resources to exploit. Trees, rocks, and even animals became objects to use and abuse.

In this sense, the climate emergency was inevitable, as soon as we shifted outside nature and lost our sense of its sacredness. Now it was possible for us to recklessly abuse and exploit nature, in the same manner that people with psychopathic traits exploit others. In fact, you could characterise our disconnected attitude to nature as *ecopsychopathy*. Ecopsychopathy can be defined as "a lack of empathy and responsibility to the natural world, resulting in its abuse and exploitation". Like psychopaths' relationships with other people, our culture's attitude to nature is based on domination and control. In the same way that men dominate women, that privileged classes dominate lower classes, and nations try to dominate each other, disconnected societies try to dominate nature, other species and the whole Earth itself.

Indigenous peoples have always recognised that modern societies suffer from ecopsychopathy, even if they wouldn't have used that term. Almost from the first moment Europeans arrived on the shores of America, Native Americans were horrified by the colonists' exploitative attitude to the land. As Chief Seattle is reported to have said in 1854, "His [the white man's] appetite will devour the Earth and leave behind only a desert."[23] At a meeting with US government representatives in 1877, a Nez Perce chief, Tuhulkutsut, voiced his misgivings about selling his tribe's land. "The earth is part of my body," he said. "I belong to the land out of which I came. The earth is my mother." Tellingly, the government representative's reply was: "Twenty times over [you] repeat that the earth is your mother... Let us hear it no more, but come to business."[24]

The inevitable end point of our exploitative attitude towards nature is the complete disruption of the fragile ecosystems on which our life depends. This disruption is already well underway, resulting in more extreme weather events such as floods and hurricanes and the mass extinction of other species. If this process isn't checked, life on Earth will become more and more challenging, until the human race becomes another extinct species.

Fortunately, there has been a growing wave of resistance to

this process, as a part of the movement towards connection. As we've seen, a new empathic attitude to nature began to emerge about 250 years ago (as evidenced by the Romantics). In recent decades, environmental awareness has grown massively, and a wide range of social movements and groups have challenged ecopsychopathic attitudes. This is another aspect of the culture wars: a struggle between disconnected people who still feel a psychopathic attitude to nature and continue to abuse the Earth for profit, and connected people who feel empathy and responsibility to the natural world.

So it may be that – at least in part – an evolutionary movement towards connection is an adaptive process which is necessary for our survival. It's certainly difficult to see how we'll survive without this evolutionary shift. We can't predict what the outcome of our culture wars will be, or whether the shift will occur in time, before irreparable damage is done. The future of the human race hangs in the balance, between disconnection and connection.

Chapter 11

Altruism: When Human Beings Connect

In 2018, I was invited to speak at a conference on "Living Kidney Donation" in Manchester, England, to mark the 50th anniversary of kidney transplants in the city. The organisers wanted me to speak about the psychology of altruism – specifically, about why people are willing to anonymously donate one of their kidneys to people who need a transplant.

While most kidney donors are deceased people, over a third are "living donors". As you might expect, most of these donors are relatives of patients. But 11% are "non-specified" donors who have no connection to any patients. They usually don't find out who has received their kidney, or even whether the transplant operation has been successful. They have simply decided to make a sacrifice to help relieve the suffering of their fellow human beings.

What would motivate a person to go through major surgery – with potential health complications – to donate an organ to a patient they have never met, and probably will never meet? Significantly, many unspecified donors are people who have had recent crises in their lives. Sometimes they are soldiers who have returned from conflict zones, where their lives were in danger. Sometimes they are people who have recovered from serious illness or who have suffered a bereavement. Their own experiences of suffering fill them with a desire to help others, both to alleviate other people's suffering and to give meaning and purpose to their lives.

Instinctive Altruism

Living kidney donation is an unusual (and especially heroic) form of altruism because it is premeditated. Most altruistic acts are spontaneous. They occur as an instinctive response to danger and suffering, without any conscious thought.

You might find it difficult to conceive of donating one of your kidneys to a stranger, but consider the following scenario. You're standing on a train platform. The person next to you suddenly faints and falls on to the track, unconscious. In the distance, you can see a train approaching. What would you do? Would you be too shocked to react and stand frozen as the train approaches? Or would you jump down to try to save the person?

You might doubt whether you would act heroically in this situation. But don't underestimate yourself. A friend of mine was waiting for a train at a station near London, when an old lady next to him had a seizure and fell down on to the track. Suddenly, before he had the chance to think, my friend found himself on the track, picking up the lady and lifting her to safety, with the aid of another man on the platform. The train arrived seconds later.

The incident changed my friend's life. He had never thought of himself as a particularly brave or kind person, and never dreamed he was capable of such heroism. He realised that he had been underestimating himself, and that he wasn't living as fully as he ought to be. At the time, he was working behind the counter at a betting shop, but soon he gave up the job and decided to go to university.

You might be surprised to find out how common such heroic acts are. If you google "person jumps down on to train track to save life" you'll find dozens of cases, including some moving video footage. There is a recent video from the New York subway, when a wheelchair-bound man fell on to the track. A bystander immediately jumps down, pushes the wheelchair to one side, and hauls the man up, with the help of others on the platform. A train arrived just ten seconds later.

In an especially striking example from the New York subway, in 2007 a man named Wesley Autrey was waiting for a train when the man next to him had an epileptic seizure and fell on to the track. Autrey could hear the approach of a train, and impulsively jumped down to try to save the man. Realising that the approaching train was moving too fast, Autrey jumped on top of the man and pushed him down into a ditch between the tracks. Five of the train carriages passed over them, but they were both miraculously unharmed.

In fact, dangers and crises of all kinds often give rise to acts of spontaneous altruism. In 2015, on a main road in London, a cyclist was trapped under the wheel of a double-decker bus. A crowd of around 100 people quickly gathered, and in an amazing act of coordinated altruism, lifted the bus so that the man could be freed. According to a paramedic who treated the man, this was a "miracle" which may have saved his life. (I'm reluctant to encourage you to put down this book and look at your computer, but you can google video footage of the incident, along with a few similar incidents from around the world.) Similarly, in 2013, there was a tragic accident in Glasgow, Scotland, when a helicopter crashed into a pub, killing ten people. Straight after the crash, people rushed towards the scene, and formed a human chain, passing wounded and unconscious victims out of danger and into the hands of the emergency services.

Of course, most acts of altruism are on a much smaller scale than this. They fill most people's lives on an ongoing basis: giving money or food to homeless people, stopping to help people who have fallen over or had an accident, doing the shopping for elderly neighbours, supporting friends who are in difficulty, donating to charities and so on.

Pure Altruism

Some modern scientists find altruism difficult to explain, because it contradicts their assumption that human beings are essentially selfish. According to the materialist view which pervades modern secular cultures, human behaviour is determined by our genes, which only care about survival and replication. In Richard Dawkins's terminology, we are "survival machines" who compete for survival with other survival machines. In these terms, it's difficult to understand why human beings are so willing to help strangers, especially if there is a risk to their own lives. Why would selfish survival machines behave so unselfishly?

Such scientists have made many attempts to explain altruism in a way that fits the materialist worldview. Some have suggested that altruism is based on "kin selection", which means that evolution has primed us to be altruistic to people who are closely genetically related to us, because this means that we're helping our own genes to survive. It's true that we tend to be most altruistic towards close relatives. After all, what could be more altruistic than parents devoting themselves to caring for their children for 18 years, or an adult child who cares for their elderly parent during his or her final years?

However, our altruism often extends far beyond people who are related to us. Why should we feel a strong impulse to help people we've never met before, who have no connection to us – even to risk our lives for their sake? Even more puzzlingly, we are often altruistic to animals – and not just to our own pets. If you were walking down your street one morning, and found an injured hedgehog that had been hit by a car, or a bird that had been mauled by a cat, what would you do? Most of us would stop and tend to the animal, perhaps find a towel and take it indoors, or drive it to the local vet or animal sanctuary. In other words, kin selection isn't an adequate explanation for human altruism.

There is another view that altruism is a form of disguised selfishness, which always brings us hidden benefits. For example, altruistic acts might enhance our social status, or even improve our reproductive possibilities by making us seem more attractive. They might enhance our self-esteem by showing off to others or proving to ourselves that we are good people. A further explanation is that altruism is essentially reciprocal – we do favours for other people in the instinctive expectation that at some point they will do favours in return.

These theories make some sense, and undoubtedly do apply to some (perhaps many) altruistic acts. But they certainly can't account for the full extent of human altruism. They certainly can't explain why people risk their lives for strangers, or why some people anonymously donate kidneys. They can't explain many of the quiet, anonymous acts of altruism that many people perform on a day-to-day basis without any expectation of gratitude or reward. Altruistic acts can be *pure*, without any hidden egoic motives.

In 1984, the rock singer Bob Geldof was horrified by a BBC TV report about a famine in Ethiopia and decided to record a song to raise money for the cause. A few months later, Geldof organised a massive concert in London, called Live Aid. Parallel concerts were held around the world, most notably in the US. The record and concerts raised around £150 million, much of which went directly to non-governmental organisations in Ethiopia. The events brought about a new awareness of humanitarian issues, putting them at the centre of government policy for the first time.

While many people praised Geldof's altruism, others were more cynical. They suggested that he was trying to raise the profile of his band, who weren't selling many records anymore. (After all, his band the Boomtown Rats performed at the UK concert.) Perhaps he was reacting to the waning of his own celebrity by placing himself at the forefront of such a major cause and event. Even more cynically, some people claimed that he was syphoning off some of the money into his own bank account. (I remember my own father suggesting this.)

However, the real answer was undoubtedly more

straightforward: Geldof was simply responding with empathy and compassion to extreme human suffering, and reacting with indignity to the moral failings of Western governments, who were stockpiling years' supplies of grain while other people in the world were starving. In fact, Geldof devoted so much time and energy to famine relief that his musical career came to a standstill. He had financial problems because he was no longer earning money of his own. His actions were undoubtedly the result of pure altruism.

Innate Altruism from Innate Connection

The significance of pure altruism is that it is a direct consequence of a fundamental connection between human beings. It's important to note that most altruistic acts are impulsive and spontaneous, in response to crises or emergencies. This indicates that altruism is natural to us, arising unconsciously and directly from the deepest levels of our being. It suggests in turn that disconnection arises at a more superficial mental or egoic level. We may be selfish and even callous at the level of the ego, but beneath the ego there appears to be a deep layer of interconnection which gives rise to empathy and pure altruism.

In fact, if we look at the cultural evolution of the human race – as we did in the last chapter – it makes complete sense that altruism should be innate to us. Many Neo-Darwinists and evolutionary psychologists believe that human beings have evolved to be selfish because of survival pressures. Because our ancestors had to struggle to survive, they naturally became competitive and ruthless. However, in the last chapter, we saw that this is a complete misconception. For the vast majority of our time on this planet, our species has lived in peaceful, egalitarian and cooperative societies. Survival was easy, as populations were very small and resources were abundant. There is nothing about our species' history that would predispose us to selfishness and competitiveness. However, these are exactly the kind of conditions – particularly cooperation and egalitarianism – that would give rise to altruism.

However, there is another even more fundamental reason why altruism is innate to human beings: because connection itself is innate.

Pure altruism is possible because, unlike people with dark triad traits, most of us are fundamentally connected to each other. Although we may sometimes – even frequently – be self-absorbed and selfish, we feel a fundamental connection which enables us to empathise with one another. We can sense each other's suffering, which triggers altruism. We respond to other people's suffering in the same way that we respond to our own pain suffering: we feel an impulse to alleviate it, and attempt to do so, through altruistic acts. In relation to my argument in the last chapter, it makes sense that present day humans are generally more altruistic than our ancestors of a few centuries ago, because we are more connected to one another. A greater capacity for altruism is one of the fruits of the evolutionary movement towards connection.

Arguing against the notion that all altruism is egoic, the American psychologist Daniel Batson has put forward an "empathy-altruism" hypothesis. Batson suggests that people can be altruistic without gaining any benefits, out of genuine concern based on empathy. As Batson has put it (in a co-authored paper with Laura Shaw), "Feeling empathy for [a] person in need evokes motivation to help [that person] in which these benefits to self are not the ultimate goal of helping; they are unintended consequences."[1] In other words, an act of pure altruism may sometimes make a person feel better about themselves. It may increase other people's respect for them or increase their chances of being helped in return at a later date. But this isn't why they did it. The impetus for the act was an impulsive, unselfish desire to alleviate suffering.

It's also significant that, as well as arising from connection, altruism is an *experience* of connection. When we help others, there's a sense of reaching out beyond ourselves and connecting with them. An indelible bond is formed, with trust and respect. This is part of the reason why altruistic acts always feel so good. Beyond showing off or feeling good about ourselves, altruism brings well-being because it shifts us out of ego-separation, into connection with others. If we've become self-absorbed or self-centred, we may feel a sense of relief and rightness, like a traveller who returns to his family. In some cases, we may not just feel connection to a specific person, but a more general feeling of connection – perhaps to the human race as a whole, or to a spiritual force or shared consciousness of some form.

This is also why just *witnessing* altruistic acts brings a powerful sense of well-being. Consider how you felt as you watched the footage of bystanders climbing down to save people who had fallen on to train tracks, or dozens of people gathering to lift a bus to free a cyclist. No doubt you felt touched and uplifted, perhaps even moved to tears. The psychologist Jonathan Haidt has referred to this experience as "elation" – the warm, uplifting feeling of witnessing acts of kindness, which gives rise to, in Haidt's words, "a sensation of expansion in [the] heart, an increased desire to help, and increased sense of connection with others."[2] On one level, elation stems from a renewed faith in human nature, an awareness of the essential goodness of human beings. But as Haidt suggests, it's also due to a sense of connection. In this sense, any act of altruism has a three-way connective effect: between the person who performs it, the person who receives it, and anyone who witnesses it.

The Fundamental Source of Connection

If there is a fundamental connection between human beings, what is the nature of that connection? What exactly is it that connects us to one another? When we sense each other's pain and suffering (or each other's joy), what is the basis of this shared experience? If we can attune to one another's feelings, what exactly are we tuning into?

Here I'm going to address what philosophers call "metaphysical" issues – that is, questions about the nature of reality, and the nature of human beings. We'll discuss whether connection or disconnection is the fundamental reality of the world.

The standard worldview of our culture is materialism (or physicalism, to use a more modern term), which assumes that disconnection is fundamental. At the most fundamental level, the universe consists of tiny particles of matter – billiard ball-like particles which are the building blocks of all physical forms and living beings. All living beings are separate entities too – biological machines made up of selfish genes. We can communicate with one another through language and other signals, and we can touch each other's physical forms, but we're all essentially separate and alone. We're both fundamentally separate and fundamentally selfish.

These assumptions have had a disastrous cultural effect. They have encouraged a cut-throat competitive culture in which disconnected people thrive. They have helped to justify the worst excesses of the capitalist system, by encouraging corporations and governments to act ruthlessly, and to exploit other people and the natural world. They have encouraged a cultural nihilism that assumes there is no meaning or purpose to life, and that while we're here we should simply try to enjoy ourselves as much as we can and take as much as we can from the world, without considering the consequences.

However, I believe that connection is fundamental, not separateness. In my book *Spiritual Science*, I describe a philosophical approach that I call *panspiritism*, which is based on the principle that the fundamental reality of the world is not matter, but consciousness, or spirit. At the most basic level, the universe doesn't consist of material particles and physical forces but a non-material quality which pervades all space and all physical structures. I usually refer to this quality as "fundamental consciousness" (or sometimes simply as "spirit"). Fundamental consciousness is everywhere around you right at this moment. It pervades the space around you and all the physical things around you. Like water in a sponge, it pervades the chair you're sitting on, the walls around you, and the trees and flowers in your garden. It also pervades the physical stuff of your body – your muscles, bones and skin right down to every cell and molecule and atom inside you. In addition, fundamental consciousness constitutes the essence of your mind, or inner being. Your own consciousness is an "influx" or emanation of universal spirit.[3]

Of course, these aren't just my own views. There are many philosophical and spiritual traditions based on the same principles. In Indian philosophy, the ultimate reality of the universe is *brahman*, a radiant spiritual force which is everywhere and in everything. Our own inner being or spirit, *atman*, has the same nature as *brahman*, so that we are essentially one with the universe and everything in it. In Western philosophy, there is a philosophical approach called idealism, with many variants that suggest that mind or consciousness is fundamental to the universe, and that material things are emanations or manifestations of mind. Many indigenous cultures have a similar concept of an all-pervading spiritual force – for example, in North America, the Lakota Indians use the term *wakan-tanka*, while the Hopi refer to it as *maasauu*.

According to panspiritism, the brain doesn't produce consciousness, but acts as a kind of receiver which transmits and canalises fundamental consciousness (or spirit) into our own being. Neuroscientists sometimes compare the brain to a computer, but it's probably more like a radio, which doesn't actually produce the programmes it broadcasts, but receives and transmits them. Via the brain (not just the human brain, but that of every other animal), the raw essence of fundamental consciousness is canalised into our own individual consciousness. And because the human brain is so large and complex, it is able to receive and canalise consciousness in a very intense and intricate way, so that we are (probably) more intensely conscious than most other animals. (In fact, every cell in our bodies canalises fundamental consciousness, which we can feel inside us as what Taoism refers to as *chi* or "life-energy." But the brain is the main group of cells through which canalisation occurs, which is why we associate it with consciousness.)

From this point of view, human beings are more than just biological machines, made up of building blocks of atoms and molecules. Our inner beings are expressions of spirit, like channels that flow inland from the same ocean. We share the same fundamental being, beneath our individual psychological traits and physical differences.

Altruism is the natural consequence of our fundamental oneness. As suggested earlier, altruism stems from empathy, and empathy is the *experience* of our fundamental connection. Because we share the same fundamental consciousness, we can sense each other's suffering, which generates an impulse to alleviate that suffering. This applies to other living beings too, since we also share fundamental consciousness with them.

In this sense, connection is innate not just because of our cultural history as a species, but because it is *the nature of reality*. The fundamental nature of reality – of consciousness, living beings and the universe – is connection. All things are expressions of the same fundamental consciousness. Disconnection is an aberration that occurs when our egos grow too strong and separate, and we misperceive ourselves as autonomous individuals, living in duality to others and the world.

It is not altruism that needs to be accounted for, but

selfishness. It's not goodness that needs to be accounted for, but evil. Goodness is natural, evil is not. The altruistic acts we've examined in this chapter flow directly from the essence of reality. We become altruistic when we *tap into* our fundamental connection, through empathy – in other words, when we *attune* to the essence of reality. We become selfish and callous when we lose touch with our fundamental connection, and become alienated from the essence of reality, due to an illusory sense of separation.

Chapter 12

Hyper-Connected People

Many of us veer between disconnection and connection, and between selfishness and altruism. We're altruistic in our highest moments, when we respond to other people's suffering, or when we react instinctively to crises or emergencies. However, some people are *always* attuned to their fundamental oneness with others, and so feel a constant sense of empathy and compassion. For such "hyper-connected people" altruism doesn't occur in isolated incidents but pervades their whole life. It doesn't just arise spontaneously in moments of crises, or in response to obvious suffering, but is the main motivating factor of their lives. These are people who live lives of service, who devote all their energies to supporting and helping others, or to helping the world in general.

Here we move towards the right side of the continuum of connection, far away from the selfishness and brutality of hyper-disconnected people. Hyper-connected people are the polar opposites of the psychopaths and narcissists we looked at in earlier chapters of this book, so different that they could almost be members of a different species. Whereas the main goal of hyper-disconnected people's lives is to take as much as they can from the world (and unconsciously, to inflict as much damage on it as possible), the main goal of hyper-connected people is to *give* as much as they can to the world, and to help heal it.

Think back over the whole of your life. Who are the most impressive people you have ever met? Are they powerful, charming, or beautiful people who become the centre of attention wherever they go? Or are they selfless and benevolent people, who devote themselves to helping others?

I would hazard a guess that it's the latter. Perhaps the most impressive person I've known personally is a man called Russel Williams, an English spiritual teacher who died in 2018. I've written about Russel in previous books (and helped Russel to write his own book)[1] so I won't describe his story in detail here. But aside from the fact that he was an extremely wise man, what was most impressive about Russel was his selflessness. He was the complete opposite of the narcissistic and corrupt spiritual teachers we looked at in Chapter 8. For almost 60 years, he held meetings – usually twice a week – at the premises of the Buddhist Society of Manchester. (Russel didn't consider himself a Buddhist but was a great admirer of the Buddha.) At the meetings, he didn't give talks so much as respond to people's queries and problems. Often, if people had serious issues, he would go into another room and talk to them alone, to offer more focused support. He also did this whenever new people visited the group. Outside the meetings, Russel spent a lot of time speaking to people on the phone, offering support and guidance.

Russel didn't expect anything in return for his support. As a point of principle, he believed that the meetings should be free of charge and open to everyone. During his earlier years, he had a full-time job, and later a pension, but he certainly wasn't wealthy, and lived very modestly and simply. Even when I helped him write a book, he told me he didn't want the royalties. (He wanted me to have them, but I have donated them to the Buddhist Society.) The book – published when he was 93 years old – was the first time that Russel had publicised his teachings. He had no need whatsoever for attention or adulation. He simply wanted to help other people, to further their spiritual development and alleviate their suffering.

While Russel took on the role of spiritual teacher, hyper-connected people may follow a variety of roles in order to serve others. They might be charity workers, counsellors, youth leaders, or nurses. You don't *have* to be highly connected to do these jobs, but such roles are attractive to connected people in the same way that the corporate and political worlds are attractive to hyper-disconnected people. Certainly, it would be difficult for hyper-disconnected people to perform such altruistic roles, because of their selfishness and malevolence.

Other highly connected people may be intensely sensitive to the suffering caused by a specific social or political issue – such as racial injustice, honour killing, domestic violence, the oppression of a minority group – and devote their lives to campaigning against it. In highly disconnected societies, such people often face harassment, with the danger of imprisonment and even death.

Let me mention a couple of examples, from the countless number of such activists around the world. One is the Iranian women's rights activist, Dr. Rezvan Moghaddam, who has founded a number of organisations to oppose discrimination and violence against women, including the "All Against Acid Attack" and "Stop Honor Killings" campaigns. There were a reported 8000 honour killings in Iran between 2010 and 2014, although the real figure is probably much higher (as some women commit suicide before they are killed, and some deaths are reported as due to illness rather than murder).[2] In recent years, Dr. Moghaddam has been documenting cases of honour killing, and campaigning for legislation against them. In response to her activism, the pathocratic Iranian government has arrested and imprisoned her several times, including a sentence of six months' imprisonment and ten lashes.

Another example is Paul Diwakar, who was born as a *Dalit*, or untouchable, in India. The country's 215 million Dalits face constant discrimination and are often the victims of hate crime or mob violence. Most work in low status jobs, usually in sanitation work, as garbage collectors, road sweepers or drain cleaners. In rural India, they are often ostracised by the rest of the community, and not allowed to use the village well, or general eating places, schools or temples. Diwakar has spent most of his life campaigning for the rights of Dalits, and against the caste system in general, leading organisations such as the National Campaign on Dalit Rights.

Other highly connected people may be journalists in pathocratic regimes, risking their lives to campaign against corruption and to uphold the principle of freedom of speech. One example is the Russian journalist Dmitry Muratov, who was awarded the Nobel Peace Prize in 2021. Since 1995, Muratov has been chief editor of the newspaper *Novaya Gazeta*, which has resolutely exposed state malevolence and corruption in the face of persecution and violence. Hyper-disconnected people in positions of power will go to any lengths to suppress criticism, and over the years, six of *Novaya Gazeta*'s journalists have been killed. Muratov shared the Nobel Prize with another campaigning journalist, Maria Ressa, who has exposed the malevolence of one of the world's most severe present-day pathocracies, the regime of President Duterte in the Philippines.

Other hyper-connected people may prefer to avoid the complex, disconnected world of humans altogether, and work altruistically with animals, at animal sanctuaries or on conservation projects. Others may feel a passionate altruistic impulse to protect the natural world and ensure the future survival of the human race and other species, which impels them to devote their lives to environmental campaigning.

The Psychology of Hyper-Connection

In psychological terms, the significant thing about hyper-connected people is that their identity isn't enclosed inside their own mental space, but expands outside them, into the beings of others. Their being has soft and fluid boundaries, like a river that flows into other streams and tributaries. This creates a feeling of *identification* with other people and living beings. For them, the sense of identification and affection that most people feel towards their spouse or family extends to the human race as a whole – and even beyond, to other species, and the whole Earth itself. Hyper-connected people love *all* human beings in the same way that other people love their children. They feel the same sense of responsibility towards the whole human race that other people feel just for their families.[3]

This high degree of empathy and identification inevitably gives rise to ongoing altruism and a life of service. In fact, one of the difficulties faced by highly connected people – especially when they're young – is to find an appropriate channel for their altruistic impulses. Before this, they may feel overwhelmed by their awareness of other people's suffering and frustrated by their inability to alleviate it. But once they do find an appropriate outlet, they usually feel a strong sense of mission. Their lives flow easily and powerfully, as if they are channels of a higher force.

Their lack of separation means that hyper-connected people are free of the need to *accumulate*. In contrast to hyper-disconnected people, they feel no need to strengthen their egos with power or wealth. Like Russel Williams, they are usually content to live quietly and simply, without drawing attention to themselves, or trying to gain credit for their good deeds. Their lives are not about accumulation, but *contribution*.

One query that might arise about the idea of service is: what about people who selflessly serve pathocratic regimes or terrorist groups? What about people who devote their lives to cult leaders or corrupt gurus? Millions of Germans selflessly supported and served the Nazis, with a powerful sense of connection to their nation and to the Nazi regime. Suicide bombers regularly sacrifice their lives for their cause, while some cult members commit murders or kill themselves in service of their leaders.

Here we need to distinguish between benevolent and malevolent service. It certainly is possible to selflessly serve malevolent people and ideologies. However, this type of service doesn't stem from empathy, but from group identity. It doesn't stem from oneness with others, but from an abstract attachment to the ideology of a group. It doesn't arise from transcendence of the ego, but from the *subsuming* of the ego within a larger, group identity. Pathocracies or extremist groups constitute a giant group-ego, which is as highly disconnected as any person with dark triad traits. Such group-egos have the same accumulative impulse as individual disconnected egos, striving to increase their power and prestige and to dominate and suppress competing groups. Like individual disconnected egos, they need conflict with other groups to sustain their sense of identity.

In other words, this type of service has nothing to do with altruism, but all to do with disconnection.

Hyper-Connected Leaders

We're so accustomed to disconnected leaders and managers that the idea of a selfless and benevolent leader – who serves rather than dominates and bullies people – seems almost like a romantic ideal. However, in psychology, a great deal of attention has been paid to the notion of "ideal management". The American psychologist Abraham Maslow conceived of an ideal society (or "eupsychian society", in his terminology) where institutions and companies were run by "enlightened managers". These are managers who trust and respect their employees and create a sense of group harmony, They recognise that employees need to feel that they are unique or autonomous to some degree and that they are doing meaningful work.[4] Similarly, the psychologist Robert Greenleaf developed a concept of "servant leadership". Far from trying to control and command their followers, the "servant leader" tries to meet their needs and encourages them to develop their full potential. The servant leader builds consensus, encouraging followers to reach decisions democratically.[5] Another model of "ethical leadership" was put forward by a group of psychologists, emphasising the importance of honesty, trustworthiness and fairness. Ethical leaders establish moral frameworks and encourage others to follow them, partly by acting as role models. Employees are sanctioned negatively or positively according to whether they meet ethical standards.[6]

In Chapter 3, I suggested three different types of leaders: hyper-disconnected, involuntary (including privileged or meritorious leaders) and altruistic leaders. Of these three, altruistic leaders are probably the least common, but even they are not unusual, particularly in less disconnected societies. As I noted earlier, most connected people aren't particularly interested in power. On the one hand, they have no psychological need for power because they don't experience separation. At the same time, they don't like being elevated above other people, standing at the top of a hierarchy, instructing and delegating to others as if they were minions. Connected people usually prefer to remain "on the ground", interacting with others at the same level. To become a leader would mean breaking – or least weakening – their connection to others.

However, some hyper-connected people do gravitate towards positions of power, *due to* their burning desire to alleviate oppression and injustice, or to help solve social and global problems. They feel impelled to attain positions of power in order to enact change and serve other people most effectively.

Such altruistic leaders are often very successful, because of their selfless determination and courage, and the positive changes they initiate. Their passion gives them great energy and massive reserves of resilience to overcome obstacles. Of course, disconnected people do everything they can to undermine them and to obstruct their positive actions. And like gurus who begin with good intentions, some connected leaders may fall victim to the leadership trap and become narcissistic and corrupt. Having said that, I think that the *more* connected a person is, the less vulnerable they are to the leadership trap. In my view, the most connected people are essentially incorruptible, no matter how much power they attain.

Some Examples of Hyper-Connected Leaders

The more disconnected a society, the less likelihood there is of highly connected people attaining power and influence. However, hyper-connected leaders sometimes do have a profound impact on disconnected societies. These leaders are especially heroic, because of the personal dangers that they face, and the obstacles they have to overcome.

One example is Joaquim Chissano, former president of Mozambique. In 1992, Mozambique's civil war came to an end, after 15 years of devastation and around a million casualties. The country was completely broken, showing all signs of being trapped in the conflict and corruption which has engulfed many African countries, leading inevitably to pathocracy. However, rather than trying to shore up his own power base and taking revenge on his former enemies, Chissano made compromises and promised there would be no prosecutions or punishments. Rather than trying to crush the rebels, he began to work with them. He offered them half of the places in the Mozambiquan army and encouraged them to start their own political party, giving them the chance to gain power through legitimate means.

Two years later, Mozambique's first ever multi-party elections were held, and Chissano and the former rebel leader came face to face in the polls. Chissano won and set about the task of establishing lasting peace by reducing poverty. Between 1997 and 2003, almost three million people were rescued from extreme poverty, out of a total population of almost 20 million. There was a 35% decrease in the number of children dying under the age of five, and an increase of 65% in the number of children going to primary school. Through Chissano's ability to set aside differences and connect with his former enemies, Mozambique was brought back from the brink of self-destruction and has instead become one of Africa's most stable and peaceful countries.

Significantly, Chissano's approach was influenced by meditation, which he learned in 1992. After quickly becoming aware of the benefits of the practice, he taught it to his family and cabinet ministers. In 1994, all military and police recruits were required to meditate twice a day. Chissano himself is in no doubt that this collective meditation was responsible for the peace and increasing prosperity of the country. As he said, "The result has been political peace and balance in nature in my country... The culture of war has to be replaced by the culture of peace. For that purpose, something deeper has to be changed in our mind and in our consciousness to prevent the recurrence of war."[7]

In 2004, Chissano's second term in office came to end. Rather than pursuing a third term – as he was legally able to do – he stepped aside. Since then he has been active as an elder statesman, campaigning for peace and working as an envoy and negotiator for the United Nations. In 2007, on his 68th birthday, he was awarded Africa's equivalent of the Nobel Prize, the $5 million prize for Achievement in African Leadership.

Chissano's ethical style of leadership is reminiscent of Abraham Lincoln, who was undoubtedly a highly connected person. Lincoln believed that the whole purpose of government was to serve the people. As he put it, "The legitimate object of government, is to do for a community of people, whatever they need to have done, but cannot do, at all, or not, so well do, for themselves."[8] Lincoln emphasised the importance of cooperation and consensus and upholding moral principles. Rather than surrounding himself with acolytes, he offered senior government positions to rivals, including figures who thought they had a better claim than him to be president. As a result, he gained the respect of his rivals – for example, Senator William H. Steward of New York, who referred to Lincoln as "the best and wisest of men" with a "superhuman" magnanimity. Lincoln spoke of the "monstrous injustice" of slavery, aware of the hypocrisy of the United States Constitution declaring that all people are free and equal while being the largest slaveholding nation in the world. As a result, Lincoln fought with great determination for the abolition of slavery, at the same time as struggling to keep the United States united as one country.

Like Gandhi – another example of a hyper-connected leader, as we saw at the beginning of this book – Lincoln wasn't perfect. Some historians blame him for the Civil War, arguing that it was unnecessary, and that slavery would have naturally come to an end. However, Lincoln was certainly much further along the continuum of connection than the vast majority of other US presidents. It's because of this that he is often ranked as the greatest ever US president.

There are many similar examples of highly connected leaders. One is Lech Walesa, former president of Poland, who guided his country to democracy and pluralism after decades of communist pathocracy. A similar example is Mikhail Gorbachev, who presided over the final years of the Soviet Union. There is also the former president of Liberia, Ellen Johnson-Sirleaf. Like Joaquim Chissano, she came to power after a long period of unrest, and devoted herself to peacebuilding, economic recovery and encouraging social tolerance. As a result of these efforts, she won the Nobel Peace Prize in 2011.

At the end of the Apartheid era, South Africa was fortunate enough to have two highly connected leaders: Nelson Mandela and Archbishop Desmond Tutu. Desmond Tutu had always been a steadfast opponent of the Apartheid regime, which he called "evil and unchristian." Influenced by Gandhi, he advocated non-violent resistance and encouraged other countries to boycott South Africa. Once the Apartheid regime came to an end, Mandela asked Archbishop Tutu to chair the Truth and Reconciliation Commission. As a highly spiritual person, Tutu constantly emphasised the importance of forgiveness and cooperation, and warned against the consequences of revenge. Together with Mandela, he helped to ensure a peaceful transition to democracy, and continued to advocate for forgiveness and reconciliation around the world. As he wrote, "If peace is our goal, there can be no future without forgiveness."[9]

The fact that many of the above leaders are "former presidents" tells its own story. Hyper-disconnected leaders never give up power of their own free will. They hold on to it until they die or are overthrown or killed. If the constitution states that a president can only serve a certain number of terms, they simply change the constitution (as Xi Jinping of China did in 2018) or find a constitutional loophole to avoid stepping down (as President Putin did when his second term as president ended in 2008). However, connected leaders know that to cling to power spuriously would cause serious long-term political damage, no matter how keen they might be to continue with their reforms. To them, moral principles are much more important than personal interest.

Connected leaders are a source of hope. They prove that it's not inevitable that power falls into the hands of disconnected people. Sometimes power can be used for benevolent purposes, by benevolent people. Such leaders point towards a different kind of society, beyond pathocracy and disconnection, in which justice, equality and harmony are not utopian ideals but natural and normal.

Women as Connected Leaders

During the COVID pandemic of 2020-21, the world's female leaders took a different approach to most of their male counterparts. They reacted more quickly and decisively and locked down earlier. A study found that the world's 19 countries (out of 194) with female leaders – such as Germany, New Zealand, Denmark, Finland and Taiwan – had "systematically and significantly better" outcomes, with half as many deaths as the countries led by men. One of the leaders of the study, the economist Supriya Garikipati, suggested that female leaders were "risk averse with regard to lives" while male leaders were more focused on economic considerations.[10]

This outcome isn't surprising. I've already suggested – in the introduction and Chapter 2 – that women are generally further along the continuum of connection than men, with higher levels of empathy and altruism. We'd therefore expect female leaders to be generally more connected than their male counterparts, and to be more ethical and responsible. As I suggested earlier, this is the main reason why such a small proportion of crimes are committed by women (especially violent crimes, including murder) and also why women are much less likely to have psychopathic traits.

No doubt these differences are partly due to social conditioning. As we've seen, in disconnected societies, men are conditioned to be ruthless and individualistic, and to suppress emotion and empathy. Nevertheless, I believe that women's higher level of altruism and empathy has a psychological basis too. I believe that women are *innately* more connected than men. This is because they generally experience a lower degree of ego-separation, with a softer and more fluid sense of self.

I think it's likely that these gender differences didn't exist – at least to the same extent – until relatively recent times. Anthropological evidence suggests that in indigenous cultures, differences between the male and female psyche are not particularly marked. For example, the anthropologist Robert Levy found that "men in Tahiti were no more aggressive than women, nor were women gentler or more maternal than men."[11] At the same time, male and female roles tend to be flexible and interchangeable. For example, men and women of the Copper Eskimos culture (of Northern Canada) would often swap their roles, so that women would go hunting while the men stayed to cook and look after the children.[12] Similarly, when the British anthropologist Bronislaw Malinowski studied the Trobriand Islanders (close to New Guinea) in the 1920s, he was struck by their lack of sex specialisation. Men frequently helped with domestic chores and played a large part in childcare.[13] In pre-colonial Africa, the concept of female domesticity didn't exist, and women were extremely active in economic affairs.[14]

It appears that the fall into disconnection affected men much more than women, resulting in a new psychological gulf between genders. Perhaps women never became as disconnected as men partly due to their emotional bond to their children, which maintained a flow of empathy and a sense of connection. Perhaps biology was also a factor. Female biological processes are more active and pronounced than male processes, with the cycle of menstruation and the processes of pregnancy and lactation. This may have stopped the female ego becoming too disconnected from the body, and from nature as a whole.

However we explain it, women's higher level of connection means that they are more likely to be ethical and altruistic leaders. This certainly doesn't mean that all female leaders are connected. In highly disconnected societies, it's impossible for women to become leaders, as they have such low status. But in less disconnected societies, women with an unusually high level of disconnection may attain power, and act as malevolently as any male leader. (In fact, such female leaders may be even more disconnected than their male counterparts, as they may learn to be especially ruthless and manipulative in order to overcome gender bias.)

The longest serving UK prime minister of the 20th century was Margaret Thatcher, who held power for 11 and a half years. On the surface, the UK might feel entitled to celebrate the egalitarian achievement of a woman leading the country for so long. However, in practice Thatcher lacked any connective "female" traits such as emotion and empathy. As her nickname of the "Iron Lady" showed, she was a highly disconnected person, who made political decisions without considering their human cost.

The more connected a society is, the better chance there

is of altruistic and ethical women becoming leaders. The fact that there are so few female leaders – 19 out of 194 – is a good indication of the low level of connection around the world generally. But as the movement towards connection continues, we should expect more women to occupy leadership positions, creating more social harmony.

Chapter 13

Spiritual Connection

Altruism and service are the main outward ways in which hyper-connection expresses itself. Inwardly, hyper-connection manifests itself in terms of spirituality. Spirituality is synonymous with connection. When we talk about "spiritual" people – or "awakened" or "enlightened" people – we're essentially referring to people who exist in a state of intense connection, without a sense of separation. When we talk about spiritual development (or awakening) we're referring to a progression towards increasing connection. Spiritually awakened people are therefore the polar opposite of hyper-disconnected people, or dark triad personalities. The state of "wakefulness" (or enlightenment) is the polar opposite of psychopathy and narcissistic personality disorder.

This is why spirituality is so closely linked to altruism. All spiritual traditions emphasise the importance of altruism and service, and spiritually developed people are always highly empathic and altruistic. This applies to all the hyper-connected people we looked at in the last chapter. In some cases, the link between spirituality and altruism is obvious, as in the cases of Russel Williams, Desmond Tutu and Joaquim Chissano (whose altruistic leadership was inspired by his practice of meditation). Other people – such as Abraham Lincoln and Ellen Johnson-Sirleaf – may not have been spiritual in any obvious outward sense. Nevertheless, they clearly had/have a natural spirituality which expressed itself through service and altruism.

The Beginnings of Spirituality

The world's first spiritual traditions began as a reaction against disconnection.

2500 years ago, most of the Eurasian landmass – Europe,

the Middle East and Asia – was in a state of extreme social disconnection. For all but a tiny minority of aristocrats or nobles, life was extremely hard and brutal. The ease and leisure of the hunter-gatherer way of life had been replaced by a constant struggle to survive in the face of poverty, illness and oppression. It's likely that most people lived in a state of chronic anxiety and insecurity. Violence was a constant feature of their lives – the indirect violence of oppression and poverty, and the direct violence of warfare, assault, murder and rape. In such societies, empathy and altruism were probably very rare, at least outside people's own families or clans.

However, a small number of exceptional people responded to the suffering and brutality around them in a radical way: by rejecting violence and advocating compassion and altruism. Somehow, amid extreme disconnection, they oriented themselves at the opposite end of the continuum of connection, and taught values of peace, equality and love.

In India, the Buddha was the most well-known exponent of this new outlook. Almost nothing is known about the Buddha as a historical person, but there's no doubt that he was a hyper-connected person, who felt intense compassion for the suffering of his fellow human beings. He was also undoubtedly a highly intelligent person, with an acute analytical mind. His compassion and intellect combined to create an intricate and methodical path of self-development, designed to help free human beings from suffering.

It is difficult to imagine how radical the Buddha's teachings must have seemed to his contemporaries. 2500 years before Gandhi, the Buddha taught compassion and altruism in the face of violence. As he advised in the Kutadanta Sutta, "In times of war, give rise in yourself to the mind of compassion, helping living beings. Abandon the will to fight." The Buddha established five precepts for his followers to abide by, the first of which is to abstain from "killing or causing harm to other living beings". This precept includes animals too, which led early Buddhists to oppose animal sacrifice and establish a tradition of vegetarianism.

The Buddha also spoke of "four sublime states" which he advised his followers to cultivate. Three of these were related to empathy and altruism. The first is *metta* – usually translated as loving-kindness – which means that one should, in the Buddha's own words, "cherish all living beings; radiating kindness over the entire world" just as "a mother protects with her life her child, her only child, so with a boundless heart."[1] The second sublime state is *karuna*, or compassion, which the Buddha defines as sensing the suffering of others. The third state is sympathetic joy, which means sharing the well-being and happiness of others. (The fourth sublime state is equanimity.)

Around 500 years later, Jesus taught a similar message of radical compassion and benevolence. As with the Buddha, Jesus's contemporaries must have been puzzled – perhaps even offended – by some of his teachings. At a time when his people were living under brutal Roman occupation, Jesus advocated peaceful non-resistance. He proclaimed, "blessed are the peacemakers," and advised would-be aggressors to "put your sword back into its place; for those who live by the sword, die by the sword." Perhaps some of his contemporaries could understand the logic of non-resistance as a way of breaking the cycle of violence, but did Jesus really expect them to *love* their brutal Roman occupiers? Did he really expect them to "do good to those who hate you, bless those who curse you, pray for those who abuse you"?

The Buddha and Jesus mean many things to their followers, but I see them as heroic revolutionary figures who resisted and transcended the insane brutality of their cultures and created a new vision of a harmonious, connected world. Although they wouldn't have used the term themselves, they were essentially spiritual teachers, who knew from their own experience that the suffering and discord of disconnection could be transcended.

Their teachings flowed from a high level of psychological connection, which they aimed to impart to others.

Hyper-Connection as Spirituality

I would define spirituality in two terms: expansion and connection. As described at the beginning of Chapter 8, spiritual awakening is a process of expanding (and intensifying) awareness. I break this down into four different types of awareness. First, there is perceptual awareness, when the world around us becomes more vivid. Then there is subjective awareness, when we become more aware of our own inner being. There is also intersubjective awareness, when we become more empathic and compassionate to others. Finally, there is conceptual awareness, when our perspective on reality grows wider, moving from an egocentric to a worldcentric outlook.

At the same time, spiritual awakening can be seen as a process of increasing connection. As our awareness expands, we become more connected. In perceptual terms, we become more connected to our surroundings, including the natural world. In subjective terms, we become more connected to our own being. As our intersubjective awareness expands, we become more connected to other living beings (and to the natural world). As our conceptual awareness expands, we become more connected to the human race and the world as a whole.

Alternately, we can see spiritual development as a process of transcending *dis*connection. The fundamental obstacle to spiritual development is our sense of separateness, when we experience ourselves as an ego that lives inside our minds and bodies, in separation from a world that seems to be "out there", on the other side. As we undergo spiritual awakening, we become aware that this sense of separateness is an illusion. Our solid, rigid sense of identity begins to soften. Our identity begins to merge with the world, and with other living beings. We become aware of a sense of kinship – or even oneness –

between ourselves and the rest of the world, sensing that we share the same essence as all other things.

It's important to note that we're not talking about religion here. As the Spiritual Continuum of Connection (in Appendix 3) makes clear, religion and spirituality belong to different sides of the continuum of connection. Fundamentalist religion is all about disconnection. If spirituality is about transcending the ego, fundamentalist religion is about supporting and strengthening it. In fact, as we saw in Chapter 8, fundamentalist religious groups are hyper-disconnected communities, with high levels of hierarchy, patriarchy, authoritarianism and sexual repression.

Of course – as also noted in Chapter 8 – religion and spirituality often merge. Some religious people are genuinely spiritual and altruistic, using the principles and teachings of their religion as a framework for spiritual development. In Christianity, these are the tolerant and liberal Christians who attempt to apply Jesus's teachings of compassion and forgiveness to their day-to-day lives. In Judaism, these are the members of the "Reform Judaism" movement which is inclusive and socially progressive, and places less emphasis on ceremony and ritual.

In terms of the spiritual continuum of connection, there is a large "middle ground" where religion and spirituality overlap. However, as we move to the right of the continuum, we leave religion behind and enter the realm of pure spirituality, which isn't attached to any particular belief system. Pure spirituality is based on experience rather than belief. It's not about worshipping a divine figure or following a set of lifestyle guidelines. It's about experiencing a more expansive awareness of reality. As a lifestyle, it's about self-transformation – specifically, about transcending separateness and expanding awareness, moving towards greater connection with the world, our own being and other living beings, at the same time as expressing this connection through service and altruism.

Awakening Experiences

Sometimes spirituality occurs in a temporary form – as spiritual or mystical experiences, in which our awareness briefly expands and intensifies, giving us access to an intensely real and beautiful world, filled with harmony and meaning.

Spiritual experiences are by no means uncommon. Surveys suggest that around a half of people have had them at least once.[2] They are by no means restricted to spiritual seekers or monks and mystics. In fact, most spiritual experiences happen to ordinary people in the midst of everyday life, rather than in the meditation room or the temple. They happen when we're walking in the countryside, watching a sunset or staring up at the stars on a clear night. They happen when we're swimming in the ocean or running in the park, while we're making love, helping other people, or even while giving birth.

I've spent around 20 years collecting and analysing reports of spiritual experiences – or "awakening experiences" as I prefer to call them. In such experiences, it's as if our consciousness temporarily opens up, as if limitations or filters fall away, allowing us to perceive reality more fully. There is a sense of revelation, as if we're seeing things as they really are. In comparison, our normal awareness seems limited, like looking at a blurred black and white photograph compared to a bright colour image. Awakening experiences may only last for a few seconds or minutes, but they usually have powerful long-term effects. They bring a new sense of optimism, trust and humility, with an awareness that life is more meaningful than we previously assumed. There are different intensities of awakening experiences, ranging from mild experiences of beauty and wonder to intense experiences of complete oneness with the universe.

Sometimes the experiences occur spontaneously, for no apparent reason, but in most cases, they are linked to specific activities and situations. In particular, there is a strong link to psychological turmoil. In 2017, I conducted a study of awakening experiences with my co-author Krisztina, and we found that their most significant trigger was psychological turmoil, including stress, depression, loss, bereavement, combat. Of the 90 experiences we studied, 37 were linked to psychological turmoil. Other significant triggers were contact with nature (23 of 90), spiritual practice (21) and reading spiritual literature (15). (Note: some of the experiences had more than one trigger.)[3]

In terms of my argument in this book, the important thing about awakening experiences (or, if you prefer, spiritual experiences) is that they are essentially experiences of connection. In fact, a viable alternate term for them is "connection experiences". They are moments in which our normal sense of separateness fades away, in which we are no longer isolated egos living inside our mental space. We feel a sense of connection (or even oneness) to nature, to other human beings or with the whole world in general. We may also sense connection in the objects and natural phenomena around us. In some way, all things – both natural and man-made objects – seem to be interrelated, as if they are part of a network of being, or all manifestations of something deeper, like plants that grow out of the same roots underground.

Different Modes of Connection

One of the most common features of awakening experiences is a sense of connection to nature. This is certainly true of my own experiences. For example, I often feel a sense of connection to nature when I'm walking in the woods or the hills. At a certain point – usually when my thoughts have slowed down and I feel relaxed – the trees, grass and stones or rocks around me become more real. They seem to become sentient beings, with their own identity. I have the same feeling when I look above me at the sky. It's as if I'm part of nature rather than just an observer of it. I am *inside* the landscape.

I often have this type of experience when I go swimming

outdoors, in a lake or in the sea. I feel completely at home and at ease in the water, as if I've returned to a place where I was always meant to be. In the ocean, I feel that I've become one with the whole Earth, as if I can feel myself part of this giant mass of water that covers the majority of the planet's surface. When I look up at the sky above, or the coastal landscape around me, I feel that all things are interconnected, part of something deeper and greater than their individual forms.

These types of experiences were often described by Romantic poets such as Wordsworth and Shelley. Wordsworth often described his sense of connection to nature, together with an awareness that *something deeper and greater* was expressing itself through natural forms. As he wrote in his autobiographical poem "The Prelude", as a young man he sensed "the sentiment of Being spread / O'er all that moves and all that seemeth still." He also described his awareness that "the great mass [of natural things] lay embedded in some quickening soul."[4] As we saw in Chapter 10, the Romantic movement was the result of an emerging new spirit of connection, so it makes sense that poets – and artists and composers too – should have described such experiences.

Other awakening experiences feature powerful connection to other human beings, with intense feelings of empathy, compassion and love. In normal circumstances, we may feel intense compassion and love for specific people, but in awakening experiences, the feelings become indiscriminate and unconditional. There is a sense of loving *everyone*, including strangers.

Here, for example, a man describes an experience that occurred when he was sitting in a waiting room at a train station, with about 20 other people. Suddenly, for no apparent reason, in his words, "I experienced in that moment a sense of profoundest kinship with each and every person there. I loved them all – but with a kind of love I had never felt before...

We were one with each other and with the Life which we all lived in common."[5] The Christian monk Thomas Merton described a similar experience when he was standing on a street corner watching people do their shopping: "I was suddenly overwhelmed with the realisation that I loved all these people, that they were mine and I theirs, that we could not be alien to one another even though we were total strangers. It was like waking from a dream of separateness."[6]

Less frequently, awakening experiences may feature a powerful connection towards animals. For example, Russel Williams (who I mentioned at the beginning of the last chapter) described a spiritual awakening that occurred while he was working as a groom at a travelling circus. He slept with horses in the stables, and one morning he woke up to find that his identity had merged with the horses. As Russel recalled:

> I was the horse. I could look through its eyes and mind. I was aware of its true nature… I looked at another horse, and another, and I was inside them as well… My own nature was just as theirs was, in a different form, with one consciousness linking us all together. They were only separate in terms of form and structure. It was the same essence, the same emptiness, in all of them – in all of us.[7]

At high intensities of awakening, there may be a more general feeling of connection to the universe as a whole. For example, a woman described an intense awakening experience that occurred in a state of intense turmoil, after the end of a long-term relationship. As she told me, "I began to experience a clearness and connection with everything that existed, with the whole Universe that felt beyond human… Out of that depth arose such a compassion and connection to everything that surrounded me that I could feel even the pain of the flowers being picked."[8] Another person described to me a powerful experience in which he became "vast and merged with the universe. No longer could I perceive myself as separate, I was in and of the universe... The sense of peace, bliss and oneness is hard to put into words."[9]

Other high intensity awakening experiences may feature a sense of connection to something *beyond* the physical world, to a spiritual essence which appears to be the source of connection, in the same way that the sun is the source of all light. This is illustrated by another example from my research, which happened to a young father who was out walking with his baby in a pram. It was the first time he had taken his son out and he felt full of love. In an enactment of the Buddha's teaching that we should love all living things as a mother loves her only child, the man described how this feeling of love expanded:

> I became aware of the feeling of unconditional love, not just toward my son but to everyone I was passing in the streets. It was as if I was giving it and receiving it at the same time. Everything was "made" of the same "stuff" and the only word I could find to describe it was love. Everything was made of love. I felt immersed in a sea of love where everyone and everything were made of this same "energy"; I was no longer a separate "ego" but was consumed by this energy of love. Everything became One and I was outside of time. I continued walking through a park with a very strong sense of compassion and love toward all that I encountered.[10]

At this intense level, awakening experiences are direct encounters with fundamental consciousness, or spirit. They are experiences of the essential oneness of the universe. In terms of Hindu spirituality, they are experiences of *atman* (or individual spirit) becoming one with *brahman* (the universal spirit). People who have intense awakening experiences sometimes describe a feeling of deep peace and ease, as if they have come home. And in a sense, this is literally true: they have returned home to the spiritual source from which we (and all other things) emerged.

Wakefulness

However, awakening isn't just a temporary experience. Less frequently, it occurs in a permanent or ongoing form. This is sometimes referred to as "enlightenment", although I prefer the term "wakefulness".

Wakefulness can be cultivated in a gradual way, through following spiritual paths or practices, or living a spiritual lifestyle of service, simplicity and detachment. Certainly, many spiritual adepts and monks who follow the paths of Buddhism, Yoga, Taoism, Sufism and the Kabbalah (and many other paths) experience a gradual awakening that becomes an ongoing state. Many people undergo the same process through the regular practice of meditation, or through following an eclectic mix of spiritual practices from different traditions.

However, spiritual awakenings also often happen to people who don't know anything about spirituality and aren't connected to any traditions. As I showed in my book *Extraordinary Awakenings*, the most common way this occurs is through psychological turmoil – for example, in the midst of intense depression, stress or addiction, or following bereavement or a diagnosis of serious illness. In these situations, what I refer to as "transformation through turmoil" may occur. The ego breaks down in the face of intense suffering. A new, spiritually awakened self emerges in its place, almost as if it was always latent, waiting for the opportunity to be born.

In terms of the continuum of connection, spiritual awakening is a shift from a point of disconnection to a point of connection. When it occurs gradually (through following practices and paths), awakening is a slow and gradual movement along the continuum. When it occurs suddenly and dramatically (usually in response to intense turmoil), it is an abrupt leap further along the continuum, to a point of much more intense connection. Not surprisingly, some people who have sudden awakenings find their new state of intense connection difficult to adjust to, especially if they don't have previous knowledge of spirituality (as is often the case). Feelings of well-being, appreciation and connection are sometimes overlaid with confusion and disorientation. It's a bit like jumping out of an aeroplane and parachuting into a strange landscape of intense beauty and meaning, without a map or a guide. On the other hand, when people undergo gradual awakening in the context of spiritual traditions, it's like exploring this landscape slowly and carefully, walking along old paths with previous explorers as your guides.

To a large extent, wakefulness shares the same characteristics as temporary awakening experiences, but established as ongoing traits. Certainly, one of the main traits of wakefulness is a wide-ranging sense of connection to nature, other people, other living beings, the world or universe in general. As one person described their ongoing wakefulness to me, "I feel a part of nature. I feel a connection with people, but I also feel connected with trees and birds and grass and hills."[11] Another person described their sense of connection in these terms: "I started seeing every single person as myself... I have a feeling of connection to everything, whether it's living or not living."[12]

After awakening, people often report feeling as if nature has become *more real*. It's as if a veil of familiarity has slipped away, revealing beauty and wonder that used to be hidden. It's as if they were previously closed off, too self-absorbed to pay real attention to their surroundings, but now their awareness is wide open. The shell of the ego has been broken, and they are somehow *outside* themselves, part of the world. For example, as one awakened person told me, "I love watching animals and insects, watching the seasons change. Before the experience, I was so immersed in myself that all those things just didn't exist for me. They were just there."[13] Another person described how

"Nature is much more important to me. Colours are brighter, and I see so much more detail. Sometimes it's almost overwhelming. Everything is much more vibrant and real. During the first two months after it happened, I had to be outside all the time. I couldn't stand being inside a building."[14]

In a similar way, their hyper-connection means that awakened individuals are more attentive and open to other people. They often report that they understand other people better, and that their relationships become harmonious, with a new depth of intimacy and authenticity. As one person put it, "I've become much more engaged with other people too. I started to really listen to them and get where they are coming from. There is a level of empathy and understanding that I didn't have before."[15] Or in another person's words, "I'm a lot more understanding rather than feeling disappointed in people. I have a much broader take on how people work. That helps me to be more supportive to those around me."[16]

Spiritual awakening changes people's lifestyles radically. Without a sense of separateness, the need to accumulate disappears. At the same time, awakened people's intense empathy brings a powerful awareness of other people's suffering, while their wide-ranging conceptual perspective gives them a clearer awareness of social and global issues. As a result, they live in a mode of contribution rather than accumulation. One person described it as "a shift in focus from what can I get from life to what I can give to life."[17] Or as another person told me, "The purpose of my life is to be here for others, to help them grow and see their own importance."[18]

Sometimes this entails a shift to a different profession, to a less accumulative and more altruistic role. For example, one woman who had a spiritual awakening after a diagnosis of cancer found that she couldn't continue in her role as an IT manager at a pharmaceutical company. When her cancer went into remission, she gave up her job and retrained as a counsellor and therapist. In other cases, people remain in the same profession but have a different attitude to their role. For example, in *Extraordinary Awakenings*, I told the story of LeeAnn, who had an awakening after the murder of a close friend. She worked as the director of practice relations for a dermatology group. Initially she struggled with some aspects of the job but adapted by changing her attitude. Now she no longer thinks in terms of profit but focuses on the well-being of patients and colleagues. As she told me, "I want to make sure that every patient that walks through the door, every employee that works there, they're always respected, valued, cared about – it's ridiculously important to me."[19]

This intense feeling of connection is the main reason why wakefulness is so exhilarating. You could compare it to release from prison. After being trapped inside a narrow world of thoughts and desires, we're suddenly free of our egos, able to connect with nature, other living beings, and the universe as a whole. Furthermore, we're like prisoners who return home straight after release. After years of being alienated, we're attuned to the fundamental oneness of all things, the source from which we emerged.

Paths of Connection

Perhaps the most important thing that spirituality can teach us is that it is possible for us to *cultivate* connection. We don't *have* to live in a state of disconnection. Spiritual traditions all include sets of practices and lifestyle guidelines designed to help us transcend separation and move towards connection. In terms of the continuum of connection, spiritual traditions teach us that it is possible to move further along the continuum, and show us methods of doing this. In this sense, spiritual paths are *paths of connection.*

The core theme of most spiritual traditions is that human suffering and unhappiness is caused by an illusory state of separateness. As we have seen, the Hindu traditions of Vedanta and Yoga tell us that *atman* is one with *brahman*. However, we lose our sense of oneness with the universe through identifying with our minds and bodies. Under the influence of *maya* – or illusion – we come to believe that we are separate and limited entities. Like a veil, *maya* covers *brahman*, hiding the reality of our essential oneness. While this state of separation and delusion exists, suffering is inevitable. We experience ourselves as incomplete and isolated fragments, broken off from the whole. Similarly, the Buddha taught that psychological suffering (or *dukkha*) is the result of perceiving ourselves as separate, autonomous beings. The Chinese philosophy of Taoism suggests that suffering and discord arise when we lose connection to the *Tao* (the universal principle of harmony that maintains the balance and order of the world) and experience ourselves as separate entities.

However, these traditions also teach that the illusion of separateness can be transcended. Spiritual geniuses like the Buddha and the Hindu sage Patanjali created extremely detailed and methodical paths of self-development, which are so effective that they are extensively used even now. The Buddha's "eightfold path" features a variety of lifestyle guidelines, covering wisdom, ethical conduct and meditation. Patanjali's "eight-limbed path" of yoga includes ethical conduct, self-discipline, yoga asanas, breath control and deepening levels of absorption and meditation. In the fertile spiritual ground of India, over the centuries the original teachings of Buddhism and Yoga were adapted in countless ways, giving rise to a host of other paths of connection, such as Tantra, Advaita Vedanta and Mahayana Buddhism.

In fact, almost every culture around the world developed their own paths of connection or adapted those of other cultures. In China, Taoists developed their own path, including ethical action, meditation, psycho-physical exercises (such as Qi Gong) and dietary guidelines. Buddhism spread to China too, as well as to Japan, where Zen is still the main national religion (along with Shinto). In the Middle East and Europe, paths of connection tended to be more esoteric and exclusive. In the Christian world, the most systematic paths of connection belonged to monastic traditions, where monks lived in voluntary poverty, silence and solitude, with long periods of prayer and meditation. Christianity also has a strong tradition of mystics – such as Meister Eckhart and St. John of the Cross – who attained a high level of wakefulness and offered guidance for others to do the same. In Jewish spirituality, there was no monastic tradition, but the esoteric teachings of the Kabbalah recommended a variety of techniques and lifestyle guidelines, such as prayer, chanting, visualisation of symbols, and contemplating the letters of the Hebrew alphabet. In the Islamic world, the Sufi tradition served a similar purpose as a path of connection.

As I've already noted, all paths of connection place a strong emphasis on altruism. They all include altruism as a *practice* which can enhance our spiritual development. Altruism and service help us transcend self-centredness and strengthen the connection to other human beings, and the world in general. Adepts are encouraged to live in service and self-sacrifice, practising virtues such as kindness, forgiveness and mercy. We've already seen that this is a strong element of the teachings of the Buddha and Jesus, and this is also true of the Sufi and Jewish paths of connection. In Sufism, for example, service is a way of opening ourselves to God. Since the nature of God is love, self-sacrifice and altruism bring us closer to Him, and attune us to His nature. In the Kabbalah, the awakened person has a responsibility to contribute to *tikkun olam* (the healing of the world). He or she serves others by sharing joy and light, which are "brought down" and spread to everyone. In this way, altruism is both the cause and consequence of spiritual development.

Meditation as a Method of Connection

However, perhaps the most important element of all paths of connection is meditation. All spiritual traditions recommend practices of quietening and emptying the mind. Meditation was central to both Buddhism and Yoga, where a wide variety of different meditative techniques developed, including "focused" meditation (usually paying attention to the breath or a mantra) and "open" meditation (simply observing whatever enters the field of awareness). In China Taoists recommended the practice of *tso-wang* – "sitting with a blank mind". Sufism and the Kabbalah both developed forms of meditation, while in the Eastern Orthodox Church the "Jesus Prayer" ("Lord Jesus Christ, son of God, have mercy on me, a sinner") was effectively used as a mantra for meditation. Western Christian monks and mystics may not have meditated in a direct sense, but no doubt attained meditative states through prayer and contemplation. Of course, nowadays it's common for people to practise meditation in a secular, standalone basis, outside the context of spiritual traditions.

Meditation is so important because it's a simple and effective method of cultivating connection, both on a short- and long-term basis. Even a single, short meditation practice can create connection. By quietening our thoughts, we soften the boundaries of our ego. Our surroundings become more real and seem somehow *closer* to us. Our awareness seems to merge with our surroundings, like a river flowing into the sea. There is an immediate sense of ease and contentment, as the stress and anxiety created by the separate ego recedes.

Usually these effects are just temporary. Perhaps after a few hours, our normal state of consciousness re-establishes itself, and our sense of connection and heightened awareness fade. However, if we meditate regularly over a long period of time – for months, years and even decades – there is a cumulative effect. Our ego-boundaries become permanently softer, and we establish an ongoing sense of connection. We undergo permanent spiritual development and move further along the continuum of connection.

Towards Union

Ultimately, all paths of connection lead to a state of union, in which human beings are no longer isolated, egoic entities but are one with the universe in general, or with God.

Different traditions conceive of union in slightly different ways. What the Yoga tradition refers to as *sahaja samadhi* (usually translated as "everyday ecstasy") is slightly different to what Taoists refer to as *ming* (when we live in harmony with the *Tao*) or what Christian mystics refer to as *theosis* or *deification* (literally, oneness with God). In Theravada Buddhism (the original form taught by the Buddha) the emphasis isn't so much on union itself but on overcoming the illusion of the separate self. *Nirvana* is a state in which our sense of individual identity is "blotted out" or extinguished (which is the literal meaning of the term), so that we no longer feel desire or create karma, and so no longer have to be reborn.

Nevertheless, all traditions agree that union means the end of suffering. As *The Upanishads* put it, "when a man knows the infinite, he is free; his sorrows have an end."[20] To transcend separation is to attain bliss. Or as I would put it in psychological terms, union means becoming free of the discord and pathology generated by disconnection. It means feeling a sense of wholeness rather than lack. It means becoming free of the desire to accumulate wealth and status which is produced by a sense of lack. It means becoming free of the need for constant activity and distraction, to escape from our discontent. It means becoming free of the need to identify with groups, and the desire to create conflict with other groups. It means experiencing a natural sense of harmony and living in a state of ease.

As stated above, there are degrees of awakening. It's quite rare for people to live in an ongoing state of union, but based on my own research, I believe that *mild* wakefulness (with an ongoing sense of connection rather than fully-fledged union) is more common than most people realise. I also have a strong feeling – again based on my research – that more and more people are moving towards wakefulness, some of them through following spiritual paths and practices, and others through a sudden shift after intense psychological turmoil.

Imagine if a *large* proportion of people began to experience a mild degree of wakefulness. On a social level, it would mean an end to oppression, hierarchy, and warfare. It would mean equality for women, humane treatment of animals, and responsible and sustainable treatment of the environment. It would mean that all societies had altruistic and empathic leaders who worked selflessly for the common good. There would be a culture of cooperation and altruism rather than ruthlessness and competition.

If the above description seems like an absurd utopian fantasy, it only shows how far into disconnection we have fallen. In fact, the summary is quite an accurate description of how our hunter-gatherer ancestors lived for tens of thousands of years. If we lived in such societies before – in fact, for the vast majority of our time on this planet – there is no reason why we shouldn't do so again.

In the last chapter of this book, we'll explore some possible measures we can take to bring about a return to such societies. We will examine what can we do, both individually and collectively, to move towards connection.

Chapter 14

Towards a Connected World

We've travelled a massive distance in this book, from the depraved depths of serial killers and psychopathic dictators to the luminous heights of spiritual awakening. If these extremes seem incongruous, remember that we've simply covered the spectrum of human nature, moving from one end of the continuum of connection to the other. Even after writing this book, I find it astonishing that humans are capable of such extremes of behaviour, from Hitler and Stalin orchestrating the deaths of millions of people to Gandhi or Martin Luther King Jr. risking their own lives to campaign against injustice. If you were on a small airplane with 100 other people, you would almost certainly be sitting a few feet away from at least one hyper-disconnected person who habitually exploits and abuses other people. But on the same airplane, there would also probably be at least one hyper-connected person who devotes their life to serving others. The other people on the plane – probably including you – would be situated somewhere between these two extremes, at various points along the continuum of connection.

However, at least now we understand why these vast differences in human behaviour occur. They're the result of variations in connection, the degree to which humans feel connected or separate to one another and the world. Hopefully we also now understand how human behaviour and human society can be improved. Both individually and collectively, progress means moving further along the continuum of connection. Progress means becoming less separate and selfish, and more empathic and altruistic. It means transcending the illusion of separation and uncovering our innate oneness.

As I suggested in Chapter 10, a collective process of increasing connection has been underway for at least 250 years, leading to significant social progress. At present there is also an ever-growing number of people who are following individual paths of connection, via spiritual paths and practices. Nevertheless, there is no doubt that, overall, we still live in a disconnected world. Although pathocracy has diminished since its twentieth century peak, there are still many highly disconnected societies in the world. According to a "democracy index" published by *The Economist* magazine, in 2020, there were only 23 full democracies in the world, along with 52 "flawed democracies", 35 "hybrid regimes" (that is, countries with some degree of democracy combined with authoritarianism), and 57 fully authoritarian regimes.[1] Roughly speaking, we could replace the term "democracy" with "connected" here, which would suggest that there are just 23 connected societies in the world, compared to 57 highly disconnected. (Significantly, in Chapter 12, we saw a similar figure of only 19 female leaders out of 194 countries.)

But of course, democracy isn't the only measure of connection. On a global scale, there are many issues which illustrate that the human race exists in a general state of disconnection. These include the climate emergency, the mass extinction of other species, warfare, terrorism, the mass production and sale of weapons, mass movements of populations due to war and poverty, international political conflict, and so on. These problems are caused by disconnection, and they can only be solved through connection. The only guarantee of our future welfare, and even our survival, is for us to move collectively towards connection.

In this final chapter, I'm going to suggest how we might do this, from both a psychological and social perspective.

Switching on Empathy

To begin with, let's return to the world of criminality and psychopathy. In the first half of this book, we examined the enormous suffering and chaos caused by hyper-disconnected people, particularly when they enter their preferred career avenues of crime, the business or corporate world, or politics. We saw then that the essential problem with hyper-disconnected people is an absence of empathy, which enables their brutality and abuse.

In physical terms, when a disease causes great suffering, we seek a cure. So perhaps we should do the same for hyper-disconnected people. Is it possible to cure their pathology? Or most specifically, is it possible to heal their lack of empathy?

In fact, psychologists have long debated whether personality disorders such as psychopathy and narcissistic personality disorder can be cured. The consensus opinion is that they are incurable, and it's true that there are very few cases of psychopaths and narcissists responding to treatment, or of psychopathic prisoners becoming rehabilitated. However, I believe that, in principle, hyper-disconnection *is* curable. Since connection is so fundamental to human beings (and to reality), it should be possible to reconnect anyone, no matter how disconnected they have become. In practice though, hyper-disconnected people rarely accept that there is anything wrong with their personality or behaviour. Their condition convinces them they're superior to everyone else, even that they are completely without faults. The very notion that they might be imperfect is an insult to them, so they rarely agree to therapy, or engage in rehabilitation.

Nevertheless, there are some cases of hyper-disconnected people becoming reconnected. One striking case I have come across – as featured in my book *Extraordinary Awakenings* – is an American man called Edward Little, who was convicted of murder while still just a child. Little had a horrific upbringing, in which he was conditioned to view violence as normal. His mother was a violent and unstable woman who went to prison for killing her husband (not Little's father, with whom he had no contact). After four years of foster care, his mother was let out of prison, and Little was sent back to live with her. But mostly he was shunted back and forth between her different boyfriends and husbands, one of whom was physically abusive. The only person Little felt he could trust was his older brother, who was a drug addict and criminal and led him into a life of crime. At the age of 15, Little held up a store with an accomplice. He brandished a gun and shot and wounded the store clerk. Later a policeman stopped them in their stolen car. As the policeman turned to walk back to his car, Little and his accomplice decided to run away, and Little shot at the policeman as they fled. The policeman died. In 1980, Little was found guilty of capital murder, and only spared the death penalty because the jury was moved by his childhood of neglect, abuse and addiction.

Eight years into his prison sentence, Little started to meditate to try to calm his mind. He vividly described to me how, one day during a meditation, his empathy suddenly switched on:

> I started crying for the first time I could remember, and it was like a light coming on inside my mind, allowing me to understand what I had done. I cried silently for a long time, trying not to let anyone hear me. I felt so much sorrow for the suffering I had caused and for my family and also for myself. It was that day that transformed me. I started searching for understanding, and so much new information started flowing into my life along with new people.[2]

If a person as intensely disconnected as Edward Little can experience a "switching on" of empathy, then there is surely hope for others. If hyper-disconnected people could somehow be encouraged to participate in therapy or to practise meditation, then they might undergo the same transformation.

At the very least, many people who exist in a state of *shallow* disconnection can – and do – undergo transformation. As described in Chapter 2, shallow disconnection is when people become disconnected due to addiction or environmental influences (for example, a deprived and hostile environment that encourages ruthlessness and violence). Another form of shallow disconnection is when young men adopt an extremist ideology that switches off their empathy to other national or religious groups who they perceive as enemies. (I referred to this specifically as "selective disconnection".)

In shallow disconnection, a person's empathy and conscience may only be temporarily "switched off", covered up by a superficial layer of callousness that leads to delinquency and crime. As we also saw in Chapter 2, some offenders who participate in restorative justice programmes experience a "switching on" of empathy, when they meet the victims (or relatives of their victims) of their crimes. They come to understand the consequences of their actions, and the suffering they have caused. To this end, restorative justice programmes should be used much more extensively throughout the justice system, with the specific aim of switching on empathy in offenders.

As Edward Little's example shows, meditation is also a powerful way of switching on empathy. In the UK, an organisation called the Prison Phoenix Trust runs yoga and meditation sessions in over 80 prisons, at the same time as offering general support for the spiritual development of prisoners. In the organisation's newsletter, many prisoners describe the transformative effects of meditation and yoga. For example, one prisoner described spending three days trying to release a moth from his cell window, when previously he would have killed it without thinking. Another prisoner described how he reacted when he saw a watch fall out of another prisoner's pocket. Rather than pocketing the watch himself (as he would have done previously), he heard himself shout, "Hey – you've dropped your watch." More generally, prisoners report changes in behaviour and attitude, becoming less self-centred, more tolerant, empathic and emotionally sensitive. One person described, "There is a deeper me who is not [the] ego and is kind, compassionate, and cares about people."[3]

These reports emphasise the point I made in the last chapter: that meditation is an incredibly effective method of creating connection. In view of this, meditation classes should be a standard part of the prison system, and the school curriculum too. The practice should be encouraged and expanded throughout society as much as possible. After all, as we saw in Chapter 12, this was a key part of the "empathic revolution" in Mozambique under Joaquim Chissano's leadership, when he encouraged his ministers and military and police recruits to meditate.

Protecting Ourselves from Pathocracy

Since it's unrealistic to hope to cure all hyper-disconnected people, we should also consider how we can protect ourselves from them – in particular, how we can restrict their access to power and minimise their influence. We also need to make positions of power less attractive to them, and more accessible and attractive to connected people. We need fewer psychopathic and narcissistic leaders, and more altruistic and ethical leaders.

In the first half of this book, we saw that hyper-disconnected people are strongly attracted to positions of power and find them easy to attain. As the originator of the concept of pathocracy, Lobaczewski, noted, pathocracies only emerge because we don't take sufficient measures to protect ourselves from the pathological minority who are drawn to power. To some extent, this has always been the goal of democracy: to protect the mass of people from the oppression and abuse of authoritarian leaders. This is why, as we noted in Chapter 7, hyper-disconnected leaders hate democracy. Democracy limits their power, obstructs their ambitions for complete dominance, and leaves them open to criticism. As a result, hyper-disconnected leaders do everything possible to undermine democracy.

However, even some of the world's most democratic countries (such as the United States or the UK) are presently unable to prevent hyper-disconnected people gaining high level political positions. The problem is that, while democratic systems provide checks and balances that limit the power of tyrants, they do little to prevent hyper-disconnected people attaining power in the first place. Most modern democracies are representative (or elective). Rather than directly participating in government, ordinary people elect representatives (such as members of Parliament, senators or congresspeople) to govern on their behalf. Representative democracy would work well if we could ensure that our representatives were altruistic and responsible. But in the present system, there are no checks on the people who put themselves forward as representatives. We simply end up with a House of Representatives or House of Commons with a high proportion of hyper-disconnected people. If the purpose of democracy is to protect us from tyrants, modern democracy is failing.

Psychological Assessment

Hunter-gatherer groups were keenly aware of a simple truth that has apparently not occurred to modern democracies: people who have a strong desire for power are the least suitable to hold power. As we saw in Chapter 10, hunter-gatherer societies take measures to prevent disconnected people gaining power, in order to preserve the equality and harmony of the group. Dominant people are barred from consideration as leaders. If they try to assert their dominance, the whole group takes action against them. They gang up against the dominant person, and ostracise or desert him.

In my view, we should follow their example. We should bar hyper-disconnected people from positions of power. Here the expertise of psychologists and other mental health professionals would be essential. In my view, every government (and indeed every organisation) should employ psychologists to assess the personality and behaviour of leadership candidates, and hence determine their suitability for power. At the simplest level, potential leaders should be assessed for empathy. If they are found to lack empathy, they should be barred from positions of power. As awareness of the problem of "corporate psychopathy" has grown, some psychologists have suggested that human resources should – in the words of Clive Boddy – "screen leadership candidates for psychopathy because organisational success and psychopathy are inimical."[4] So why shouldn't we do the same for political candidates? To paraphrase Boddy, we need to screen political candidates for psychopathic traits because societal success and psychopathy are inimical.

There are a range of assessments that psychologists use to test for psychopathy and narcissistic personality disorder, as well as broader personality traits. However, since hyper-disconnected people are manipulative and dishonest, such self-report inventories probably won't be reliable. But there are many other types of assessments. For example, when self-reports are unsuitable, psychologists sometimes use "observer ratings", where a person's personality is assessed by their peers, such as supervisors and co-workers. Psychologists could also examine the person's life history, looking for evidence of empathy and compassion (or their reverse). They could interview past acquaintances, former schoolteachers or university tutors, and so on. Since most people with psychopathic traits show signs of cruelty and callousness while children, early teachers and childhood friends or relatives of political candidates could also be interviewed.[5]

Some psychologists might feel reluctant to take on a political role, but there is a precedent. After the Second World War, psychologists routinely conducted assessments as a part of an effort to "denazify" Germans. Most assessments were by necessity rudimentary, since there were still so many Nazis in Germany at large after the war. However, there were some rigorous assessments of high-level Nazis, such as Rudolf Hess.[6] There were also attempts to understand the mass psychology of Hitler's and the Nazis' appeal, in the hope of ensuring that mass fascist movements wouldn't re-emerge. In addition, some psychologists studied German opponents of Nazism, to try to understand why some people were resistant to fascist ideology and authoritarian leaders.[7]

One criticism might be that these measures would give too much power to psychologists, who would effectively become kingmakers, and perhaps become vulnerable to corruption and narcissism themselves. In the worst-case scenario, the assessor roles would become attractive to hyper-disconnected people, and another form of pathocracy would emerge. However, measures could easily be taken to mitigate against this. Following the democratic principles of Ancient Athens (which we'll examine in a moment), decisions would be taken by boards, and the assessing psychologists could be selected by sortition, and only serve for a limited period.

Even if imperfect, it's clear that some action is necessary. Representative democracy can only work if candidates are carefully screened, and hyper-disconnected people are excluded. Nothing could be worse than the present situation, when there is no regulation at all to stop hyper-disconnected people laying claim to positions of power. In the same way that corporations can be brought to their knees by the behaviour of a small number of disordered high level managers, entire societies – and the world itself – are being badly damaged by the actions of a small number of disordered politicians. And more than anyone else, psychologists and other mental professionals have a moral duty to help.

A Different Kind of Democracy

Another possibility is that, instead of trying to improve representative democracy, we should adopt different democratic processes, or a different democratic system altogether. Here we can take further guidance from simple hunter-gatherer groups. Most groups do have a leader of some form, but their power is usually limited, since most decisions are made by consensus. People don't volunteer themselves as leaders but are chosen by the rest of the group, on the basis of wisdom and experience, or because a person's ability and wisdom suit a particular situation. Leaders can easily be deposed if the rest of the group are dissatisfied with them. In some societies, the role of leader is not fixed, but rotates according to different circumstances. As the anthropologist Margaret Power has noted of simple hunger-gatherer groups in general, "The leadership role is spontaneously assigned by the group, conferred on some members in some particular situation... One leader replaces another as needed."[8]

In contrast, in modern democracies, power is not assigned, but *sought*. Anyone can put themselves forward as a member of Parliament, or a senator or congressperson. Since hyper-disconnected people are drawn to power (and find it easy to attain), they are much more likely than psychologically normal people to put themselves forward as representatives. And once they become representatives, there is a good chance that they will ascend quickly through the hierarchy of their political parties or governments and become dominant figures. As noted already, most connected people aren't particularly interested in power. So this leaves the positions free for disconnected people, who gladly occupy them.

Perhaps, then, we should emulate hunter-gather groups by *assigning* leadership roles, rather than leaving them open to volunteers. No one should be able to put themselves forward as a representative, or a prime minister or president. Citizens' assemblies (themselves randomly selected) could nominate wise, experienced and altruistic individuals as local representatives. The individuals may not particularly desire positions of power, but the representative role should be seen as a mandatory public duty, like jury service, which people are obliged to perform for a certain amount of time.

Here we can learn from another early form of democracy: Ancient Athens. Admittedly the Athenian concept of democracy was very limited, since it didn't include women or slaves. As we noted above, Ancient Greece was in many ways a highly disconnected society. However, the Athenians developed a sophisticated political system that was more genuinely democratic than the present-day UK or US. As the historian Paul Cartledge has pointed out in his book *Democracy: A Life*, the modern concept of democracy is a degradation of the original Greek concept and has very little in common with it. Whereas modern democracy is merely representative, the Ancient Greeks practised *direct* democracy. It literally was "people power".

Like hunter-gatherer groups, the Ancient Athenians were very aware of the danger of corrupt and callous people attaining power. Their standard method of selecting political officials was sortition, or random selection by lot. This ensured that ordinary people were represented in government, and safeguarded against corruption and bribery. The Athenians knew there was a risk of handing responsibility to incompetent people but mitigated this by ensuring that decisions were made by groups, or boards. Different members of the group took responsibility for different areas and acted as a check on each other's behaviour.

Athenian democracy was direct in other ways too. Political decisions – such as whether to go to war, the election of military leaders or the nomination of magistrates – were made at massive assemblies, where thousands of citizens would gather. (A minimum of 6000 citizens was required to pass any legislation.)

Citizens usually voted by showing hands – sometimes with stones or pieces of broken pottery – and decisions were carried by simple majority. The Ancient Athenians also had a system of ostracism, not dissimilar to hunter-gatherer groups. Ostracisms took place annually, when disruptive people who threatened democracy were nominated for expulsion. If a sufficient number of citizens voted in favour, they would be banished from the city for ten years. (This is where the English word *ostracise* comes from.)

Again, I believe we should emulate some of these ancient democratic principles. Sortition is still used in modern democracies, most notably in jury service, but it needs to be much more widespread. In fact, in recent years, many political thinkers have recommended reviving sortition in government. In 2014, Alexander Guerrero – professor of philosophy at Rutgers University – published an influential paper advocating what he called *lottocracy* as an alternative to representative democracy. In this system, government is done by "single-issue legislatures", assemblies that focus on specific issues such as agriculture or health care. Members of the legislatures are chosen by lot and make decisions after consulting relevant experts. Another political philosopher, Helene Landemore, advocates a similar model in which assemblies of randomly selected citizens (ranging in size from 150 to a thousand) make political decisions. Landemore's model of "open democracy" also includes referendums and "crowd-sourced feedback loops" (when large numbers of people discuss policies on Internet forums, and the feedback is evaluated by legislators). Similarly, an earlier political philosopher, John Burnheim, used the term *demarchy* for a political system made up of small randomly selected "citizens' juries" who discuss and decide public policies.

All of these measures would be extremely welcome, to reduce the likelihood of hyper-disconnected people attaining power. Significantly, such measures will make leadership positions less *attractive* to hyper-disconnected people. Direct democracy means less individual power, and more checks and limitations to individual authority. Governments and organisations become less hierarchical and more cooperative, based on partnership rather than power. There is much less opportunity for hyper-disconnected people to satisfy their craving for dominance and express their malevolence.

Empathocracy

Perhaps even more important than these political and social measures are the steps we can take as *individuals* to move towards connection.

We can do this by following spiritual paths of connection, by undergoing a journey of self-development that leads us beyond selfishness towards selflessness. For some, this might mean following a specific spiritual path like Buddhism or Sufism. For others, it might mean creating an eclectic individual path made up of elements from different traditions. For others, it might simply mean regularly meditating, or following a life of service. The type of path we choose isn't so important, although some may suit our personality and our developmental needs better than others. All the paths lead in the same direction: towards connection.

As I suggested earlier, there is an interweaving, mutually reinforcing relationship between individual and social connection. The further we move towards connection as individuals, the more our societies move towards connection. And as societies become more connected, the easier it becomes for individuals to move towards connection. A feedback process begins, moving towards greater and greater connection. Eventually we may reach a threshold when human beings' normal state is one of empathic connection towards other people, other living beings and the natural world.

At this point, human societies will transition to a radically new form of government. After centuries of oppressive monarchies, brutal pathocracies and malfunctioning democracies, we will finally live in *empathocracies*. Empathocracy is the form of government that naturally arises in highly connected societies. It is the polar opposite of pathocracy, in the same way that wakefulness is the opposite of psychopathy. In an empathocracy, a government is made up of empathic and altruistic people, who govern selflessly for the common good. The link between power and malevolent personalities disappears. Power is no longer sought by corrupt people, and no longer corrupts once it has been attained. It is simply used to organise and administrate, to help generate and maintain harmony.

The only issue is whether there is enough time left for us to reach a collective state of connection. Thousands of years of disconnection are heading towards a catastrophic conclusion. The crises we are facing now are the logical culmination of a pathological ego-separateness that has disconnected us from our environment, each other, and even our own bodies. For the last few thousand years, the human race has been suffering from a collective, life-threatening illness: the disease of disconnection. We're now in a critical condition. However, like our bodies, the human race has collective self-healing powers, which have begun to take effect. Whether or not we survive is a question of whether the healing process can overcome the disease in time.

As individuals, we're all potentially part of the healing process, and we all have a responsibility to contribute to it. We have a responsibility to heal ourselves through following paths of connection, and so contribute to the collective process of connection, helping to ensure our future welfare as a species, and the welfare of the Earth itself.

Connection doesn't mean losing our individuality and identity. Connection and individuality aren't mutually exclusive. You can be an individual without experiencing a sense of separation to the world. In fact, this is the ideal human state – to possess individual identity at the same time as feeling our essential oneness with the whole world, and with all other individual forms. In this state, the self exists without boundaries, in a fluid dynamic relationship to other beings and the world, without losing its own form. You could compare to it to a wave and the ocean: a wave has its own individual form but is part of the whole of the ocean. It is one with the whole ocean. The problem arises when the wave perceives itself as separate and independent and loses awareness of its oneness with the ocean.

In connection, we don't lose our identity, but gain it – that is, we gain our *real* identity. We were never meant to live as disconnected selves, with an illusory sense of separation. It's because our disconnected identity is false that it feels uncomfortable and creates anxiety. It doesn't feel right, because it's wrong. In contrast, connection feels deeply *right*, because it's our true nature.

Connection isn't a quality that we cultivate so much as one that we *uncover*. As this book has shown, goodness is innate to human beings, because connection is innate. Despite the appalling brutality that some human beings are capable of, evil is not innate, but an aberration that arises from an unnatural state of disconnection. Since all our beings arise from the same fundamental source, we are always interconnected. Love, empathy and altruism are simply pure, unadulterated expressions of our fundamental oneness, like fresh water that flows from a spring.

Even at our most isolated and divided, we are always one. We only need to remember what we have always known. We only need to become what we have always been.

Appendix 1

The Continuum of Connection

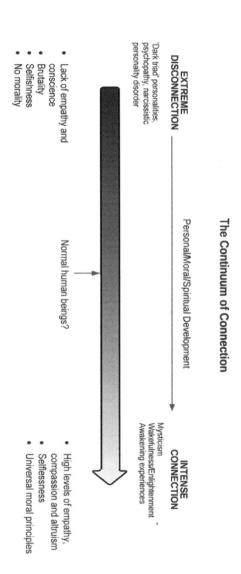

The Continuum of Connection

Personal/Moral/Spiritual Development

EXTREME DISCONNECTION

'Dark triad' personalities, psychopathy, narcissistic personality disorder

- Lack of empathy and conscience
- Brutality
- Selfishness
- No morality

Normal human beings?

INTENSE CONNECTION

Mysticism
Wakefulness/Enlightenment
Awakening experiences

- High levels of empathy, compassion and altruism
- Selflessness
- Universal moral principles

Appendix 2

The Social Continuum of Connection

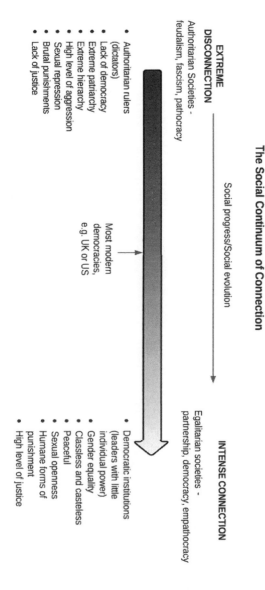

The Social Continuum of Connection

Social progress/Social evolution

EXTREME DISCONNECTION

Authoritarian Societies - feudalism, fascism, pathocracy

- Authoritarian rulers (dictators)
- Lack of democracy
- Extreme patriarchy
- Extreme hierarchy
- High level of aggression
- Sexual repression
- Brutal punishments
- Lack of justice

Most modern democracies, e.g. UK or US

INTENSE CONNECTION

Egalitarian societies - partnership, democracy, empathocracy

- Democratic institutions (leaders with little individual power)
- Gender equality
- Classless and casteless
- Peaceful
- Sexual openness
- Humane forms of punishment
- High level of justice

Appendix 3

The Spiritual Continuum of Connection

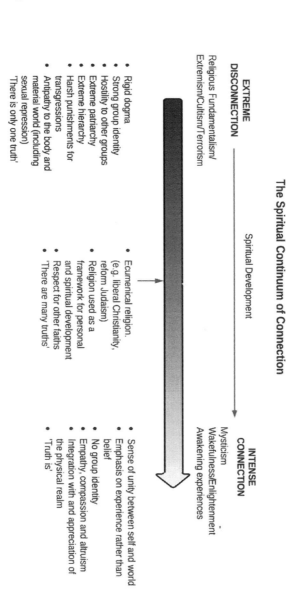

The Spiritual Continuum of Connection

Spiritual Development

EXTREME DISCONNECTION

Religious Fundamentalism/
Extremism/Cultism/Terrorism

- Rigid dogma
- Strong group identity
- Hostility to other groups
- Extreme patriarchy
- Extreme hierarchy
- Harsh punishments for transgressions
- Antipathy to the body and material world (including sexual repression)
- 'There is only one truth'

- Ecumenical religion. (e.g. liberal Christianity, reform Judaism)
- Religion used as a framework for personal and spiritual development
- Respect for other faiths
- 'There are many truths'

INTENSE CONNECTION

Mysticism
Wakefulness/Enlightenment
Awakening experiences

- Sense of unity between self and world
- Emphasis on experience rather than belief
- No group identity
- Empathy, compassion and altruism
- Integration with and appreciation of the physical realm
- 'Truth is'

249

Appendix 4

Answers to Statements of Pathocratic Leaders

1. Silvio Berlusconi
2. Donald Trump
3. Caligula
4. Muammar Gaddafi

Acknowledgements

This book grew organically over several years, beginning with blog articles I published with *Psychology Today* and later with *The Conversation*. It began to take real shape once the psychotherapist Elizabeth Mika read one of my articles and recommended the work of Andrzej Lobaczewski, including his concept of pathocracy. My thanks to Elizabeth, and also to my editors at *Psychology Today* and *The Conversation*. Thanks also to Edward Hoffman, who edited a special issue of the *Journal of Humanistic Psychology*, including my essay "Towards a Utopian Society", which also inspired and shaped this book. Finally, thanks to my son Hugh Taylor, who designed the "Continuum of Connection" diagrams.

Notes

Introduction

1. Gandhi, 2021a.
2. Gandhi, 2021b.
3. Iwamoto et al., 2020.
4. Wlodarczyk et al., 2016.
5. Brañas-Garza et al., 2018.
6. Sanz-García et al., 2021.
7. Baron-Cohen, 2003, p. 1.

Chapter 1

1. Paulus & Williams, 2002.
2. Baron-Cohen & Wheelwright, 2004.
3. Hare, 1993.
4. Simon Baron-Cohen (2003) makes a similar connection between a lack of empathy and cruelty in his book *The Science of Evil*. He suggests that there is an "empathy circuit" in the brain which can malfunction, causing an absence of empathy. He also suggests that the term "evil" should be replaced with "empathy erosion". Controversially (and falsely, in my view), Baron-Cohen believes that autism is linked to a lack of empathy, and so he also associates autism with a malfunction of the "empathy circuit".
5. Preston, 2021, p. 132.
6. ibid.
7. Tiihonen et al., 2020, p. 1.
8. Bowlby, 1969.
9. I've always been a big music fan, and one of my favourite albums is Pink Floyd's *The Wall*. The album is a thinly veiled depiction of Roger Waters' – Pink Floyd's main songwriter – own experiences. It describes a person responding to trauma by building an armour (or wall, in this case)

around himself, and disconnecting from the world. The main character, Pink, has a traumatic childhood: his father dies in the Second World War, and he is terrorised by his teachers at school. As a result, he starts to build a wall around himself, brick by brick. The wall protects him from the world, but also isolates him. Despite becoming a famous rock star, he feels embittered and depressed. He loses the ability to feel anything, becoming "comfortably numb" (as the title of one of the album's best-known songs describes it). He becomes violent and abusive and contemplates suicide. Eventually he becomes so disconnected from the world that he goes insane, fantasising that he is a fascist dictator. The album ends with the wall being torn down, exposing Pink to the world again, and forcing him to face reality. This is an excellent description of the armouring process that many people undergo in response to early emotional deprivation and trauma. (The fact that Pink fantasises about becoming a fascist dictator also highlights the link between disconnection and authoritarian leaders, which is one of the topics of Chapters 4-8.)

10. Vronsky, 2018.
11. Dawkins, 1976, p. 66.

Chapter 2

1. Kiehl & Hoffman, 2011.
2. Saladino et al., 2021; Warren et al., 2002.
3. "Statistics on Women and the Criminal Justice System", 2019.
4. Elliott & Bailey, 2014; "Global study on homicide", 2022.
5. Smithyman, 1979.
6. Thornhill & Palmer, 2001.
7. Marono et al., 2020.
8. Silke, 2003; Victoroff, 2005.

Chapter 3

1. Wilson & McCarthy, 2011; Hassall et al., 2015.
2. Croom, 2021.
3. Boddy, 2011.
4. Preston, 2012, p. 97.
5. Martin, 2014, p. 131.
6. Haslam et al., 2011.
7. In relation to politics, the British ex-politician and medical doctor David Owen has identified a similar "hubris syndrome". Owen believes that many leaders are drawn to power by their dark triad traits. However, in his view the most serious damage occurs once they attain power. Their dark triad traits quickly intensify, due to the intoxicating thrill of power, the constant attention of the media, alongside the stress and pressure of their roles. Owen mentions a number of UK and US leaders who were affected by the hubris syndrome, such as Tony Blair, Bill Clinton, and less recent figures such as Richard Nixon and Lyndon Johnson. And no doubt the hubris syndrome could be applied to many pre-modern politicians too.

Chapter 4

1. Lobaczewski, 2022, p. 187.
2. Montefiore, 2003.
3. Domitian, 2021.
4. Herodian, 2021.
5. Hibbert, 1966, p. 44.

Chapter 5

1. Hobsbawm, 1994.
2. Leitenberg, 2006.
3. Travis, 2013.

Chapter 6

1. This was a controversial issue, as there is a convention in the US that mental health professionals shouldn't diagnose public figures. This convention came about in 1964, when *Fact* magazine sent questionnaires to thousands of psychiatrists about presidential candidate Senator Barry Goldwater. The consensus opinion was that Goldwater was mentally unfit for office, which may have helped the democratic candidate, Lyndon Johnson, to a landslide victory. After the election, Goldwater successfully sued the magazine. Ever since, the American Psychiatric Association has advocated the "Goldwater Rule" that it is unethical for psychiatrists to voice their professional opinion about public figures whom they haven't examined in person. However, in Trump's case, many health professionals felt justified in overriding the convention, believing that as psychiatrists and psychologists they had a moral duty – and a moral right – to use their professional expertise to warn others. They also pointed out that, while the Goldwater Rule is an important safeguard against "armchair psychiatry", it may not apply in all cases. It was designed to prevent psychiatrists from voicing their opinions in a haphazard, uninformed way, without proper assessment. But in the case of Trump, there was much more evidence – from his biography, his own statements, people close to him, and observable behaviour — than could ever be gleaned from a clinical setting.
2. Trump, 2020, pp. 12-13.
3. ibid., pp. 23-24.
4. Bures, 2003; Morris et al., 2003.
5. Gillath & Keefer, 2016.
6. Of course, hyper-disconnected leaders often claim to be altruistic too. Like Hitler and Stalin, they love to project the image of a benevolent father who is looking after his

people. But this is simply propaganda. Their relationships – both to individuals and to the nation as a whole – are purely transactional. As I'll suggest in the next chapter, pathocrats only care about their countries as a way of enhancing their own power and prestige, or of supplying them with the adulation they crave.

Chapter 7

1. Khan, 2021.
2. Fromm, 1964/2021, p. 23.
3. Gooch, 2020.
4. Fromm, ibid.
5. Doder and Branson, 1999, p. 272.
6. ibid., p. 253.
7. LeBor, 2003, p. 184.
8. Dutton, 2013.
9. At the same time, some of Nietzsche's ideas didn't fit at all with Nazi philosophy, such as his denunciations of anti-Semitism.

Chapter 8

1. Cohen, 1992, p. 128.
2. in Benjamin, 2022.
3. Wilber, 2022.

Chapter 9

1. Wilber, 1997.
2. Clark, 1993.
3. Zablocki, 1998, p. 232.
4. Galanter, 1993.

Chapter 10

1. The cultural historian Riane Eisler (1987) has a similar concept of "partnership" and "dominator" societies. In

her classic book *The Chalice and the Blade*, she suggests that "partnership" societies were common throughout Europe until around 5000 years ago, when "dominator" societies arose and became the standard social model.

2. Galtung, 1969.
3. Lee, 1979.
4. Haas & Piscitelli, 2013.
5. Slingenbergh, 2013.
6. Haas & Piscitelli, 2013.
7. Ferguson, 2013.
8. Haas & Piscitelli, 2013, p. 176.
9. Burch & Ellanna, 1994, p. 61.
10. Fry and Soderberg, 2012.
11. Ferguson, 2013, p. 79.
12. Woodburn, 1982, p. 437.
13. Knauft, 1991.
14. Ingold et al., 1998.
15. Bird & Bird, 2008.
16. Boehm, 2001, p. 64.
17. ibid., p. 69.
18. Ferguson, 2013.
19. Boehm, 2001, p. 38.
20. Kramer, 1969, p. 16.
21. Hawkes, 1973, p. xxv.
22. Conway Morris, 2006, p. 327.
23. in McLuhan, 1971, p. 36.
24. ibid., p. 61.

Chapter 11
1. Batson & Shaw, 1991, p. 14.
2. Haidt, 2002, p. 864.
3. For further details on panspiritism, see Taylor, 2020.

Chapter 12

1. Williams, 2015.
2. Karami et al., 2019.
3. The psychologist Abraham Maslow also identified a general sense of kinship as a characteristic of "self-actualized" people. Maslow saw self-actualization as the goal of human development, after more basic physiological and emotional needs have been satisfied. Self-actualized people are characterised by their strong sense of appreciation and gratitude, their greater than normal need for peace and solitude, and their sense of duty or mission beyond their own personal ambitions. They also possess, in Maslow's words, "a deep feeling of identification, sympathy and affection... Because of this [self-actualizers] have a genuine desire to help the human race. It is as if they were all members of a single family" (Maslow, 1954, p. 217). In my view, the self-actualized state is essentially the same as the hyper-connected state. Significantly, some of the examples I give of hyper-connected people – such as Gandhi and Abraham Lincoln – are also cited by Maslow as examples of self-actualized people.
4. Maslow, 1965.
5. Greenleaf, 1977.
6. Brown et al., 2005.
7. "How Peace Was Brought To War-Torn Mozambique in the 1990s", 2022.
8. "Selected Quotations by Abraham Lincoln", 2022.
9. Tutu, 2022.
10. Garikipati & Kambhampati, 2020.
11. in Wade & Tavris, 1994, p. 124.
12. Service, 1978.
13. Malinowski, 1932.
14. Falola, 2000.

Chapter 13

1. "Metta Sutta", 2022.
2. Taylor, 2021a, p. 140.
3. Taylor & Egeto-Szabo, 2017.
4. Wordsworth, 1994, p. 648.
5. in Johnson, 1959, pp. 83-84.
6. Merton, 1966, p. 140.
7. Williams, 2015, pp. 76-77.
8. Taylor & Egeto-Szabo, 2017, p. 61.
9. ibid., p. 54.
10. Taylor, 2018b, pp. 45-46.
11. Taylor, 2017a, p. 192.
12. Taylor, 2021a, p. 94.
13. ibid., p. 115.
14. ibid., p. 147.
15. ibid.
16. ibid., p. 115.
17. Taylor, 2017, p. 207.
18. Taylor, 2021a, p. 29.
19. ibid., p. 95.
20. *The Upanishads*, 1988, p. 86.

Chapter 14

1. "Democracy Index 2020", 2021.
2. Taylor, 2021a, p. 80.
3. All these quotes come from newsletters of the Prison Phoenix Trust, available at https://www.theppt.org.uk/about-us/newsletters.
4. Boddy, 2017, p. 156.
5. Salekin, 2006; Frick, 2009; Glenn, 2019.
6. Pick, 2013.
7. Levy, 1947.
8. Power, 1994, p. 61.

Bibliography

Babiak, P. & Hare, R.D. (2006). *Snakes in Suits: When Psychopaths Go to Work*. Regan Books.

Baron-Cohen, S. (2003). *The Essential Difference: Men, Women and the Extreme Male Brain*. Allen Lane.

Baron-Cohen, S. & Wheelwright, S. (2004). The empathy quotient: an investigation of adults with Asperger syndrome or high functioning autism, and normal sex differences. *J P Autism Dev Disord. 34*(2), 163-75.

Batson, C.D. & Shaw, L. (1991). Evidence for altruism: Toward a pluralism of prosocial motives. *Psychol Inq. 2*(2), 107-122, 14.

Benjamin, E. (2022). Andrew Cohen's apology. Available at http://www.integralworld.net/benjamin79.html

Bird, R.B. & Bird, D.W.W. (2008). Why women hunt. *Current Anthropology 49*(4), 655-693.

Boddy, C.R. (2005). The implications of corporate psychopaths for business and society: An initial examination and a call to arms. *Australasian Journal of Business and Behavioural Sciences 1*(2), 30-40.

Boddy, C.R. (2006). The dark side of management decisions: Organisational psychopaths. *Management Decision 44*(10), 1461-1475.

Boddy, C.R. (2010). Corporate psychopaths and productivity. *Management Services 54*(1), 26-30.

Boddy, C.R. (2011). *Corporate psychopaths: Organisational destroyers*. Palgrave Macmillan.

Boddy, C.R. (2012). The impact of corporate psychopaths on corporate reputation and marketing. *The Marketing Review 12*(1), 79-89.

Boddy, C.R. (2014). Corporate Psychopaths, Conflict, Employee Affective Well-Being and Counterproductive Work Behaviour. *J Bus Ethics 121*, 107-121.

Boddy, C.R. (2017). Psychopathic leadership: A case study of a corporate psychopath CEO. *Journal of Business Ethics 145*(1), 141-156.

Boehm, C. (2001). *Hierarchy in the Forest*. Harvard University Press.

Bowlby, J. (1969). *Attachment and Loss: Vol. 1. Loss*. Basic Books.

Brañas-Garza, P., Capraro, V. & Rascón-Ramírez, E. (2018). Gender differences in altruism on Mechanical Turk: Expectations and actual behaviour. *Economics Letters 170*, 19-23.

Brown, M.E., Treviño, L.K. & Harrison, D.A. (2005). Ethical leadership: A social learning perspective for construct development and testing. *Organizational Behavior and Human Decision Processes 97*(2), 117-134.

Burch, E.S. & Ellanna, L.J. (1994). Editorial. In E.S. Burch & L.J. Ellanna (Eds.), *Key Issues in Hunter-Gatherer Research*. Berg.

Bures, R.M. (2003). Childhood residential stability and health at midlife. *American Journal of Public Health 93*, 1144-1148.

Cassius Dio (2021). *Roman history*. Available at https://penelope.uchicago.edu/Thayer/e/roman/texts/cassius_dio/67*.html

Chabrol, H., van Leeuwen, N., Rodgers, R. & Séjourné, N. (2009). Contributions of psychopathic, narcissistic, Machiavellian, and sadistic personality traits to juvenile delinquency. *Personality and Individual Differences 47* (7), 734-39.

Clark, C.S. (1993). Cults in America. *CQ Researcher 3*, 385-408. Available at http://library.cqpress.com/cqresearcher/cqresrre1993050701

Cleckley, H. (1941). *The Mask of Sanity: An Attempt to Reinterpret the So-called Psychopathic Personality*. Mosby.

Cohen, A. (1992). *Autobiography of an Awakening*. Moksha Press.

Coid, J., Yang, M., Ullrich, S., Roberts, A. & Hare, R.D. (2009). Prevalence and correlates of psychopathic traits in the household population of Great Britain. *International Journal of Law and Psychiatry 32*(2), 65-73.

Conway Morris, S. (2006). *Life's Solution: Inevitable Humans in a*

Lonely Universe. Cambridge University Press.

Croom, S. (2021). 12% of corporate leaders are psychopaths. It's time to take this problem seriously. Available at https://fortune.com/2021/06/06/corporate-psychopaths-business-leadership-csr/

Dawkins, R. (1976). *The Selfish Gene*. Oxford University Press.

Democracy Index 2020 (2021). Available at https://www.eiu.com/n/campaigns/democracy-index-2020/?utm_source=economist-daily-chart&utm_medium=anchor&utm_campaign=democracy-index-2020&utm_content=anchor-1

Doder, D. & Branson, L. (1999). *Milosevic: Portrait of a Tyrant*. Free Press.

Dutton, K. (2013). *The Wisdom of Psychopaths*. Arrow.

Eisler, R. (1987). *The Chalice and the Blade*. Thorsons.

Elliott, I.A. & Bailey, A. (2014). Female Sex Offenders: Gender and Risk Perception. In K. McCartan (Ed.), *Responding to Sexual Offending. Palgrave Studies in Risk, Crime and Society*. London: Palgrave Macmillan.

Falola, T. (Ed.) (2000). *Africa, Volume 1: African History Before 1885*. Carolina Academic Press.

Ferguson, R.B. (2013). The Prehistory of War and Peace in Europe and the Near East. In D.P. Fry (Ed.), *War, Peace, and Human Nature: The Convergence of Evolutionary and Cultural Views* (pp. 121-240). Oxford University Press.

Frick, P.J. (2009). Extending the construct of psychopathy to youth: implications for understanding, diagnosing, and treating antisocial children and adolescents. *Canadian Journal of Psychiatry 54*(12), 803-812.

Fromm, E. (1964). Creators and destroyers. *The Saturday Review*, New York (4 January 1964), 22-25.

Fry, D.P. & Soderberg, P. (2014). Myths about hunter-gatherers redux: Nomadic forager war and peace. *J Aggress Confl Peace Res. 6*(4), 255-266.

Galanter, M. (1999). *Cults: Faith, Healing, and Coercion*. Oxford

University Press.

Galtung, J. (1969). Violence, Peace and Peace Research. *Journal of Peace Research* 6(3), 167-91.

Gandhi, M. (2021a). Letter to Adolf Hitler (1). Available at https://www.mkgandhi.org/letters/hitler_ltr.htm

Gandhi, M. (2021b). Letter to Adolf Hitler (2). Available at https://www.mkgandhi.org/letters/hitler_ltr1.htm

Garikipati, S. & Kambhampati, U. (2020). Leading the Fight Against the Pandemic: Does Gender 'Really' Matter? *Feminist Economics* 27(1-2), 401-418.

Gillath, O. & Keefer, L.A. (2016). Generalizing disposability: Residential mobility and the willingness to dissolve social ties. *Personal Relationships 23*, 186-198.

Glad, B. (2002). Why tyrants go too far: Malignant narcissism and absolute power. *Political Psychology* 23(1), 1-37.

Glenn, A.L. (2019). Early life predictors of callous-unemotional and psychopathic traits. *Infant Ment Health J.* 40(1), 39-53.

Global Study on Homicide. Available at https://www.unodc.org/documents/data-and-analysis/GSH2018/GSH18_Gender-related_killing_of_women_and_girls.pdf

Gooch, J. (2020). *Mussolini's War: Fascist Italy from Triumph to Collapse, 1935-1943.* Allen Lane.

Greenleaf, R.K. (1977). *Servant Leadership: A Journey into the Nature of Legitimate Power and Greatness.* Paulist Press.

Haas, J. & Piscitelli, M. (2013). The Prehistory of Warfare: Misled by Ethnography. In D.P. Fry (Ed.), *War, Peace, and Human Nature: The Convergence of Evolutionary and Cultural Views* (pp. 168-190). Oxford University Press.

Haidt, J. (2002). The Moral Emotions. In R. Davidson, K. Scherer & H. Goldsmith (Eds.), *Handbook of Affective Sciences* (pp. 852-870). Oxford University Press.

Hare, R.D. (1993). *Without Conscience: The Disturbing World of the Psychopaths Among Us.* Guilford.

Hart, S. & Hare, R.D. (1998). Association Between Psychopathy and Narcissism: Theoretical Views and Empirical Evidence. In E.F. Ronningstam (Ed.), *Disorders of Narcissism: Diagnostic, Clinical, and Empirical Implications* (pp. 415-436). American Psychiatric Press.

Haslam, S.A., Reicher, S.D. & Platow, M.J. (2011). *The New Psychology of Leadership: Identity, Influence and Power.* Psychology Press.

Hassall, J., Boduszek, D. & Dhingra, K. (2015). Psychopathic traits of business and psychology students and their relationship to academic success. *Personality and Individual Differences 82*, 227-231.

Hawkes, J. (1973). *The First Great Civilizations: Life in Mesopotamia, the Indus Valley, and Egypt.* Alfred Knopf.

Herodian (2021). *History of the Roman Empire since the Death of Marcus Aurelius.* Available at https://www.livius.org/sources/content/herodian-s-roman-history/herodian-1.2/

Hobsbawm, E. (1994). *The Age of Extremes: A History of the World, 1914–1991.* Michael Joseph.

Hodson, G.M., Hogg, S.M. & MacInnis, C.C. (2009). The role of "dark personalities" (narcissism, Machiavellianism, psychopathy), Big Five personality factors, and ideology in explaining prejudice. *Journal of Research in Personality 43*(4), 686-690.

Hoffer, E. (2009). *The True Believer: Thoughts on the Nature of Mass Movements.* Harper Perennial.

How Peace Was Brought To War-Torn Mozambique in the 1990s. (2022). Available at https://www.bienfaits-meditation.com/pdf/celebrities_pdf/chissano_nlpwessex.org_docs_mozambique.pdf

Ingold, T., Riches, D. & Woodburn, J. (1988). *Hunters and Gatherers, Vol. 2: Property, Power and Ideology.* Berg.

Iwamoto, S.K., Alexander, M., Torres, M. et al. (2020). Mindfulness Meditation Activates Altruism. *Sci Rep 10*, 6511.

Johnson, R.C. (1959). *Watcher on the Hills.* Harper.

Jones, D.N. & Figueredo, A.J. (2013). The core of darkness: Uncovering the heart of the dark triad. *European Journal of Personality* 27(6), 521-531.

Jones, D.N. & Paulhus, D.L. (2010). Different provocations trigger aggression in narcissists and psychopaths. *Social Psychological and Personality Science* 1(1), 12-18.

Karami, G., Maleki, A. & Zahedi Mazandarani, M. (2019). Sociological explanation of the phenomenon of honor killings (for the sake of honor) in Khuzestan Province during 2011-2015. *Quarterly Journal of Social Development* 13(3), 81-116.

Kernberg, O.F. (1998). Pathological Narcissism and Narcissistic Personality Disorder: Theoretical Background and Diagnostic Classification. In E. Ronningstam (Ed.), *Disorders of Narcissism: Diagnostic, Clinical, and Empirical Implications* (pp. 29-51). American Psychiatric Press.

Kernberg, O.F. & Caligor, E. (2005). A Psychoanalytic Theory of Personality Disorders. In M.F. Lenzenweger & J. Clarkin (Eds.), *Major Theories of Personality Disorder* (pp. 114-156). Guilford Press.

Khan, S. (2021). Many said Trump's presidency would end this way. But the warnings were ignored. *The Guardian*, 9/1/21. Available at https://www.theguardian.com/commentisfree/2021/jan/09/many-said-trumps-presidency-would-end-this-way-but-the-warnings-were-ignored

Kiehl, K.A. & Hoffman, M.B. (2011). The Criminal Psychopath: History, Neuroscience, Treatment, and Economics. *Jurimetrics* 51, 355-397.

Knauft, B.M. (1991). Violence and Sociality in Human Evolution. *Curr Anthropol.* 32(4), 391-409.

Kramer, S.N. (1969). *The Sacred Marriage Rite*. Bloomington: Indiana University Press.

Langer, W.C. (1943/1972). *The Mind of Adolf Hitler*. New York, NY: Basic Books.

LeBor, A. (2003). *Milosevic: A Biography*. Bloomsbury.

Lee, K., Ashton, M.C., Wiltshire, J., Bourdage, J.S., Visser, B.A. & Gallucci, A. (2013). Sex, power, and money: Prediction from the dark triad and honesty-humility. *European Journal of Personality 27*(2), 169-184.

Lee, R. (1979). *The !Kung San: Men, Women and Work in a Foraging Society*. Cambridge University Press.

Leitenberg, M. (2006). Deaths in Wars and Conflicts in the 20th century. Available at https://www.clingendael.org/sites/default/files/pdfs/20060800_cdsp_occ_leitenberg.pdf

Levy, D.M. (1946). The German anti-Nazi; A case study. *American Journal of Orthopsychiatry 16*(3), 507-515.

Lilienfeld, S. & Andrews, B. (1996). Development and preliminary validation of a self-report measure of psychopathic personality traits in noncriminal populations. *Journal of Personality Assessment 66* (3), 488-524.

Lincoln, A. (2022). Selected quotations by Abraham Lincoln. Available at http://www.abrahamlincolnonline.org/lincoln/speeches/quotes.htm

Lobaczewski, A. (2022). *Political Ponerology: A Science on the Nature of Evil for Political Purposes*. Red Pill Press.

Malinowski, B. (1932). *The Sexual Life of Savages*. Routledge and Kegan Paul.

Marono, A.J., Reid, S., Yaksic, E. & Keatley, D.A. (2020). A behaviour sequence analysis of serial killers' lives: From childhood abuse to methods of murder. *Psychiatry, Psychology, and Law 27*(1), 126-137.

Martin, I. (2014). *Making It Happen: Fred Goodwin, RBS and the Men Who Blew Up the British Economy*. Simon & Schuster.

Maslow, A.H. (1954). *Motivation and Personality*. Harper and Row.

Maslow, A.H. (1965). *Eupsychian Management: A Journal*. Irwin-Dorsey.

Maslow, A.H. (1968). Some fundamental questions that face the normative social psychologist. *Journal of Humanistic*

Psychology 8, 143-153.

Mathieu, C., Neumann, C.S., Hare, R.D. & Babiak, P. (2014). A dark side of leadership: Corporate psychopathy and its influence on employee well-being and job satisfaction. *Personality and Individual Differences 59*, 83-88.

McLuhan, T.C. (1971). *Touch the Earth: A Self-Portrait of Indian Existence*. Abacus.

Merton, T. (1966). *Conjectures of a Guilty Bystander*. Doubleday.

Metta Sutta (2022). Available at http://www.accesstoinsight. org/tipitaka/kn/snp/snp.1.08.amar.html

Montefiore, S.S. (2003). *Stalin: The Court of the Red Tsar*. Knopf Doubleday Publishing Group.

Morris, T.T., Manley, D., Northstone, K. & Sabel, C.E. (2017). How do moving and other major life events impact mental health? A longitudinal analysis of UK children. *Health & Place 46*, 257-266.

Nai, A. & Toros, E. (2020). The peculiar personality of strongmen: Comparing the Big Five and Dark Triad traits of autocrats and non-autocrats. *Political Research Exchange 2*, 1-24.

Owen, D. (2020). *Hubris: The Road to Donald Trump*. Methuen.

Owen, D. & Davidson, J. (2009). Hubris syndrome: an acquired personality disorder? A study of US Presidents and UK Prime Ministers over the last 100 years. *Brain 132*(5), 1396-1406.

Patrick, C., Fowles, D. & Krueger, R. (2009). Triarchic conceptualization of psychopathy: developmental origins of disinhibition, boldness, and meanness. *Development and Psychopathology 21*(3), 913-938.

Paulhus, D. & Williams, K. (2002). The Dark Triad of personality: Narcissism, Machiavellianism, and psychopathy. *Journal of Research in Personality 36*(6), 556-563.

Pick, D. (2013). *The Pursuit of the Nazi Mind*. Oxford University Press.

Pincus, A., Ansell, E., Pimentel, C., Cain, N., Wright, A. & Levy, K. (2009). Initial construction and validation of the Pathological

Narcissism Inventory. *Psychological Assessment* 21(3), 365-79.

Power, M. (1991). *The egalitarians – human and chimpanzee: An anthropological view of social organization.* Cambridge University Press.

Preston, J. (2021). *Fall: The Mystery of Robert Maxwell.* Penguin.

Redlich, F. (1998). *Hitler: Diagnosis of a Destructive Prophet.* Oxford: Oxford University Press.

Resick, C., Hanges, P., Dickson, M. & Mitchelson, J.K. (2005). A cross-cultural examination of the endorsement of ethical leadership. *Journal of Business Ethics* 63(4), 345-359.

Saladino, V., Lin, H., Zamparelli, E. & Verrastro, V. (2021). Neuroscience, empathy, and violent crime in an incarcerated population: A narrative review. *Front Psychol.* 28;12:694212.

Salekin, R.T. (2006). Psychopathy in Children and Adolescents: Assessment and Critical Questions Regarding Conceptualization. In C.J. Patrick (Ed.), *Handbook of Psychopathy* (pp. 389-414). Guilford Press.

Sanz-García, A., Gesteira, C., Sanz, J. & García-Vera, M.P. (2021). Prevalence of psychopathy in the general adult population: A systematic review and meta-analysis. *Frontiers in Psychology* 12, 661044.

Service, E.R. (1978). *Profiles in Ethnology.* Harper and Row.

Silke, A. (2003). Becoming a terrorist. In A. Silke (Ed.), *Terrorists, Victims and Society: Psychological Perspectives on Terrorism and its Consequences* (pp. 29-53). Wiley.

Slingenbergh, J. (2013). World livestock: Changing disease landscapes. Food and agriculture organization of the United Nations. Available at https://reliefweb.int/sites/reliefweb.int/files/resources/World%20Livestock%202013.pdf

Smithyman, S.D. (1979). Characteristics of "undetected" rapists. In W.H. Parsonage (Ed.), *Perspectives on Victimology* (pp. 99-120). Sage.

Statistics on Women and the Criminal Justice System. (2019). Available at https://assets.publishing.service.gov.uk/

government/uploads/system/uploads/attachment_data/file/938360/statistics-on-women-and-the-criminal-justice-system-2019.pdf

Taylor, S. (2017). *The Leap: The Psychology of Spiritual Awakening*. New World Library.

Taylor, S. (2018a). *The Fall: The Insanity of the Ego in Human History and the Dawning of a New Era* (2nd edition, with Afterword). John Hunt Books.

Taylor, S. (2018b). *Spiritual Science*. Watkins.

Taylor, S. (2019). The puzzle of altruism: Why do "selfish genes" behave unselfishly? *Explore 15*, 5, 371-375.

Taylor, S. (2020). An introduction to panspiritism: An alternative to materialism and panpsychism. *Zygon 55*(4), 898-923.

Taylor, S. (2021a). *Extraordinary Awakenings: When Trauma Leads to Transformation*. New World Library.

Taylor, S. (2021b). Toward a utopian society: From disconnection and disorder to empathy and harmony. *Journal of Humanistic Psychology*, June 2021.

Taylor, S. & Egeto-Szabo, K. (2017). Exploring awakening experiences: A study of awakening experiences in terms of their triggers, characteristics, duration and aftereffects. *The Journal of Transpersonal Psychology 49*(1), 45-65.

Thornhill, R. & Palmer, C.T. (2001). *A Natural History of Rape: Biological Bases of Sexual Coercion*. MIT Press.

Tiihonen, J., Koskuvi, M., Lähteenvuo, M. et al. (2020). Neurobiological roots of psychopathy. *Mol Psychiatry 25*, 3432-3441.

Travis, H. (2013). *Genocide, ethnonationalism, and the United Nations: Exploring the causes of mass killing since 1945*. Routledge.

Trump, M. (2020). *Too Much and Never Enough*. Simon & Schuster.

Tutu, D. (2022). Truth and Reconciliation. *Greater Good Magazine*. Available at https://greatergood.berkeley.edu/article/item/truth_and_reconciliation

The Upanishads (1988). Ed. and trans., J. Mascaro. Penguin.

Victoroff, J. (2005). The mind of the terrorist: A review and critique of psychological approaches. *Journal of Conflict Resolution 49*(1), 3-42.

Vronsky, P. (2018). *Sons of Cain: A History of Serial Killers from the Bronze Age to the Present*. Berkley.

Wade, C. & Tavris, C. (1994). The Longest War: Gender and Culture. In W.J. Lonner & R.S. Malpass (Eds.), *Psychology and Culture*. Allyn and Bacon.

Wade, J. (2019). Get off the mountaintop and back into the marketplace: Leadership as transpersonal psychology's highest calling. *Transpersonal Psychology Review 21*(1), 22-39.

Warren, J.I., Burnette, M., South, S.C., Chauhan, P., Bale, R. & Friend, R. (2002). Personality disorders and violence among female prison inmates. *J Am Acad Psychiatry Law 30*(4):502-9.

Wilber, K. (1997). *The Eye of Spirit: An Integral Vision for a World Gone Slightly Mad*. Shambhala.

Wilber, K. (2022). An update on the case of Adi Da. (August 28, 1998.) Retrieved from http://www.adidawilber.com/update_on_case_of_adi_da/

Williams, R. (2015). *Not I, not other than I: The Life and Teachings of Russel Williams*. O-Books.

Wilson, M.S. & McCarthy, K. (2011). Greed is good? Student disciplinary choice and self-reported psychopathy. *Personality and Individual Differences 51*(7), 873-876.

Wlodarczyk, A., Basabe, N., Páez, D. et al. (2016). Communal Coping and Posttraumatic Growth in a Context of Natural Disasters in Spain, Chile, and Colombia. *Cross-Cultural Research 50*(4), 325-355.

Woodburn, J. (1982). Egalitarian societies. *Man 17*(3), 431-451.

Wordsworth, W. (1994). *The Works of William Wordsworth*. Wordsworth Editions.

Zablocki, B. (1998). Exit cost analysis: A new approach to the scientific study of brainwashing. *Nova Religio 1*(1), 216-249.

ACADEMIC AND SPECIALIST

Iff Books publishes non-fiction. It aims to work with authors and titles
that augment our understanding of the human condition, society and
civilisation, and the world or universe in which we live.
If you have enjoyed this book, why not tell other readers by posting a
review on your preferred book site.
Recent bestsellers from Iff Books are:

Why Materialism Is Baloney
How true skeptics know there is no death and fathom answers
to life, the universe, and everything
Bernardo Kastrup
A hard-nosed, logical, and skeptic non-materialist metaphysics,
according to which the body is in mind, not mind in the body.
Paperback: 978-1-78279-362-5 ebook: 978-1-78279-361-8

The Fall
Steve Taylor
The Fall discusses human achievement versus the issues of war,
patriarchy and social inequality.
Paperback: 978-1-78535-804-3 ebook: 978-1-78535-805-0

Brief Peeks Beyond
Critical essays on metaphysics, neuroscience, free will,
skepticism and culture
Bernardo Kastrup
An incisive, original, compelling alternative to current mainstream
cultural views and assumptions.
Paperback: 978-1-78535-018-4 ebook: 978-1-78535-019-1

Framespotting
Changing how you look at things changes how
you see them
Laurence & Alison Matthews
A punchy, upbeat guide to framespotting. Spot deceptions and
hidden assumptions; swap growth for growing up. See and be free.
Paperback: 978-1-78279-689-3 ebook: 978-1-78279-822-4

Is There an Afterlife?
David Fontana
Is there an Afterlife? If so what is it like? How do Western ideas
of the afterlife compare with Eastern? David Fontana presents the
historical and contemporary evidence for survival of
physical death.
Paperback: 978-1-90381-690-5

Nothing Matters
a book about nothing
Ronald Green
Thinking about Nothing opens the world to everything by
illuminating new angles to old problems and stimulating new
ways of thinking.
Paperback: 978-1-84694-707-0 ebook: 978-1-78099-016-3

Panpsychism
The Philosophy of the Sensuous Cosmos
Peter Ells
Are free will and mind chimeras? This book, anti-materialistic but
respecting science, answers: No! Mind is foundational
to all existence.
Paperback: 978-1-84694-505-2 ebook: 978-1-78099-018-7

Punk Science
Inside the Mind of God
Manjir Samanta-Laughton
Many have experienced unexplainable phenomena; God, psychic
abilities, extraordinary healing and angelic encounters. Can
cutting-edge science actually explain phenomena
previously thought of as 'paranormal'?
Paperback: 978-1-90504-793-2

The Vagabond Spirit of Poetry
Edward Clarke
Spend time with the wisest poets of the modern age and of the
past, and let Edward Clarke remind you of the importance of
poetry in our industrialized world.
Paperback: 978-1-78279-370-0 ebook: 978-1-78279-369-4

Readers of ebooks can buy or view any of these bestsellers by
clicking on the live link in the title. Most titles are published in
paperback and as an ebook. Paperbacks are available in traditional
bookshops. Both print and ebook formats are available online.
Find more titles and sign up to our readers' newsletter at
http://www.johnhuntpublishing.com/non-fiction
Follow us on Facebook at
https://www.facebook.com/JHPNonFiction
and Twitter at https://twitter.com/JHPNonFiction